THE DIVINE QUEST IN MUSIC

BY THE SAME AUTHOR

From a Music-Lover's Armchair
The Appeal of Jazz
The Soul of Music

THE DIVINE QUEST IN MUSIC

by

R. W. S. Mendl

M.A., Oxon.

WITH A FOREWORD BY

The Dean of Windsor

AND A PREFACE BY

Sir Adrian Boult

SALISBURY SQUARE · LONDON

TO MY WIFE

MADE AND PRINTED IN GREAT BRITAIN BY
LOXLEY BROTHERS LIMITED
LETCHWORTH, HERTFORDSHIRE

CONTENTS

FOREWORD

by the Right Rev. Eric K. C. Hamilton, K.C.V.O., Dean of Windsor

THAT I should have the honour of contributing a foreword to this remarkable book is mainly due to the fact that its author and I spent some of the happiest of our earlier years as fellow-undergraduates at University College, Oxford, and share nostalgic memories of lovely quiet days before the flood, when even in " the High " one could listen to the music of the spheres.

Robert Mendl has chosen a fascinating theme for this essay. It is easy for a Christian and indeed for all who believe in God to agree that He must be the source of all beauty and that those who first found out musical tunes were discovering further secrets of His unfathomable mind, but few could trace for us the process of those discoveries from the dawn of history to the present day as he can with a truly astonishing range of knowledge and detailed understanding.

In my humble opinion *The Divine Quest in Music* is a devout and learned contribution to the common weal in a dangerously materialistic age.

On one theological point I would dare to join issue with the author. In his introductory chapter he writes of " a God who *when the human part of Him* had perished. . . ." Is this compatible with the Christian belief that the manhood assumed at the incarnation was never and will never be laid aside? This being so, one may hope that something corresponding to angels' harps may yet be found among the joys of heaven.

✠ ERIC HAMILTON

PREFACE

by Sir Adrian Boult

SOME years ago I took a very famous airman to his first concert. It was a Henry Wood Promenade, and we sat where we could see the faces of those young people who were cheerfully standing up to their two hours' music in addition (most of them) to an hour or two in the queue outside. He looked at their expressions and said afterwards: " This is the next thing to an act of worship ".

Again I remember a scene during the war, in the recreation theatre of a very big Air Force station in South Wales. Twelve or fourteen hundred young airmen and W.A.A.F.s were assembled to hear the B.B.C. Symphony Orchestra, who had been brought there by ENSA. Sitting at the very back of the hall, one could hardly see the platform, so thick was the smoke. Albert Coates conducted, and the moment the music began there was a stillness that could be felt as well as seen; it was a shock to see anyone's hand go up to keep a cigarette alight or make any other movement—very few did so, and in half an hour the air in the hall was entirely clear.

These are not isolated observations; they are symptomatic of the present-day attitude to musical performance: " the next thing to an act of worship ".

Mr. Mendl's fine study approaches this phenomenon from the opposite angle, and provides an explanation for the new attitude. The question may well be asked: " Then why is it a new attitude? The music hasn't changed since it was first written down ". The answer can only be that if the music hasn't changed, the audiences have. The audience I first observed in the early years of this century was a most respectable Kensington and Bayswater community; people who would no more readily miss their concert on Sunday afternoon than they would miss being seen at church that morning—I'm afraid that was often their principal reason for attending. Now Sir Henry Wood and the " Proms " have brought up an entirely different audience, coming from schools that no longer even have a Scripture hour on Mondays. The lack of this has thrown many of those who are spiritually perceptive into the concert room instead; and Mr. Mendl has shown us by detailed analysis the inner message of many of the masterpieces and how it is they help and feed and thrill these new audiences.

That great pianist Harold Samuel used to say that in performance you have, of course, to *state* the facts of the music, and state them well, but what really matters is what you *imply*. There is so much that is implied in and by great music which is beyond what can be put into words, though there are some writers who can, in their descriptions, lift a corner of the curtain for us now and then, and at any rate one hardened executant can find them stimulating and inspiring—in fact most helpful in his preparatory work. One thinks first perhaps of Tovey's *Essays in Musical Analysis* and Neville Cardus's *Ten Composers*, and now we must add the present book to the list, for Mr. Mendl's descriptions are always illuminating, and often take us right to the heart of greatness.

ADRIAN C. BOULT

27th March, 1957.

AUTHOR'S PREFACE

THIS book is not a history of liturgical music, though it necessarily discusses, among other works, a good many compositions written for use in public worship. Nor is it intended as a work of reference. It is an essay on the relationship between music and God. It may seem strange at first sight that, in a book on this subject, less space has been given to such great masters of devotional music as Palestrina, Vittoria, Lassus, Byrd and Orlando Gibbons, for instance, than to Mozart, Berlioz and Wagner, who are not considered primarily as creators of sacred art. The answer is that just because the five first-mentioned composers unquestionably expressed religious thoughts and emotions in their work there was no need to discuss them so fully as others who either present a problem or have aroused controversy. Even Bach, who embodied the whole of Christianity in his sublime music, does not, for my purposes here, require such full treatment as certain more controversial figures. On the other hand, Beethoven, whose music embraced not only the Christian faith but all humanity, must be considered at some length. These two are the joint kings of the musical firmament; but Bach to a large extent transformed sacred words into musical counterparts, whereas Beethoven, using instruments only, created works of more profound spiritual grandeur than any other composer of instrumental music; how he did so, involves a mystery more baffling than the miracle of Bach's inspiration; his liturgical works have also presented problems, because they are affected by the question of his own religious beliefs.

The very conception of the divinity of beauty may arouse misgivings in some minds. Are we not liable, it may be asked, to attribute divinity simply to those works of nature or of art that we happen to enjoy—like the contemporary of Congreve whose comment on his play *Love for Love* was " My dear, it's *divine*!"? But the fact that the term may sometimes be misapplied should not deter us from using it in what we believe to be the right place.

. . . . . .

The version of the Homeric Hymn quoted in Chapter 2 is reproduced from *World Music* by kind permission of the late Mrs. Elizabeth Brewster, mother of the Editor, Ralph Brewster (who predeceased her). My thanks are due to Mrs. Villiers for her assent to the reprinting in Chapter 5 of the extracts from *Noonday and Nocturne*, written by her late husband George Villiers.

In addition I wish to acknowledge my indebtedness to the following: Gerald Abraham: *Tchaikovsky, a short biography*; Jacques Barzun: *Berlioz and the Romantic Century*; Paul Bekker: *Beethoven*; Ferruccio Bonavia: *Verdi*; A. C. Bradley: *Oxford Lectures on Poetry—The Sublime*; Richard Capell: *Schubert's Songs*; Neville Cardus: *Ten Composers*; E. F. Carritt: *The Theory of Beauty*; Martin Cooper: *French Music from the death of Berlioz to the death of Fauré*; E. J. Dent: *Mozart's Operas* and *Ferruccio Busoni*; R. Nathaniel Dett; Article on " Negro Music " in the *International Cyclopedia of Music and Musicians* (edited by Oscar Thompson); E. R. Dodds: *The Greeks and the Irrational*; Alfred Einstein: *Gluck, Mozart, Schubert* and *Music in the Romantic Era*; *The Encyclopaedia Britannica* (11th and subsequent editions)—passim, but particularly the articles on " Drama ", " Orpheus " and " St. Cecilia "; Newman Flower: *George Frederic Handel;* Hubert Foss: *Ralph Vaughan Williams*; Cecil Gray: *Sibelius* and *Sibelius: the Symphonies*; Sir George Grove: *Beethoven and his Nine Symphonies*; *Grove's Dictionary of Music and Musicians* (3rd, 4th, and 5th editions)—passim; Paul Hindemith: *A Composer's World*; Imogen Holst: *Gustav Holst* and *The Music of Gustav Holst*; S. R. Hopper: *The Crisis of Faith*; Fred Hoyle: *The Nature of the Universe*; Vincent d'Indy: *César Franck* (translated, with an introduction, by Rosa Newmarch); C. E. M. Joad: *The Recovery of Belief*; A. C. Kalischer: *Beethoven's Letters*, a critical edition (translated by J. S. Shedlock); Paul H. Lang: *Music in Western Civilisation*; A. D. Lindsay: *The Republic of Plato* (translated, with an introduction); Arthur Little: *The Nature of Art*; A. Macbeath: *Experiments in Living*; Basil Maine: *Elgar: his Life and Works*; Wilfrid Mellers: *François Couperin*; Edited by Donald Mitchell and Hans Keller: *Benjamin Britten—a Commentary*; M. Montagu-Nathan: *A History of Russian Music* and *Moussorgsky*; Ernest Newman: *Gluck and the Opera, Musical Studies, Hugo Wolf, The Unconscious Beethoven, The Life of Richard Wagner, Wagner Nights*, Preface to Novello's edition of Brahms' *Requiem*; *Memoirs of Hector Berlioz*, annotated and edited by Ernest Newman; Walter Niemann: *Brahms* (translated by Catherine Alison Phillips); Harold Osborne: *Theory of Beauty*; *The Oxford History of*

Music (2nd edition)—passim; *The New Oxford History of Music*, Vol. II; C. H. H. Parry: *Johann Sebastian Bach*; Guy de Pourtalès: *Chopin, a man of solitude* (translated by Charles Bayly, Jnr.) and *Franz Liszt, the man of love* (translated by Eleanor Stimson Brooks); A. O. Prickard: *Longinus on the Sublime* (a translation); Alec Robertson: *Sacred Music* and *Dvořák*; W. S. Rockstro: *Handel*; John F. Runciman: *Purcell*; Albert Schweitzer: *J. S. Bach* (translated by Ernest Newman); Otakar Šourek: *Antonin Dvořák*; Richard Specht: *Johannes Brahms* (translated by Eric Blom); Norman Suckling: *Fauré*; J. W. N. Sullivan: *Beethoven*; A. W. Thayer: *The Life of Ludwig van Beethoven*, edited by H. E. Krehbiel; Sir Donald Tovey: *Essays in Musical Analysis*—passim; Francis Toye: *Giuseppe Verdi*; Léon Vallas: *Claude Debussy* (translated by Maire and Grace O'Brien) and *César Franck* (translated by Hubert Foss); Frank Walker: *Hugo Wolf, a biography*; Bruno Walter: *Gustav Mahler*; Herbert Weinstock: *Tchaikovsky*; Werner Wolff: *Anton Bruckner, rustic genius.*

R. W. S. M.

I

INTRODUCTORY

"Now must we praise
The guardian of Heaven's realm
The Creator's might
And His mind's thought
The glorious works of the Father
How of every wonder
He the Lord Eternal
Laid the foundation.
He shaped erst for the sons of men
Heaven as their roof
Holy Creator.
The middle world He
Mankind's guardian
Eternal Lord
Afterwards prepared
The earth for men
Lord Almighty."

THIS poem is inscribed on Caedmon's cross at Whitby, in the parish churchyard, and is said to be "the first song Caedmon sang". He was the earliest English Christian poet and wrote these lines at some time in the seventh century. Thus, in the dawn of English literature, art praised a beneficent God and expressed the artist's faith in an eternal Creator, maker of a glorious Heaven and earth. According to Bede, Caedmon had left a festive company because, being an illiterate herdsman, he could not carry out the requests of each of those present to sing a song to the harp; he went home to bed, and in a dream was bidden by a mysterious stranger to sing of "the beginning of created things". The result was this poem, which he remembered after waking. The farm bailiff, under whom he worked and to whom he told his dream, took him to the neighbouring monastery at Whitby, and he subsequently became an inmate. Thus the poem, at the time when it was conceived, was not intended for any liturgical purpose. It does not mention Christ, and its message is wide enough to fit most of the great religions.

The music with which this book is concerned bears certain resemblances to Caedmon's first song. Some of it is connected with ecclesiastical purposes, but a great deal of it is not. God is often present in music which is not commonly called sacred, and the spiritual quality inherent in some of the greatest music in the world is evidence of the existence of a God who is not merely a powerful Deity but a loving one. Some music possesses a divine character so universal that it awakens a response in the minds of men of diverse faiths and even of those who have—or think they have—no faith at all.

Before we can consider the subject of God in music, it is necessary to get clear in our minds what we mean by "God", the nature of our beliefs about Him and about His relationship to art in general and to music in particular.

Now, I believe in a Christian conception of God: a God of love, who cares for the creatures and objects which He has created; who implanted in men a freedom of choice enabling them to choose whether to do that which they believe to be right or to follow the impulses which lead them into cruelty, greed or selfishness; a God who at a certain stage in history assumed human form and, as man, submitted Himself to torture and death itself for the sake of the truth and on behalf of His fellow-men, and by means of this sacrifice gave the supreme example of that love of mankind which He had enjoined as one of the two great commandments—the other being love towards God Himself; a God who, when the human part of Him had perished, came once more to life and showed that the divine power can triumph even over death; a God who lives not only in Heaven and in the person of Christ, but in the souls of men, comforting them in their sufferings and prompting them to help and care for their neighbours.

In my eyes, the differences in belief between the various sects of Christianity are today relatively unimportant. If a Roman Catholic, or an Anglo-Catholic member of the Church of England, believes that the bread and wine used in the Mass or Communion service are indeed the body and blood of Jesus, whereas others treat them as symbols of His sacrifice, this divergence is, from my standpoint, nowadays of little moment; the Roman Catholic worships the Virgin, whereas others simply revere her memory because she was Christ's human mother: this difference does not seem to me to matter greatly. What does matter is the bond of Christianity, and what matters even more is that many of the Christian beliefs and moral values are shared by Jews, Mohammedans, Buddhists and even Hindus, though all of us in our actions obviously fall short of the standards of our various faiths, in varying degrees. The great division in modern times is no longer between Christians and pagans or between Jews and Gentiles, much less between Catholics and heretics or even between Christians and infidels, but between religion and materialism. Even a religion with barbarous practices attached to it, or a primitive or superstitious faith, is better than none at all: for the practices can in time be removed by enlightenment and the superstition by education. But a materialism which abolishes belief in God altogether, thereby eliminates spiritual values from the minds of men and leaves humanity a prey to cruelty, injustice and oppression.

I am not discussing politics. It is possible that Communism may, in time, perhaps by some process of evolution, cease to be materialistic and become associated with the worship of God or even specifically with Christianity. But materialism is not only pernicious in its ethical effects; it is also based on a fallacy—the theory that the soul of man does not exist. One of the strongest proofs of the fallacy of materialism is the spiritual quality present in so many of the artistic creations that we possess, and among them in countless works of music. This quality is a witness to the existence of the soul, and thereby to the existence of God.

In one sense, God is in all music, because He is the creator of all things. But though He is a God of goodness and of love, He has created not only human beings who are for the most part good and others who are strange mixtures, but also men who are chiefly evil or who at any rate develop from innocent babies into mainly evil adults; in addition, it is presumably He who has created foul diseases and other misfortunes which beset mankind through no apparent fault of man; and though most of the works of nature seem good or beautiful, some of her manifestations are terrible, dangerous or cruel. These are the great mysteries of the Universe. But just as men depart from the divinity which is within them exactly in accordance with the extent to which they fall away from goodness, so the music which they make evinces infinite degrees of divinity or of the lack of it, ranging from that which is (unless you are an atheist) unquestionably divine at one end of the scale, to that which bears little or no trace of divine character at the other end.

The manifestation of God in music differs from the manifestation of Him in other arts, owing to a fundamental divergence between it and them. When we speak of certain works of literature as being religious, we are referring to the fact that they deal unmistakably with sacred subjects: there is no doubt that they do so, because literature employs words, which are the normal medium of communication between human beings, and thus conveys a more or less definite meaning to our minds. Thus religious dramas and poems tell their own tale. Painting, by being directly imitative, can depict Biblical scenes and, in particular, Christian subjects such as the Crucifixion, the Transfiguration, and so on, and we know that such pictures have a religious significance because they have devotional associations for us, though we may say that the actual sacred quality varies according to the nature of the artist's attitude towards religion. Painting may also express spiritual character in a portrait.

Similarly with sculpture. The *Pietà* of Michelangelo in the Cathedral at Florence does not merely depict three people supporting the body of a dead man. Its beauty in great measure consists in the expressions of infinite compassion and reverence on their faces: the religious effect is produced partly by this, partly by the noble character of the whole conception, and partly by its association in our minds with the solemn subject which it portrays.

Architecture, in the form of a great church or temple, can be a *sursum corda* in stone. The cathedral is built for worship, and the architects and builders consecrate their art accordingly.

Dancing had religious associations in ancient Greek times, partly through its connection with the drama, which in its beginnings was intimately bound up with worship, and the same can be said of early Indian dances. Modern ballet, in such creations as *Job*, *The Wise Virgins* and *The Quest*, has shown that it is still possible to express religious ideas and emotions through the medium of dancing, miming and choreography.

Music's method is different from all these. It does not necessarily rely on association. It can be religious or spiritual—and the two adjectives, though not identical in meaning, are closely connected with one another—by virtue of the intrinsic character of the composition itself. It does not actually imitate (except in so far as it can reproduce those sounds which in real life are caused by regular vibrations and are therefore themselves musical, such as the songs of birds). It represents, and this simply means that it is appropriate to the subject which the composer has in mind.

The spiritual quality in music is indefinable. Much music that is felt to be spiritual is not based on technical devices which have any religious or ecclesiastical associations. The chorales in Bach's settings of the Passion according to St. John and St. Matthew are based on old German hymn tunes, but they are not more religious than the reflective choruses, arias and duets in the same works which owe their sacred feeling to no other source than Bach's own inspiration. The spiritual flavour which is present in most of the instrumental music of Beethoven from his early works down to the profound mysteries of his third period compositions cannot be accounted for by any reference to use of sequences, rhythms or harmonies to be found in the specifically consecrated art of his predecessors or of earlier, traditional liturgy. When we say that Elgar's music in *The Dream of Gerontius* embodies the religious emotions and thoughts of Cardinal Newman's poem, or that " Nimrod " in the " Enigma " Variations is noble music expressing the noble character of the man portrayed in it, we cannot point to any actual ingredients in the score which are related to musical devices of earlier times.

Conversely, some music which is set to sacred words is not intrinsically religious in quality. Certain hymn tunes which have the square-cut rhythms and slow tempo associated with congregational worship are nevertheless banal and, frankly, not beautiful enough to be a suitable offering to God, as contrasted with the fine ones which, happily, are nowadays more frequently sung in church services, such as the Old Hundredth, "O God, our help in ages past" (the tune of which is similar to the theme of Bach's " St. Anne " Fugue for organ in E flat), " Lord, dismiss us with thy blessing " (sung to the melody of Haydn's *Emperor's Hymn*), or Parry's *Jerusalem* set to Blake's words. The music which Rossini wrote for *Stabat Mater* is charming, but differs little in character from his operatic style. Gounod's *Nazareth* is a rousing tune, but I suggest that it would not have been described as religious by anyone ignorant of the words to which it is set.

The spiritual element in music corresponds to the soul in man, though if we believe that every man has a soul (of some kind!) this statement should not be taken to imply that all music is spiritual in character. It corresponds, in the sense that you cannot analyse it or reduce it to concrete terms. The scientist who dissects the human body or examines it while life still subsists in it, will not find a soul within that he can express in scientific terms. The sceptic may argue from this that there is no such thing as a soul. Actually, he is begging the question: obviously a soul cannot be detected by natural science, because this deals only with physical things,[1] and the soul, if it exists at all, is purely spiritual and has no physical existence whatever: it is the sum of a person's character, the essence of his personality, and Heaven is not a place but a state of existence. The sceptic tries to maintain that the so-called "soul" really consists of cerebral processes—actions of the brain which cease at death. His argument is pure surmise, and one of the pieces of evidence against it is that the spiritual quality of a great deal of the music which has been composed is actually perceived and experienced by large numbers of music-lovers, even though he may not apprehend it: that experience can no more be denied than the existence of the pen with which I am writing. If this element in music were a purely cerebral one, it would not differ in kind from skill, ingenuity or craftsmanship. Yet it is clearly distinguishable from them—even in the same composition. The supreme mastery of means in the first movement of Beethoven's Seventh Symphony is distinct from the spiritual quality present in it: and even though we may rightly say that the manner in which he makes the principal theme float in on the woodwind in a minor key in the recapitulation is at once a witness to his genius for construction and to the spiritual character of his art, these two elements are nevertheless separate.

Music cannot be divided into sacred and secular, in anything like watertight compartments. The liturgical masterpieces of Palestrina, Byrd and Bach, Handel's *Messiah*, Beethoven's *Missa Solemnis*, Elgar's three great oratorios, Holst's *Hymn of Jesus*, Kodály's *Psalmus Ungaricus*, Fauré's *Requiem*, Vaughan Williams' *Sancta Civitas*, *Dona Nobis Pacem* and Mass in G minor, Bloch's *Sacred Service*, Benjamin Britten's *Rejoice in the Lamb*, and Herbert Howells' *Hymnus Paradisi*—all these aimed at being religious in character, and by general consent they achieve that object. It is difficult to draw the line between the music which manifests divine inspiration and that which does not; but whilst there are borderline cases—a kind of musical no-man's land between Heaven and Earth—there is on one side quite clearly a vast quantity of music which is so obviously mechanical, insincere, superficial or

[1] Psychology is not a branch of "natural science": William McDougall, in his book *Psychology* (Home University Library) calls it "the science of behaviour of living things": "mind" and "soul" are, in his view, words which are too vague for the purpose of psychology. I think it is clear that psychology cannot throw any light on the question whether the soul exists. And psychoanalysis is primarily a method of interview and only secondarily a body of doctrine—as was pointed out in an article on Freud in *The Times Literary Supplement* on September 4th, 1953.

meretricious, that inspiration can have played little or no part in its creation, and on the other hand a great deal which is inspired in the sense that it is either noble or spiritual in quality or expressive of deep feelings and thus partakes of the divine element in man's nature. This latter type of music is not confined to that which is specifically sacred in intention or effect. As I have indicated, most of Beethoven's instrumental art is in this category, and we can all think of countless examples in the works of other composers too.

The book of Ecclesiasticus, Chapter xliv, opens with the familiar words:

> Let us now praise famous men,
> And our fathers that begat us.
> The Lord hath wrought great glory by them
> Through his great power from the beginning.

Among these are included "Such as found out musical tunes".

2

IN THE BEGINNING

THE two earliest elements of music were rhythm and melody. Rhythm arose in man instinctively from the pulse and the heart-beat and led him to express his emotions by dancing or stamping his feet on the ground. Melody originated from the inarticulate cries with which he uttered his needs or accompanied his dance-steps. Music diverged into religious and secular in remote times, but the two types have interacted on one another throughout history. We may well regard this fact as symbolising the link between religion and the rest of human life.

Music is not essential to dancing, but it has almost invariably accompanied it, in however primitive a form—such as beating out a rhythm on a drum. A. C. Bouquet[1] thinks that dances which were a form of sympathetic magic performed by huntsmen to induce a mysterious Power to send animals to be killed for food, with the men wearing masks resembling the animals' heads, probably date back to a period between 20,000 and 12,000 B.C.: he saw modern dances of this type enacted by Tibetans, Scandinavians and (in a photograph) Englishmen (at Abbot's Bromley, Staffordshire), and considers that they had a common origin of immense antiquity.

Hymns or songs, and dances which can be presumed to have been accompanied by music, formed part of religious worship in pre-Christian times throughout the Eastern Hemisphere.

Scholars believe that the Sumerians entered Mesopotamia before 5000 B.C. In the temples which they erected there to gods who were mountain-deities or personifications of heavenly bodies, the earliest set liturgies known to history were performed, with hymns or psalms and some kind of music, both vocal and instrumental. Later, the Babylonian and Assyrian Semites took over the Sumerian pantheon, and in their temple services there were long, sung liturgies, with single songs called " ershemma " or " song to the flute", and " kishub " or "song of prostration", which were continued from the early Sumerian period. Under the last dynasty of Ur and the kings of Larsa (Sankarah) and Isin, complex musical liturgies were held for the great deities

[1] *Comparative Religion*, p. 24.

—" ershemmas " and " kishubs " being arranged so as to show the theological ideas relating to the particular deity, and all of them penitential and mournful in character. Each liturgy contained a hymn to the " Word of Wrath " of the god, except in the case of those to the mother goddess; the section called the " Titular Litany " mentioned the Sumerian names of all the main deities of the pantheon, each followed by a sad refrain; lastly came a penitential psalm begging the god for mercy and peace. The priesthood of psalmists sang these liturgies, usually to the accompaniment of the "balag", which was probably either a harp or a lyre, though some authorities think it was a drum. They were performed as regular religious duties at frequent intervals, and dealt with the universal sorrows of mankind and the dreadful vengeance of the gods, or were sometimes designed to avoid the effects of evil omens. Although they were hymns of praise to the deities, they were otherwise very cheerless.[1]

The period in which Zarathustra (=Zoroaster), the great Persian prophet of antiquity, lived, is unknown to this day. Different Greek writers placed him as early as 5,000 years before the Trojan War, 6,000 years before Xerxes and 6,000 years before Plato. These figures are almost certainly wide of the mark, but there is no doubt that his monotheistic community was recognised by Darius in the sixth century B.C. Our knowledge of the religion which he taught is largely derived from the Gathas or sacred writings—miscellaneous collections which have survived and which, in addition to prayers and instructions, include hymns: the words of five of these are said to have been his own compositions. He taught belief in a supreme, beneficent god, Ahuramazda, though there were inferior deities too. The most popular of these subsequently was Mithras, the sun-god, who later still became the chief object of worship: at his festival the king, as a form of religious ritual, became intoxicated with drink and danced the national dance.

In the ancient Chinese religion, even before 1200 B.C. there was a supreme Ruler of the universe, who did not create it but lived on high, hating wickedness and rejoicing in virtue. He was called Shang-ti, but the name T'ien also occurs in old poetry about 1100 B.C., as though he had been worshipped before then. They seem, indeed, to have been synonymous or to have signified two persons in one substance, T'ien being more abstract and Shang-ti more personal and

[1] Article on Babylonian and Assyrian religion in the *Encyclopaedia Britannica*, by Professor Stephen Langdon.

anthropomorphic. Shang-ti walked and talked, was pleased with sacrifices, even took sides in war, and enjoyed music and dancing in his honour. But in addition to this supreme, if dualistic, deity there were many inferior gods and spirits; and at the nature and fertility festivals when they were worshipped in public, the rhythms of nature are thought to have been represented in song and dance as well as in the mating of men and women.

Chinese drama arose from the combination of dance and song. It developed out of ballets and pantomimes; and the dances of trained performers, to the accompaniment of music and singing, were carried out on solemn and festive occasions, some of which had religious associations.

The ancient Indian hymns of the Rig-Veda or Royal Veda, comprising 1,028 hymns in ten books, all date from the period 1500 to 1000 B.C.[1] (other Vedic books were of later dates). These hymns first showed signs of dramatic elements and took the form of dialogues between divine persons. They were combined with dances in the festivals of the gods, and to the union of song and dance were added recitation and dialogue, first sung, then spoken. Thus music was early on the scene in the Indian drama, which, like Greek tragedy, was religious in origin, and in worship generally. A. H. Fox Strangways[2] considered it doubtful whether the ancient melody differed essentially from that still to be heard in the sub-continent, and wrote that "this music speaks the soul of a people" and "reveals man in the presence of God".

The ancient Egyptians regarded music as an important science, and their priests studied it thoroughly. They believed music to be of divine origin, and that their most sacred melodies came from Isis. In the ritual of the temples in which the Egyptian deities were worshipped, the trumpet, the flute and the harp were usually employed, but the most typical instrument was the "sistrum", which had small disks shaken on wires: (it is still used as a church instrument in Abyssinia). The priestesses sang and shook the sistrum in dances and processions.

The historical bond between religion and the early stages of music in ancient Greece is represented mythologically by the stories of Hermes, the god who created the lyre, and of Orpheus, who in Greek legend was the chief representative of the art of song and playing

[1] A. C. Bouquet, *Comparative Religion*, p. 97. The word "Veda" means "knowledge".

[2] Article on Indian Music in *Grove's Dictionary of Music and Musicians*, Vol. II (3rd edition).

on the lyre and was also an important figure in Greek worship; and by certain of the Nine Muses.

A Homeric Hymn of the sixth century B.C., tells the wondrous tale of the youthful Hermes:[1]

" Muse, sing of Hermes, the son of Zeus and Maia, lord of Cyllene and Arcadia rich in flocks, the luck-bringing messenger of the immortals whom Maia bare, the rich-tressed nymph, when she was joined in love with Zeus—a shy goddess, for she avoided the company of the blessed gods, and lived within a deep, shady cave. There the son of Cronos used to lie with the rich-tressed nymph, unseen by deathless gods and mortal men, at dead of night that sweet sleep might hold white-armed Hera fast. And when the purpose of great Zeus was fulfilled, and the tenth moon with her was fixed in heaven, she was delivered and a notable thing was come to pass. For then she bare a son of many shifts, blandly cunning, a robber, a cattle driver, a bringer of dreams, a watcher by night, a thief at the gates, one who was soon to show forth wonderful deeds among the deathless gods. Born with the dawning, at mid-day he played on the lyre, and in the evening he stole the cattle of far-shooting Apollo on the fourth day of the month; for on that day queenly Maia bare him.

" Soon as he had leaped from his mother's heavenly womb, he lay not long waiting in his holy cradle, but he sprang up and sought the oxen of Apollo. But as he stepped over the threshold of the high-roofed cave, he found a tortoise there and gained endless delight. For it was Hermes who first made the tortoise a singer. The creature fell in his way at the courtyard gate, where it was feeding on the rich grass before the dwelling, waddling along. When he saw it, the luck-bringing son of Zeus laughed and said:

" 'An omen of luck for me so soon! I do not slight it. Hail, comrade of the feast, lovely in shape, sounding at the dance! With joy I meet you! Where got you that rich gaud for covering, that spangled shell—a tortoise living in the mountains? But I will take and carry you within: you shall help me and I will do you no disgrace, though first of all you must profit me. It is better to be at home: harm may come out of doors. Living you shall be a spell against mischievous witchcraft; but if you die then you shall make sweetest song.'

" Thus speaking, he took up the tortoise in both hands and went back into the house carrying his charming toy. Then he cut off its limbs and scooped out the marrow of the mountain-tortoise with a scoop of

[1] Reproduced from *World Music*, Vol. I (see Preface).

grey iron. As a swift thought darts through the heart of a man when thronging cares haunt him, or as bright glances flash from the eye, so glorious Hermes planned both thought and deed at once. He cut stalks of reed to measure and fixed them fastening their ends across the back and through the shell of the tortoise, and then stretched ox-hide all over it by his skill. Also he put in the horns and fitted a cross-piece upon the two of them and stretched seven strings of sheep gut. But when he had made it he proved each string in turn with the key, as he held the lovely thing. At the touch of his hand it sounded marvellously; and, as he tried it, the god sang sweet random snatches, even as youths bandy taunts at festivals. He sang of Zeus, the son of Cronos, and neat-shod Maia, the converse which they had before in the comradeship of love, telling all the glorious tale of his own begetting. He celebrated, too, the handmaids of the nymph, and his bright home and the tripods all about the house and the abundant cauldrons.

" But while he was singing all these, his heart was bent on other matters. And he took the hollow lyre and laid it in his sacred cradle, and sprang from the sweet-smelling hall to a watch-place, pondering sheer trickery in his heart—deeds such as knavish folk pursue in the dark night-time; for he longed to taste flesh.

" The Sun was going down beneath the earth towards Ocean with his horses and chariot when Hermes came hurrying to the shadowy mountains of Pieria, where the divine cattle of the blessed gods had their steads and grazed the pleasant, unmown meadows. Of these the son of Maia, the sharp-eyed slayer of Argus, then cut off from the herd fifty loud-lowing kine, and drove them straggling-wise across a sandy place, turning their hoof-prints aside. Also, he bethought him of a crafty ruse and reversed the marks of their hoofs, making the front behind and the hind before, while he himself walked the other way. Then he wove sandals with wicker-work by the sand of the sea, wonderful things, unthought of, unimagined; for he mixed together tamarisk and myrtle twigs, fastening together an armful of their fresh, young wood, and tied them, leaves and all securely under his feet as light sandals. . . .

" . . . But an old man tilling his flowering vineyard saw him as he was hurrying down the plain through the grassy Onchestos. So the son of Maia began and said to him:

" ' Old man, digging about your vines with bowed shoulders, surely you shall have much wine when all these bear fruit, if you obey me and strictly remember not to have seen what you have seen, and not to have heard what you have heard, and to keep silent when nothing of your own is harmed. . . .'

" Then the strong son of Zeus drove the wide-browed cattle of Phoebus Apollo to the river Alpheus. And they came unwearied to the high-roofed byres and the drinking troughs that were before the noble meadow. Then, after he had well fed the loud-bellowing cattle with fodder and driven them into the byre, close-packed and chewing lotus and dewy gallingal, he gathered a pile of wood and began to seek the art of fire . . . For it was Hermes who first invented fire-sticks and fire.

" *Hermes now kills and roasts two of the cows, and though much tempted does not eat any of the meat, but stores all the flesh and fat away as a token of his youthful theft, destroying with fire all the hoofs and all the heads. Apollo seeking in a great state of perturbation for his lost cattle passes the old man who divulges the fact that he has seen a child driving cattle. Catching sight of a long-winged bird Apollo now realises by this omen, that the thief must be a child of Zeus, and sets forth for Maia's cave on Mount Cyllene.*

" . . . Now when the son of Zeus and Maia saw Apollo in a rage about his cattle, he snuggled down in his fragrant swaddling-clothes; and as wood-ash covers over the deep embers of tree-stumps, so Hermes cuddled himself up when he saw the Far-Shooter. He squeezed head and hands and feet together in a small space, like a new born child seeking sweet sleep, though in truth he was wide awake, and he kept his lyre under his armpit. . . .

" *When Apollo on entering the cave caught sight of little Hermes he said to him:*

" ' Child, lying in the cradle, make haste and tell me of my cattle, or we two will soon fall out angrily. For I will take you and cast you into dusky Tartarus and awful hopeless darkness, and neither your mother nor your father shall free you or bring you up again to the light, but you will wander under the earth and be the leader amongst little folk.'[1]

" Then Hermes answered him with crafty words. . . .

" ' . . . I was born yesterday, and my feet are soft and the ground beneath is rough; nevertheless, if you will have it so, I will swear a great oath by my father's head and vow that neither am I guilty myself, neither have I seen any other who stole your cows—whatever cows may be; for I know them only by hearsay.'

[1] " For those in Hades retain the state of growth in which they are at the moment of leaving the upper world."

" So, then, said Hermes, shooting quick glances from his eyes: and he kept raising his brows and looking this way and that, whistling long and listening to Apollo's story as to an idle tale.

" *But Apollo was not taken in and laughing softly said to him:*

" ' If you would not sleep your last and latest sleep get out of your cradle. . . .'

" So said Phoebus Apollo, and took the child and began to carry him. But at that moment the strong Slayer of Argus had his plan, and, while Apollo held him in his hands, sent forth an omen, a hard-worked belly-serf, a rude messenger, and sneezed directly after. And when Apollo heard it, he dropped glorious Hermes out of his hands on the ground: then sitting down before him, though he was eager to go on his way, he spoke mockingly to Hermes:

" ' Fear not little swaddling baby, son of Zeus and Maia. I shall find the strong cattle presently by these omens, and you shall lead the way.'

" *Hermes goes on protesting and denying ever having seen any cows in his short life but finally agrees to let the dispute be taken before Zeus. They wander across the sands, Hermes leading the way towards Olympus, where they find the immortal gods assembled. Zeus asks Apollo why he is driving before him a child with the look of a Herald. Whereupon Apollo tells his father the whole story. Then Hermes speaks to his father and still denies the whole thing complaining of Apollo's pitiless inquisition, appealing for help, on the grounds that while Apollo is big and strong, he was born only yesterday. Zeus is amused at the child's cunning and tells the two boys to be of one mind and to go together in search of the cattle, Hermes leading the way. So they set off to sandy Pylos and reach the byre where the beasts were kept at night time. While Hermes goes into the cave to drive out the cattle, Apollo sees the cow-hides on the rock, and asks Hermes:*

" '. . . How were you able, you crafty rogue, to flay two cows, new-born and babyish as you are?'

" *Apollo tries in vain to bind Hermes with withes of osier, which only fall from Hermes and start growing, so quickly that they soon cover the herd. But Hermes, realising that he is found out, quickly thinks of some way to placate Apollo.*

" Very easily he softened the son of all-glorious Leto as he would, stern though the Far-Shooter was. He took the lyre upon his left arm and tried each string in turn with the key, so that it sounded awesomely at his touch. And Phoebus Apollo laughed for joy; for the sweet throb of the marvellous music went to his heart, and a soft longing took hold on his soul as he listened. Then the son of Maia, harping sweetly upon his lyre, took courage and stood at the left hand of Phoebus Apollo; and soon, while he played shrilly on his lyre, he lifted up his voice and sang, and lovely was the sound of his voice that followed. . . .

" . . . But Apollo was seized with a longing not to be allayed, and he opened his mouth and spoke winged words to Hermes:

" 'Slayer of oxen, trickster, busy one, comrade of the feast, this song of yours is worth fifty cows, and I believe that presently we shall settle our quarrel peacefully. But come now, tell me this, resourceful son of Maia: has this marvellous thing been with you from your birth, or did some god or mortal man give it you—a noble gift—and teach you heavenly song? For wonderful is this new-uttered sound I hear, the like of which I vow that no man nor god dwelling yet on Olympus ever yet has known but you, O thievish son of Maia. What skill is this? What song for desperate cares? What way of song? For verily here are three things to hand all at once from which to choose—mirth, and love, and sweet sleep. And though I am a follower of the Olympian Muses who love dances and the bright path of Song—the full-toned chant and ravishing thrill of flutes—yet I never cared for those feats of skill at young men's revels as I do now for this: I am filled with wonder, O son of Zeus, at your sweet playing. But now, since you, though little, have such glorious skill, sit down, dear boy, and respect the words of your elders. For now you shall have renown among the deathless gods, you and your mother also. This I will declare to you exactly: by this shaft of cornel wood I will surely make you a leader renowned among the deathless gods, and fortunate, and will give you glorious gifts and will not deceive you from first to last.'

"Then Hermes answered him with artful words: 'You question me carefully, O Far-Worker; yet I am not jealous that you should enter upon my art: this day you shall know it. For I seek to be friendly with you both in thought and word. . . .

" ' . . . Now, you are free to learn whatever you please; but since, as it seems, your heart is so strongly set on playing the lyre, chant, and play upon it, and give yourself to merriment, taking this as a gift from me, and do you, my friend, bestow glory on me. Sing well with this clear-voiced companion in your hands; for you are skilled in good, well-ordered utterance. From now on bring it confidently to the rich feast and lovely dance and glorious revel, a joy by night and by day. Whoso with wit and wisdom enquires of it cunningly, him it teaches through its sound all manner of things that delight the mind, being easily played with gentle familiarities, for it abhors toilsome drudgery;

but whoso in ignorance enquires of it violently, to him it chatters mere vanity and foolishness. But you are able to learn whatever you please. So then, I will give you this lyre, glorious son of Zeus, while I for my part will graze down with wild-roving cattle the pastures on hill and horse-feeding plain: so shall the cows covered by the bulls calve abundantly both males and females. And now there is no need for you, bargainer though you are, to be furiously angry.'

" When Hermes had said this, he held out the lyre: and Phoebus Apollo took it, and readily put his shining whip in Hermes' hand, and ordained him keeper of herds. The son of Maia received it joyfully, while the glorious son of Leto, the lord far-working Apollo, took the lyre upon his left arm and tried each string with the key. Awesomely it sounded at the touch of the god, while he sang sweetly to its note.

" Afterwards the two, the all-glorious sons of Zeus, turned the cows back towards the sacred meadow, but themselves hastened back to snowy Olympus, delighting in the lyre. Then wise Zeus was glad and made them both friends. And Hermes loved the son of Leto continually even as he does now, when he had given the lyre as token to the Far-Shooter, who played it skilfully, holding it upon his arm. But for himself Hermes found out another cunning art and made himself the pipes whose sound is heard afar.

" Then the son of Leto said to Hermes: ' Son of Maia, guide and cunning one. I fear you may steal from me the lyre and my curved bow together; for you have an office from Zeus to establish deed of barter amongst men throughout the fruitful earth. Now if you would only swear me the great oath of the gods, either by nodding your head, or by the potent water of Styx, you would do all that can please and ease my heart.'

" Then Maia's son nodded his head and promised that he would never steal anything of all the Far-Shooter possessed, and would never go near his stronghouse; but Apollo, son of Leto, swore to be fellow and friend to Hermes, vowing that he would love no other among the immortals, neither god nor man sprung from Zeus, better than Hermes: and the Father sent forth an eagle in confirmation."

. . . . .

The name of Orpheus was probably connected with " orph- " (" dark "). Thus he may originally have been a god of darkness or the liberator from the power of darkness by his gift of music, or he may have got his name because his rites were celebrated at night. Pindar

(522-442 B.C.) called him " son of Apollo " and "the father of song", and from the sixth century onward he was regarded as one of the leading poets and musicians, who perfected the lyre, and by his music and singing not only charmed wild animals but even drew trees and rocks from their places and stopped rivers in their courses. He was believed to have taught mankind medicine, writing and agriculture, practised astrology, founded or propagated religious cults such as those of Apollo and Dionysus, established mystic, initiatory, and purificatory ritual, and visited Egypt, where he became acquainted with the writings of Moses and the faith in a future life.

It is unlikely that he was a historical character. According to one tradition he was the son of Oeagrus, King of Thrace, and the muse Calliope, and joined the expedition of the Argonauts, whose leader Jason had been told by Chiron, with his prophetic gift, that only by the aid of Orpheus would they be able to get past the Sirens.

His wife, Eurydice, roaming in the fields one day, was bitten by a snake and died. Orpheus descended into Hades and by his music so charmed the Eumenides, Pluto and Persephone, that they allowed him to take her back to earth. According to a later version of the legend, however, this was subject to the condition that he walked in front and did not look back at her until he had reached the upper world, but in his anxiety he broke his word, and Eurydice died again.

After her death, he shunned the love of womankind, and the jealous Thracian women, during the Bacchic rites, tore him limb from limb in their frenzy. His head and lyre floated down the river Hebrus to the sea. According to Lucian, the head floated on the lyre, singing Orpheus' dirge as it went, with the winds blowing an accompaniment on the strings. Eventually they reached Lesbos, where the inhabitants buried the head and built a shrine in honour of Orpheus near Antissa, and the nightingales sang there twice as sweetly as anywhere else. Legend tells us that the lyre was carried to heaven by the Muses and placed among the stars.

The story of the death of Orpheus has counterparts elsewhere. Osiris also was torn to pieces and his head floated down every year from Egypt to Byblus. A similar fate was also told of Dionysus, whose head was said to have been carried by the waters to Lesbos. A close connection obviously exists between Orpheus and Dionysus. Frazer (in *The Golden Bough*) suggests that stories such as these (Pentheus, king of Thebes, and Lycurgus, king of the Thracian Edonians, both of whom were torn to pieces for their impious opposition to the vine-god

Dionysus; and Orpheus, who was dismembered by Bacchanals), may be " distorted reminiscences " of a custom of sacrifice of human beings, and especially divine kings, in order to ensure fertility in the animal and vegetable worlds. Orpheus in his death personated Dionysus and represented the god torn to pieces every year, a ritual performed by the Bacchae from earliest times with a human victim, and later with a bull to symbolise the bull-formed god. The rite included " Omophagia " (eating the flesh of the victim raw) by which the participants believed that they took into themselves the god represented by the victim and thus became inspired with the divine ecstasy.

Orpheus was just as important in Greek religious history as he was for the legends connected with him and for his name as a musician. He was the mythical founder of a school of worship observable from the sixth century B.C. onwards and based partly on the Thraco-Phrygian cult of Dionysus with its orgies, mysteries and purifications, and partly on speculation regarding the character and relations of the various gods which was fostered by contact with Egypt and the Orient and by the closer intercourse between the many tribes and religions within Greece. Until comparatively recently it was believed by scholars that Orphism inculcated abstinence from beans, flesh and certain kinds of fish, and the wearing of special sorts of clothes; its doctrines included the homogeneity of all things living, original sin, the transmigration of souls, and the belief that the soul can reach perfection during its association with a number of bodies: and that when fully purified, it will be freed from the " circle of generation " and will become divine once more, as it was before it first entered a mortal frame. Nowadays, the authorities are not certain about all these factors, but there is no doubt about the importance of Orphism in ancient Greek religion.

The ritual contained libations and sacrifices (without blood), prayer and purification, the symbolisation of sacred myths, the rape of Persephone, the descent into Hades, the rite of "Omophagia", and liturgical formulae to guide the dead person's soul on its way to Hades and to act as credentials to the gods there.

Professor E. R. Dodds suggests a connection between Orpheus and the shamans.[1] He describes a shaman as " a psychically unstable person who has received a call to the religious life". As a result of his call he undergoes rigorous training—solitude and fasting, and possibly a psychological change of sex. From this religious " retreat " he emerges

[1] *The Greeks and the Irrational*, Chapter v. The remainder of this paragraph is either a reproduction or paraphrase of passages from that chapter.

with the power of passing at will into a state of mental dissociation. His own soul is thought to leave its body and travel to distant parts, most often to the spirit world. He may thus be seen simultaneously in different places. From these experiences, narrated by him in extempore song, he derives the skill in divination, religious poetry and magical medicine which make him socially important—for his supernormal wisdom. In Scythia, and probably in Thrace, the Greeks came in contact with peoples influenced by shamanistic culture. That culture—embodying belief in a detachable soul or self which by suitable techniques can be withdrawn from the body even during life, a self which is older than the body and will outlast it—still exists in Siberia. It started in Scythia, crossed the Hellespont into Asiatic Greece, was perhaps combined with some remnants of Minoan tradition surviving in Crete, emigrated to the Far West with Pythagoras and had its last outstanding representative in Empedocles (who was a scientist and a magician as well). Now, Orpheus lived in Thrace, was the worshipper or companion of a god whom the Greeks identified with Apollo; was poet, magician, religious teacher and oracle-giver; like certain legendary shamans in Siberia, he could by his music summon birds and beasts to listen to him; like shamans everywhere, he visited the underworld—and, as so often with shamans, to recover a stolen soul. Moreover, his magical self lived on as a singing head, which continued to give oracles for many years after his death: "that too", says Professor Dodds, "suggests the North: such mantic heads appear in Norse mythology and Irish tradition", and he calls Orpheus "a mythical shaman or prototype of shamans" in Thrace.

This theory, if we accept it, provides a further link between Orpheus, the musician, and ancient religious beliefs.

Clearly, the bond between music and religion was personified in Orpheus, though in musical history of the Christian era—apart from such songs as Sullivan's and Vaughan Williams' settings of Shakespeare's words in *Henry VIII*, Act III, scene I, about "Orpheus with his lute"—he figures chiefly in the story of his love for Eurydice, which gave rise to a number of operas, the two most famous being those of Monteverdi and Gluck.

In Greek mythology, the Muses (or thinkers) were originally nymphs of springs, then goddesses of song, and later, of the various kinds of poetry and of the other arts and sciences. Homer, without giving them names or a number, treated them as goddesses of song, dwelling among the gods on Mount Olympus, where they sang at banquets under the leadership of Apollo. Hesiod (who is thought to have lived in the eighth century B.C.) is the first author in whom we find their names and their number given as nine (in his *Theogony*). Some authorities, however, consider that there were only three Muses at the outset, and that the number was increased to nine through their being arranged in three groups of three persons each in the sacred choruses. Around Zeus' altar they sang of the origin of the world, of gods and men, and of the wonderful deeds of Zeus. They honoured the great heroes, and celebrated the marriages of Cadmus and Peleus, and the death of Achilles. As goddesses of song, they protected those who recognised their superiority, but punished those who were so presumptuous as Thamyrus, the Thracian bard, for example: he claimed to be their equal, and therefore forfeited his sight and power of song.

Certain of the Nine Muses were, in the minds of the ancient Greeks, associated with " music " in our modern sense of the term, as distinct from the wider meaning of it to include all the arts, which we find in Plato. Euterpe was connected with lyric poetry and represented with a double flute. Erato, the Muse of erotic poetry, carried a small lyre. Polyhymnia, a veiled figure in a thoughtful attitude, stood for sacred hymns.

Now, Greek drama, in its beginnings and throughout its course, was closely connected with the national religion, and music was one of the ingredients in the drama.

The worship of Dionysus, introduced into Greece by the Phoenicians as that of the sun-god who was adored with loud cries, and the god of generation and production, became linked with the Dorian religion of the sun-god Apollo. The Pelasgian and Achaean deities of sun and moon were replaced by the Phoenician Dionysus and Demeter. Dionysus, worshipped also as a wine-god, was attended by deified representations of his original devotees, who wore the skin of the goat (" tragos ") sacrificed to him: these were the satyrs. It was out of the related worships of Dionysus, Apollo and Demeter that Greek drama began.

Aristotle tells us in the *Poetics* that tragedy originated from the leaders of the dithyramb. The Greeks in the Dorian states, whose life was arranged on a military basis, used to offer thanks to the gods by means of hymns and dances in public places. Their dances either taught or initiated the movements of soldiers, and their hymns were martial chants. Thus began the " chorus " and its songs or " paeans ", accompanied by the phorminx and later by the flute. From the " paeans " various types of choral dancing arose. Eventually, the dithyramb came into being, at first a song of revellers, probably led by a flute-player and accompanied by other Eastern instruments, in which the birth of Bacchus (=Dionysus) was celebrated in Crete. The "coryphaeus", or leader, most likely represented the wine-god, with his followers carrying the vine-clad "thyrsus". Arion of Lesbos, early in the seventh century B.C., formed the dithyramb into a regular type of poem: the worshippers became a formal chorus of attendants on Dionysus—a chorus of satyrs, i.e. a "tragic" or goat chorus—and Arion invented a suitable kind of music and called the songs "tragedies" or "goat-songs".

The recitation of poetry by wandering minstrels, called "rhapsodes", began in Ionia, and became popular at Attic festivals: their practice of mutually emulating one another in reciting long epic poems resembled theatrical dialogue, and so also did the iambic poems in metres invented by Archilochus in the eighth century and frequently in the form of an address in the second person. The rhapsodes were almost actors, and it was the merging of their types of recitation with the lyrical "tragedies" of Arion that produced the tragic drama proper. Thespis, in the sixth century, is said to have been the inventor of this: he introduced an actor ("hypocrites", literally an "answerer"), who instead of merely alternating his recitations with the songs of the chorus, conducted a kind of dialogue with its leader.

The importance of music in the ancient Greek drama therefore stems, so far as tragedy is concerned, from the vital rôle which it played in the sources from which the drama sprang. Aristotle describes "melody" as the greatest of the pleasurable accessories of tragedy. In the Athenian drama, the choruses were sung to the accompaniment of instruments; and in the dialogues either the actors, though speaking much of the verse, broke into song occasionally, or else their voices continuously rose a little above a sing-song, slightly enhancing the inflexions of speech; in any case, the "aulos" (flute) was played during the action.

Comedy, according to Aristotle, originated from those who led the phallic songs. The first writer of it is said to have been Susarion, born in Doric Megaris, whose natives were celebrated for their coarse humour, which spread from them to their own and other Dorian colonies in Sicily. In the country festivals in honour of Bacchus bands of revellers ("comoi") went about in carts or on foot, carrying the phallic emblem and indulging in amusing ribaldry. This may not sound very religious to us, but it has to be remembered that the phallus, or male organ of generation, was an object of worship in primitive times. From the songs sung on these occasions the Bacchic reveller was called a " comoedus " (" comus "-singer), and from these processions sprang the old Attic comedy. Music continued to play an important part in the comedies of Aristophanes, which almost corresponded to the Gilbert and Sullivan operas of our nineteenth-century England.

Thus, music was associated with religion in the ancient Greek drama, to a strong extent in the case of tragedy, but in a lesser degree as regards comedy. Assuming, as we can, that the character of the music was in some sense appropriate to the words, we can here discern, perhaps, a distinction somewhat similar to the contrast between religious and secular music in later times and among the ancient Hebrews.

It is true that it is the origins of Greek tragedy which were so thoroughly religious: but even in its subsequent development it continued to be bound up with the national religion and therefore its music was also. Sacred myths often formed the basis of its plots, and gods figured in the story and in the " dramatis personae " to an extent rare in the dramatic art of other peoples. This is especially the case in Aeschylus and Sophocles, in whose plays the conflict is often between gods and men or between divine ordinances and human beings, rather than between men themselves. In Euripides, though the part played by deities is still important, the emphasis is starting to shift; there is a tendency towards scepticism regarding the authority of the gods; and the conflict of human wills and characters begins to form the basis of drama as it was subsequently to become in Shakespeare and other writers.

The association of music with religious ritual in ancient Greece is shown also in the rites of the maenads. The Greek cult of Dionysus had a cathartic, or purifying, function—i.e. for effecting cures of the afflicted; and that of the corybantes, who were originally the attendants of the Asiatic mother of the gods, Cybele, was similar. As Professor Dodds[1] says: " Both claimed to operate a catharsis by means of an infectious 'orgiastic' dance accompanied by the same kind of 'orgiastic' music—tunes in the Phrygian mode played on the flute and the kettle-drum." The dancers worked themselves into a state of frenzy, which had, however, it was claimed, an ultimately salutary effect. They were possessed by a god—and the wild dancing and music of the maenads in Euripides' *Bacchae*, and shown, with the musical instruments, on Greek vases, give vivid pictures of women in the grip of this orgiastic religion.

[1] *The Greeks and the Irrational*, Chapter III, p. 78.

Among the excavations at Delphi various inscriptions were found on the walls of the Treasury of the Athenians, and two of them were hymns to Apollo with music. Both refer to the destruction of the Gauls at Delphi and must therefore have been written after 279 B.C. The second was written after 146 B.C., as it calls for a blessing on the Roman Empire. Both hymns mention the Athenian Guild of Artists. These guilds, which included poets, actors, singers and musicians, were to be found in many parts of the Hellenic world. An inscription of about 125 B.C. in the Athenian theatre of Dionysus, who was the patron god of such guilds, gives a decree of the Amphictyonic Council at Delphi that the Guild of Artists was to enjoy certain privileges throughout Greece, unless the Romans objected. Later, the Roman emperors became patrons jointly with Dionysus, and the guilds became very powerful. They controlled all the music at the great festivals, and therefore indirectly had an influence on the music of the early Christian Church.

In very early times in Italy, a mixture of dance, song, speech and dialogue was accompanied by the music of the flute (" tibia ") at religious celebrations, especially weddings. The Salii, who were a college of priests at Rome dedicated by King Numa to the service of Mars, used to carry in procession the " ancilia " (or copies of the sacred shield which was said to have fallen from heaven) and sang and danced as they moved about the city. Broadly speaking, however, though the Romans doubtless had their own folk-songs, ancient Roman music was largely Greek music transplanted to Rome and developed there. Music was used in Rome on all public occasions, whether religious or theatrical, but there was no difference between sacred and secular music.

The association of music with worship among the ancient Hebrews is mentioned in countless passages of the Old Testament. The invention of musical instruments is attributed in Genesis iv, 21, to Jubal, " the father of all such as handle the harp and organ "; and the reference to " songs, with tabret and with harp " in Genesis xxxi, 27, shows that the people were familiar with the art before their sojourn in Egypt. Philo, the Alexandrian Jew, tells us that the Egyptian priests taught Moses metre and music, in addition to arithmetic and geometry. Instances of the religious use of instruments—cornet, cymbal, harp, psaltery, timbrel and trumpet—as well as of singing, abound in the books of Exodus, Numbers, Chronicles and Nehemiah.

Exodus xv tells of the great song of thanksgiving which Moses and the children of Israel sang to the Lord after the crossing of the Red Sea; and how Miriam, the prophetess, took a timbrel in her hand and all the women went out after her with timbrels and with dances and sang to the Lord.

The Shofar, or ram's horn, is still blown in the synagogue services, several times at the Festival of New Year and at the end of the Day of Atonement, in accordance with the institution set up in Leviticus xxv, 8–10, and Numbers xxix, 1. In the Authorised Version it is translated " trumpet ".

Three Old Testament passages describing the religious power of music are worth quoting:

(1) In *I Samuel, x*, 5, 6, Samuel utters these words in addressing Saul after anointing him:

" After that thou shalt come to the hill of God, where is the garrison of the Philistines: and it shall come to pass, when thou art come thither to the city, that thou shalt meet a company of prophets coming down from the high place with a psaltery, and a tabret, and a pipe, and a harp, before them; and they shall prophesy."

(2) *Ibid., xvi*, 15–16: " And Saul's servants said unto him, Behold now, an evil spirit from God troubleth thee. Let our lord now command thy servants, which are before thee, to seek out a man who is a cunning player on an harp: and it shall come to pass, when the evil spirit from God is upon thee, that he shall play with his hand, and thou shalt be well." Saul assented, and they brought to him David, who " took an harp, and played with his hand: so Saul was refreshed, and was well, and the evil spirit departed from him " (*ibid., xvi*, 23).

(3) *II Kings, iii*, 15. Elisha said " But now bring me a minstrel. And it came to pass, when the minstrel played, that the hand of the Lord came upon him."

I Chronicles xiii tells how David fetched the Ark with great solemnity from Kirjath-jearim, and how he " and all Israel played before God with all their might, and with singing, and with harps, and with psalteries, and with timbrels, and with cymbals, and with trumpets." In Chapter xv we hear of the singers and instrumentalists who accompanied the bringing-up of the Ark from the house of Obed-edom to the tent pitched by David. Three singers apparently led the choir and " were appointed to sound with cymbals of brass "; and Chenaniah, chief of the Levites, was " the master of the song " and " instructed about it, because he was skilful ". The next chapter describes the service of song with instruments, and sets out the words of the psalm of thanksgiving to the Lord for the victories over the Philistines and for His " marvellous works among all nations".

In I Chronicles xxiii, 5, we read how, at the census of the Levites, David, who, in his old age, had made his son, Solomon, king over Israel, selected 4,000 to perform the religious music; and Chapter xxv gives details of this enormous choir and orchestra.

After David's death, Solomon built the great Temple at Jerusalem, and its consecration was celebrated with sacred music rendered by " the Levites which were singers . . . with their sons and their brethren . . . having cymbals and psalteries and harps . . . and with them an hundred and twenty priests sounding with trumpets " (II Chronicles v, 12–13; vii, 6).

After the death of Solomon and the partition of the kingdom, and during the exile, the liturgical music was maintained, and Nehemiah vii, 44, records that 148 singers of the Asaph family came back from Babylon; chapters xi, 17–23, and xii, 27–29, show that the musical services were restored at Jerusalem (cf. Ezra iii, 10–11): they continued until the destruction of the Temple under the Emperor Titus.

The Psalms, both those written by David and those credibly attributed by scholars to other hands, were chiefly sung, and some were accompanied by stringed instruments (" Neginah " or " Neginoth " in the title), and others by wind instruments (" Nehiloth "). Some titles are probably the names of tunes, e.g. " The hind of the morning " (Psalm xxii), " Destroy not " (Psalms lvii–lix; lxxv), " The silent dove of them that are afar off" (Psalm lvi), and " Lilies " (Psalms xlv, lxix).

The book of Daniel (iii, 5–15) in a famous passage describes the various kinds of instruments which were used by the heathen, also, in worshipping the golden image and at the sound of which Nebuchadnezzar bade Shadrach, Meshach and Abed-nego worship it too and serve his gods: " the cornet, flute, harp, sackbut, psaltery, dulcimer and all kinds of music."

Thus we find that in various civilisations throughout the pre-Christian era, music, though it had many secular uses—warlike, festal or domestic—was intimately bound up with religious observance.

3

AS TIME WENT ON

A STUDY of the ethics of so-called "primitive" tribes shows that some of them regarded many, or even most, of their rules of life as having a supernatural sanction, whilst others did not do anything of the kind. Professor A. Macbeath, in his book *Experiments in Living*,[1] draws the conclusion that morality is in origin and authority independent of religion. To those who have been brought up in the Christian or Jewish faiths this notion seeems strange at first sight, but among the earliest Greeks there was no vital bond between theology and morality. Gods were powerful and had to be placated by sacrifice; some might protect men, but others had what seem to us today very obvious human failings and vices. Among the Greeks, it was only later, and gradually, that religion and ethics became linked together, and in Plato's eyes the conception of a god who does wrong is completely fallacious; hence his reluctant banishment of the poets, including even Homer, from his ideal Republic, for presenting unworthy stories about Divine Beings.

It is therefore relevant to the question of the relationship between music and religion to recall that Plato[2] would only admit art to his Republic in so far as it had an ethical purpose. For instance, the contents, form and style of poetry must be such as would produce honest, brave and steadfast characters in the children to whom it was taught. Beauty, harmony and rhythm in nature corresponded to, and resulted in, grace and harmony in the soul, and by constant association with beautiful things the souls of children would be unconsciously shaped to the beauty of reason. Applying this principle to the art of music (in its narrower, modern meaning), Plato admitted only two modes: "one will fittingly imitate the tones and accents of a man brave in battle and in every difficult and dangerous task; the other would imitate a man in the actions of peace, where his choice has scope and

[1] A study of the Nature and Foundations of Ethics or Morals in the light of recent work in social anthropology. The Gifford Lectures for 1948-9, delivered in the University of St. Andrews (MacMillan).

[2] In this paragraph I am indebted to A. D. Lindsay's introduction to and translation of Plato's *Republic*.

he is free from compulsion; when he is persuading or entreating a god in prayer, or a man by instruction and advice . . . ; it shall imitate a man who . . . is ever prudent and restrained." Moreover, the rhythms of music must be those " of an orderly and brave life".

The theme of the relationship between religion, or morality, and music, recurs constantly throughout history. For the Neo-Pythagoreans, represented chiefly by Nicomachus of Gerasa in the second century A.D., music and its acoustical laws were theological and metaphysical symbols; " the music of the spheres " in their revolutions consisted of eight melodies, the ninth being the diapason; music was solely a means of religious experience, not an end in itself. Philo of Alexandria utterly rejected the notion of music as giving pleasure to the senses. The Neo-Platonists Plotinus and Porphyry, in the third century A.D., similarly regarded it solely as an approach to the Divine through a condition of " ecstasy " or " enthusiasm", and objected to the secular music performed in the theatre and at banquets. Their attitude was warmly approved by the Fathers of the Church, for example St. John Chrysostom, who was Bishop of Constantinople at the close of the fourth and the beginning of the fifth centuries. Church music should, in their view, help to lift the souls of men towards God: it should not entertain them.

Now, the New Testament, like the Old, treated music as sacred. Whether the " Magnificat " uttered by Mary before the birth of Jesus, and the words of the heavenly host to the shepherds just after that event, were spoken or sung (St. Luke i, 46–55; ii, 13 and 14), it is recorded in St. Matthew xxvi, 30 and St. Mark xiv, 26 that after the Last Supper our Lord and the disciples sang a hymn. James (v, 13) bids his readers sing psalms when they are merry, and St. Paul enjoins the Ephesians (v, 19) to speak to themselves " in psalms and hymns and spiritual songs, singing and making melody in your heart to the Lord"; similarly he tells the Colossians (iii, 16) to teach and admonish one another " in psalms and hymns and spiritual songs, singing with grace in your hearts to the Lord".

Although the early Christians inherited the Hebrew use of music in ritual and received these specific dedications of the art to the worship of God, the Church soon found itself involved in a problem, which in one form or another persisted through the Middle Ages. Music affected the soul and must be employed for truly religious purposes; yet it did exert a sensuous, carnal influence which must be resisted.

St. Augustine (A.D. 354–430), in his Confessions, expressed this conflict in eloquent words:[1]

> So often as I call to mind the tears I shed at the hearing of Thy Church songs, in the beginning of my recovered faith, yea, and at this very time, whenas I am moved not with the singing, but with the thing sung (when namely they are set off with a clear and suitable modulation), I then acknowledge the great use of this institution. Thus float I between peril and pleasure, and an approved profitable custom: inclined the more (though herein I pronounce no irrevocable opinion) to allow of the old usage of singing in the Church; that so by the delight taken in at the ears, the weaker minds be roused up into some feeling of devotion. And yet again, so oft as it befalls me to be moved with the voice rather than with the ditty, I confess myself to have grievously offended: at which time I wish rather not to have heard the music.

The Fathers of the Church, and those who followed them, thus felt bound to resist the intrusion of secular music into worship. We today may find it difficult to sympathise with this austere attitude, but without it, plainchant (which is generally assumed to have been systematised by St. Gregory about the end of the sixth century) would not have retained its simple, devout beauty, with its rhythms those of speech, not metrical or dance-rhythms, and its monodic melody untrammelled by any accompaniment of other voices or of instruments. St. Bernard of Clairvaux, in the twelfth century, wrote of it: "Let the chant be full of gravity; let it be neither worldly, nor too rude and poor . . . Let it be sweet, yet without levity, and, whilst it pleases the ear, let it move the heart. It should alleviate sadness, and calm the angry spirit. It should not contradict the sense of the words, but rather enhance it. For it is no slight loss of spiritual grace to be distracted from the profit of the sense by the beauty of the chant, and to have our attention drawn to a mere vocal display, when we ought to be thinking of what is sung."

Thus, more than 700 years after St. Augustine, we find St. Bernard giving expression to that same conflict which was felt to exist between aesthetic beauty and religious emotion—even though he was writing about so pure a form of music as plainchant, which contained no admixture of secular elements.[2]

[1] Translated by William Watts (Loeb Classical Library), Book 10, Chapter xxxiii, p. 165.

[2] Father G. B. Chambers, in his book, *Folksong-Plainsong*, suggests that plainchant itself originated in folk-song. However that may be, as time went

It is not known for certain at what stage men discovered the pleasing effects obtainable from the simultaneous performance of notes of different pitch; the division of men's voices into tenor and bass, which nature imposed, made it also easier for them to sing the same chant at the pitch that suited them. Thus the earliest " organum " or polyphony in the Church was in two parts, with the Gregorian melody simply reproduced at an interval below. Later on, it came to be repeated a fourth above and an octave below. In turn, this led to "descant", which may be said to have corresponded to the Gothic cathedrals with their soaring, elaborate architecture in contrast to the broad, simple Romanesque style: counter-melodies were composed to be sung at the same time as the main chant, and eventually popular melodies from songs and dances outside the Church began to encroach into liturgical music. Once this tendency started, it became impossible to preserve a rigid separation between sacred and secular music.

Polyphonic music, through the art of such masters as Dunstable, Dufay and Josquin des Prés, enriched the Catholic liturgy so much that when the Council of Trent, convened in the middle of the sixteenth century to consolidate the results of Catholic Reform, came to deliberate about the state of church music, it resisted the attempt of its more extreme members who wanted to eliminate polyphonic music entirely, and contented itself with recommending that anything inconsistent with the dignity of the ritual should be avoided. Thus Palestrina could consecrate his art to church worship through the medium of polyphony. Yet even he made use of a secular song, *L'Homme armé*, and set it to sacred words, as had been done by other composers, including Dufay, before his time. For the most part, however, his liturgical compositions had no secular element in them whatsoever: employing either plainchant melodies or those of his own invention, and treating them contrapuntally, he created music of the utmost purity, tenderness and devotion.

No music ever written is more intensely religious than that of Palestrina. The vast bulk of it is church music, but he was also a composer of beautiful secular madrigals, which seem, as it were, to have fertilised the seraphic quality of his liturgical compositions with a warmth of human emotion, so that his Masses, culminating in the great *Missa Papae Marcelli*, his motets, his settings of the *Stabat Mater*,

---

on it became so completely imbued with the character of the liturgy that any remote secular origins were not intrinsically discernible in it.

of the Lamentations of Jeremiah and of the Song of Songs, are not the remote utterances of some disembodied spirit, but the fervent expressions of the beliefs of a deeply devotional man. His art reflects the unquestioning faith of a soul no less serene than Bach's; but in Bach there was a strong sense of the mystery of things, as we can tell, for instance, from his setting of the " Et Incarnatus " in the B minor Mass and parts of the St. Matthew Passion. Palestrina's music diffuses into our minds a celestial, yet human, radiance.

Both Palestrina and his Spanish contemporary Vittoria, whose motets are deeply religious in feeling, were children of the Renaissance more as a matter of chronology than of character. Orlandus Lassus, the great Flemish composer of the same period, was a more typical offspring of the Renaissance: it was only in the midst of his career that he devoted his art to the Catholic Counter-Reformation, and even then he employed secular melodies in his liturgical works, but imbued them with a devotional spirit.

Carols have always stood, as it were, on the borderline between liturgical and secular music. Today we associate them mainly with Christmas, and they are sung either in church services in place of hymns or by parties of singers in the streets. But in the Middle Ages they dealt not only with the Nativity but also with subjects such as morals, allegory, politics and agriculture. Dr. R. L. Greene in *The Early English Carols* defined the carol up to 1550 as " a song on any subject composed of uniform stanzas and provided with a burden", and he dates the form from about 1350. The performers used to dance to it, and the burden (as contrasted with the verse which told the story) was the point at which they started to dance and was a distinct part of the whole. Byrd's 1589 series of madrigals contained one—" From Virgin's womb "—which he rightly described as " a carowle for Christmas Day", as it contained a separate burden, " Rejoice, rejoice".

The relationship between music and religion had naturally taken a different turn outside the Catholic Church from the time of Luther onwards. He himself composed popular melodies as well as chorales, though the Reformed Church still included in its services plainchant and motets in the old style; but the " chorale concertato " in the Lutheran liturgy, containing an instrumental continuo part which was no longer optional as it had been in the motet, but obligatory, was a significant feature: for it was symptomatic of the increasing importance of instrumental music.

Heinrich Schütz, in the seventeenth century, who had set the Psalms to music in the declamatory style which he had learnt from his first visit to Italy, embodied instrumental parts in the second and third groups of his *Symphoniae Sacrae*, such as the " Lament for David over Absalom " (for bass solo with four trombones), " Saul, Saul, was verfolgst du mich? " (for six soloists, two choruses, two violins and organ), and " Mein Sohn, warum hast du uns das gethan? " Similarly his noble oratorio *The Story of the Resurrection of Jesus Christ* is both vocal and instrumental. In his later settings of the Passions, however, he gave up the use of instruments. His art combines the merits of the new dramatic character that was then entering into religious music with those of the older polyphonic style—thereby anticipating, in their different ways, the work of Bach and Handel.

Meanwhile, Monteverdi, one of the greatest and most revolutionary composers of opera and a supreme master of the madrigal, was almost equally eminent as a creator of devotional art. He wrote a great deal of church music; his setting of the Vespers (1610) was, however, not meant for liturgical purposes, but was a " concerto ecclesiastico ". It is therefore not surprising that it contains an interesting combination of styles. The " Nigra sum "—both music and words—is completely secular in character and fits oddly into a mainly religious composition: " Nigra sum, sed formosa, filia Jerusalem: ideo dilexit me Rex et introduxit me in cubiculum suum " (" I am dark, yet comely: a daughter of Jerusalem; therefore hath the King loved me and admitted me to his couch "). The coloratura and trills which figure, for instance, in the "Duo Seraphim" and elsewhere, are also distinctly operatic in flavour. But most of the music is not only spiritual, but devotional in essence. Thus in general the work might be said to be midway between the completely liturgical music of Palestrina or Byrd or the entirely religious creations of Bach on the one hand and the distinctly operatic, secular-flavoured *Stabat Mater* of Rossini on the other. Poles though they are apart, Verdi's *Requiem*, which combines drama with religion and is, like Monteverdi's *Vespers*, the work of a man chiefly noted for composing operas, has this in common with it, that both were mainly, but not completely, devotional in character. Monteverdi's later liturgical works—settings of the Mass and motets—were mostly less devout in style, but the whole " Magnificat " section of the Vespers is serenely religious, with no admixture of operatic flavour.

The Reformation affected music in England more vitally than in any other country. The dissolution of the monasteries, each of which had a regular choir and one or more organists, involved a great destruction of music. Yet this period and that which followed was an age of great English composers, who reacted to the political-religious upheaval in the most varied ways. John Taverner, after composing large quantities of Catholic church music, turned into a violent persecutor of monasteries and, according to John Foxe (author of *Actes and Monuments*) "repented him very much that he had made Songes to Popish Ditties in the time of his blindness". Merbecke, organist of St. George's Chapel, Windsor, and one of the earliest composers of music for the Anglican liturgy, subsequently went so far as to denounce all church music as "vanity" and thenceforward devoted himself to writing pamphlets. Christopher Tye wrote a six-part Mass called *Euge Bone* in traditional polyphonic form, but his work *The Acts of the Apostles* was one of the first important musical products of the Reformation. Thomas Tallis, having begun as a creator of Roman Catholic church music, had no difficulty in switching over to the greater simplicity of the Protestant style. William Byrd, the greatest English composer of this "Golden Age", was a Roman Catholic who produced superb Masses and motets for his own Church, and Queen Elizabeth was wise enough not to interfere with him, but the remarkable thing is that he also composed a great deal for the Reformed Church, including the Great Service, one of his finest works. He has been described as an English Palestrina, but the expression has no more meaning than similar ones applied to other creative geniuses have had. He was even more versatile than the great Italian, for Byrd was a supreme master of every form of the art which existed in his day, apart from opera which only came into existence in Italy in the later part of his life: madrigals and other secular works for voices, instrumental compositions, and liturgical music of all kinds. His works equal those of Palestrina in profundity and devotional feeling, but differ from them in style. Tallis and Orlando Gibbons are the only English composers among his contemporaries who approached his level as a composer of liturgical art. Unlike the other composers mentioned, all Gibbons' sacred works were written only for the ritual of the English Church.

From the standpoint of musical history, however, one of the most important features of this period both in England and on the Continent was the rise of instrumental music unconnected with voices. The delightful pieces for virginal by Byrd, Bull, Morley, Philips, Tallis and Dowland contained in the Fitzwilliam book and Lady Nevill's book, and the consorts for viols or other instruments, which constituted the chamber music of those days, the instrumental "canzone", the polyphonic "ricercar", its more elaborate successor the "fantasy", and the development of the "toccata" from the drum accompaniments of the late medieval brass fanfares into elaborate keyboard pieces, show how instrumental music had advanced in variety and scope from the dances, or even suites of dances, of an earlier age. From the sixteenth century onwards—and particularly from the beginning of the seventeenth century when opera began in Italy and thus produced the operatic overture which paved the way for the symphonies of the future—instrumental art gradually acquired an importance equal to that of vocal music. And just as music for voices had been both sacred and secular, so instrumental music might evince a spiritual quality or not, according to its intrinsic nature.

In the past, even allowing for the beauty and variety of the madrigals and other secular vocal forms produced on the continent of Europe and in England, most of the finest music had been liturgical, and the character of that which was used for the purposes of ritual was a matter for the Church to control according to its convictions or its ability to do so. But in future, the relationship between music and religion, which had been largely internal to the Church, was to assume a more complex shape because instrumental art began to make a claim to men's attention commensurate with that of music for voices. The degrees in which various vocal compositions are sacred in character continue to present a never-ending problem; but the question whether this or that purely instrumental work reveals the finger of God is even more subtle, because without the presence of words which can at least guide us as to the composer's intentions, we have to deal with music as an entirely distinct language. All music, except that which is directly imitative of actual sounds in the external world, is independent: even when it is expressing the meaning of words, it can be no more than appropriate to the sense of them; but where it is not tied to words at all, its " meaning " is inextricably wrapt up in the music itself.[1]

[1] A fuller account of the independence of music is contained in Chapter iii of my book *The Soul of Music*.

4

SAINT CECILIA

IN considering the relationship between music and religion down to the time of the Reformation, I have not hitherto mentioned St. Cecilia, because the period at which she was first regarded as the patron saint of music is uncertain. She was a girl of noble Roman birth, educated as a Christian, and vowed to lead a celibate life and to devote herself to religious service. However, her parents forced her to marry Valerianus, a noble young Roman pagan, but by her strength of character she not only persuaded him to respect her vow but converted him and his brother to Christianity. All three were therefore brought before the pagan authorities, and as they refused to give up their faith, were condemned to death. The two men were beheaded, and Cecilia was placed in a dry bath with fire below it, but as she did not die as quickly as her persecutors wished, her head also was cut off. These events are now thought to have occurred, not at Rome about A.D. 230 under the Emperor Alexander Severus, as was believed at one time, but in Sicily under Marcus Aurelius between 176 and 180. A church in her honour at Rome existed from about the fourth century, and her remains, together with those of Valerianus, his brother, and other martyrs, were transferred to it in 821. The church was repaired and richly ornamented in 1599, when a monument to St. Cecilia was built there.

Early writers do not refer to her musical skill,[1] and even a long Italian poem by Castelletti, " La trionfatrice Cecilia, vergine e martire Romana", written in 1594, says nothing about it. Yet in 1502 a musical society had been founded at Louvain under the patronage of St. Cecilia. Legends tells that an angel who visited her was attracted to earth by her lovely singing, and that she praised God by instrumental as well as vocal music. This last feature is significant, for it links both forms of the art to religion in the person of a saint and martyr.

For hundreds of years Cecilia has been the patron saint of music and the blind in the Roman Catholic Church, and Christian music-lovers

[1] In the Second Nun's Tale, which contains the story of her life, the only reference which Chaucer makes to music is to the organ's melody played at her wedding (l. 134).

have united in honouring her on November 22nd by musical performances, sometimes under the auspices of societies formed expressly for the purpose. "Le Puy de Musique", the earliest of these which has been traced, was formed at Evreux in Normandy on October 12th, 1570: services with music were held in the cathedral, and a banquet took place at which prizes were given for the best motets, airs, sonnets and part-songs. Orlandus Lassus was one of the prize-winners. In London, in 1683, "The Musical Society" started holding annual celebrations on St. Cecilia's day, with choral and orchestral performances forming part of a service in church, followed by a concert, usually in Stationers' Hall, where an ode in praise of music was performed, the words and the composition being specially written for the occasion. The celebrations ultimately became less frequent, but were revived by the Musicians' Company in London in 1903. Sir Henry Wood fostered the practice of honouring St. Cecilia regularly each November, and the custom has continued since his death. London has not been the only centre for these festivities in England, for Oxford, Winchester, Gloucester, Devizes and Salisbury have also played their part, and at various times the day has been celebrated musically in Edinburgh, Dublin, Paris and elsewhere in France, Italy and Germany. The Cecilia Society, of Boston, Massachusetts, formed in 1874, has paid homage to the saint from whom it took its name by giving its members the opportunity of hearing modern choral compositions particularly.

Odes for the English celebrations of St. Cecilia's day have been composed at different stages of history by Purcell, Handel, Boyce, Samuel Wesley, Parry, Gerald Finzi, Benjamin Britten and others.

Purcell wrote two Cecilian odes: "Welcome to all the pleasures" (1683), to words by Christopher Fishburn, is a delightful little work, though inevitably overshadowed by "Hail, Bright Cecilia" (1692), which is one of his most vivid and splendid creations, with its impressive choruses and its delicate and beautiful solo parts. This was set to an ode by Nicholas Brady, which acclaims Music as "Nature's voice" and "soul of the world", pays homage to Cecilia as Music's "great patroness" and speaks of it as her "celestial art".

Handel composed magnificent music for both of the odes of Dryden which were associated with the saint. *Alexander's Feast*, or *The Power of Music* (written in 1697 and set by Handel in 1737) was called by the poet an ode in honour of St. Cecilia's day, but most of it tells of the songs which Timotheus sang to the lyre " amid the tuneful choir " at the triumphant feast of Alexander the Great; it is only towards the end that we read:

> At last divine Cecilia came,
> Inventress of the vocal frame;
> The sweet enthusiast, from her sacred store,
> Enlarged the former narrow bounds,
> And added length to solemn sounds,
> With nature's mother-wit, and arts unknown before.
> Let old Timotheus yield the prize,
> Or both divide the crown;
> He raised a mortal to the skies,
> She drew an angel down.

Dryden's earlier *Song for St. Cecilia's Day* (1687) was the subject of Handel's later ode (1739) and is short enough to be quoted in full:

> From harmony, from heavenly harmony,
> This universal frame began:
> When nature underneath a heap
> Of jarring atoms lay,
> And could not heave her head,
> The tuneful voice was heard from high,
> Arise, ye more than dead.
> Then cold, and hot, and moist, and dry,
> In order to their stations leap,
> And Music's power obey.
> From harmony, from heavenly harmony,
> This universal frame began:
> From harmony to harmony,
> Through all the compass of the notes it ran,
> The diapason closing full in Man.
>
> What passion cannot Music raise and quell?
> When Jubal struck the chorded shell,
> His listening brethen stood around,
> And, wondering, on their faces fell
> To worship that celestial sound.
> Less than a God they thought there could not dwell
> Within the hollow of that shell,
> That spoke so sweetly and so well.
> What passion cannot Music raise and quell?
>
> The trumpet's loud clangor
> Excites us to arms,
> With shrill notes of anger,
> And mortal alarms.

The double double double beat
Of the thundering drum
Cries, hark! the foes come;
Charge, charge, 'tis too late to retreat.

The soft complaining flute
In dying notes discovers
The woes of hapless lovers,
Whose dirge is whisper'd by the warbling lute.
Sharp violins proclaim
Their jealous pangs, and desperation,
Fury, frantic indignation,
Depth of pains, and height of passion,
For the fair, disdainful dame.

But oh! what art can teach,
What human voice can reach,
The sacred organ's praise?
Notes inspiring holy love,
Notes that wing their heavenly ways
To mend the choirs above.

Orpheus could lead the savage race;
And trees uplifted left their place,
Sequacious of the lyre:
But bright Cecilia raised the wonder higher:
When to her organ vocal breath was given,
An angel heard, and straight appear'd
Mistaking earth for heaven.

Grand Chorus
As from the power of sacred lays
The spheres began to move,
And sung the great Creator's praise
To all the bless'd above;
So when the last and dreadful hour
This crumbling pageant shall devour,
The trumpet shall be heard on high,
The dead shall live, the living die,
And Music shall untune the sky.

Handel set this ode to vivid, grand and varied music, for soprano and tenor soloists, chorus, organ and orchestra: the latter has an important part to play throughout, including a long overture in three sections.

Pope also wrote an *Ode on St. Cecilia's Day*, which was set to music, among others by Parry, for soloists, chorus and orchestra in 1889. In it he invokes the Nine Muses, dwells on the soothing effect of music and its power of encouraging and exalting the spirit, and tells the story of Orpheus and Eurydice. He concludes with lines which contain an echo of Dryden:

> Of Orpheus now no more let Poets tell,
> To bright Cecilia greater power is given;
> His raised a shade from hell,
> Hers lifts the soul to heaven.

In our own day, the saint has been celebrated by Gerald Finzi and Benjamin Britten. Finzi's Ceremonial Ode *For St. Cecilia*, with words by Edmund Blunden, appeared in 1947: it opens exultantly in praise of the saint, pays homage to Byrd, Dowland, Purcell and other English musicians, and tells that man martyred Cecilia, yet is himself comforted by her in his own martyrdom; at the end it returns to the joyful mood of the beginning. Britten's music is a choral setting of the *Hymn to St. Cecilia* by W. H. Auden. It begins:

> In a garden shady this holy lady
> With reverent cadence and subtle psalm,
> Like a black swan as death came on
> Poured forth her song in perfect calm:
> And by ocean's margin this innocent virgin
> Constructed an organ to enlarge her prayer,
> And notes tremendous from her great engine
> Thundered out on the Roman air.

In a later stanza, the poet invokes the saint by name:

> Blessed Cecilia, appear in visions
> To all musicians, appear and inspire:
> Translated Daughter, come down and startle
> Composing mortals with immortal fire.

Elsewhere, the words are secular in character. The music is very original and beautiful; though modern in idiom, it has its roots in the past; in some passages, the voices imitate instruments—violin, flute, or drums.

The words of these odes by Fishburn, Brady, Dryden and Pope are not, for the most part, actually devotional, nor is the music composed for them. Blunden's is somewhat more so, Finzi's setting matches it in character, and they alone treat of Cecilia's martyrdom—in moving accents. In general, the poets and composers seem to have regarded her as having shown the divinity which inspired her by blessing mankind with the gift of music, without its being necessary for them to dwell on the martyrdom which won her sainthood.

The true significance of Cecilia for the relationship between music and religion is this: that whether the compositions directly associated with her are specifically devotional or not, she unites in herself a double personality, on the one hand a tremendously brave and devout woman, who died rather than renounce her faith, and, on the other, the patron saint of vocal and instrumental art. Thus the godlike nature of great music, both that which is avowedly "sacred" and that which is not, reflects the character of music's own votaress who lived about 1,800 years ago.

5

THE DIVINITY OF BEAUTY

PURCELL has been described[1] as a secular, even a pagan, composer. It is admitted that, having been born the son of a Gentleman of the Chapel Royal and himself sung there as a choirboy, he eventually became organist of Westminster Abbey and composed a great deal of church music—anthems, settings of the " Te Deum " and the " Jubilate "—but it is said that he only had one style, a secular style. King Charles did not like the old Catholic music, nor the Puritan singing of psalms. He wanted cheerful tunes to which he could beat time in church; he loved the theatre, and if music for worship was like that of the stage, so much the better. Pelham Humphry, who had become " master of the children " of the Chapel Royal, had been sent by Charles to Paris to study foreign ways, and had learnt much from Lulli who was to become famous as a great operatic composer even if no operas of his had been produced up to that time; Humphry returned, according to Pepys, " mighty great " with the King, and was thus encouraged to introduce into religious worship a style of music that would be more attractive in Charles' ears. Humphry died prematurely when Purcell was only sixteen, and as John Blow, who succeeded him, knew practically nothing about the foreign methods that Humphry had acquired, it was clearly from Humphry that Purcell learnt them.

Nevertheless, Purcell's liturgical music does seem to us today to be intrinsically religious. At times it is extremely moving—for instance, his setting of the words " Thou art he that took me out of my mother's womb " in the anthem " In thee, O Lord, do I put my trust ". Elsewhere it expresses great happiness or thanksgiving, and does so in music which is supremely apt for the words. If it were trivial, insincere, or frivolous (as some of his more austere comtemporaries in the Church contended), then the accusation of composing secular music for religious purposes might have been justified. It is truer to say that a great deal of his non-liturgical work was, in the broader sense of the term, sacred.

This raises a much deeper question than that of the ordinary distinc-

[1] e.g. by John F. Runciman in *Purcell* (Bell's Miniature Series of Musicians), p. 10.

tion between sacred and secular—the question of the real relationship between beauty and divinity, which concerns not only music but other arts, and not only art but nature.

Science can tell us how the colours of a sunset are formed, how the rainbow comes to assume its particular pattern, or why the trees and grass and hills in a landscape show their varied shades of green in an almost endless pageant of subtleties against a background of sky ranging from deep blue overhead to a distant, delicate paleness, with clouds now white and fleecy, now grey and solemn. But it cannot explain the splendour of the sunset, the charm of the rainbow, or the beauty of the landscape. Nor are these mere attributes of our minds, for if the landscape's beauty were something put into it by human intelligence, we could not account for the fact that this loveliness is recognised by the minds of millions, each working independently, and must therefore have an existence external to them. Beauty is not solely in the eye of the beholder. It is an attribute of the object itself, not explicable by science and not, on the other hand, merely the result of the application of men's intelligence to it.

A short digression is necessary on this subject of the objectivity of beauty, which is one of the main contentions in Harold Osborne's book, *Theory of Beauty*. (Actually he is discussing artistic beauty, but if his argument is sound, it applies with even greater force to the beauty of nature.) "Education of taste", he says (p. 89), "is justified only on the supposition that one man's taste and appreciation is superior to another's. . . . Unless this were presumed, all educational . . . activities would be an impertinent endeavour to foist one's own emotional reactions upon others. . . . That presumption, which is the justification of education in relation to beauty and its appreciation, is implicitly denied in the subjective theory of beauty." He says that in the enjoyment of beautiful things there is a sort of emotional state, not evoked by other things; and that such an emotional state *ought* to be experienced only towards certain objects. "There is presumed to be in the appreciation of beauty a rightness or appropriateness between the response and the object towards which the response is experienced." And this "notion of rightness or appropriateness implies that there is in the beautiful object some quality, which it possesses in itself, which renders certain reactions appropriate and certain others inappropriate, in virtue of which it *ought to control* the reactions of the appreciator. Such a view of beauty is objective in that the beauty of any object for any observer does not depend upon the emotions which he does actually experience towards it, but upon the response which he ought ideally to experience towards it. And the qualities of the object itself determine what this response ought ideally to be."

Now, in the case of music, all that a sound-producer does is to cause vibrations, which are transmitted through the air, received by the ear and communicated to the brain, which transforms them into sound. It might therefore be argued that, as sound does not exist in the absence of ears and a brain to change the vibrations into sound, music itself has no objective existence but only a subjective one and therefore that musical beauty, in turn, must be subjective. This contention, however, would be fallacious. For the sounds have not really been created by the brain of the recipient, but previously by the sender of the vibrations, and he—the performer—in turn, has been told by the composer by means of symbols what to sing or play. Thus the composer has originated the cause of the sounds and is the real creator of the music. And once he has created it, that music and its beauty remain objective realities, ready to be made audible by the action of performers and listeners.

To say at this stage of our argument that the beauty of nature is divine would be begging the question, when we are trying to ascertain whether there is such a thing as divinity; and to call it spiritual would be to employ a term which is more usually applied to human qualities, or to superhuman influences, assuming that we believe that there are such things. Yet, as natural science has nothing to do with it, and as, according to the argument set out above, it exists objectively, outside our minds, we are led to the conclusion that it is evidence of the reality of a Power which is neither materialistic nor human.

The assertion that beauty is an indication of the existence of God does present certain difficulties, but these are not insuperable. The cynic may ask whether it is not rather absurd to suggest that there is anything divine in the beauty of the colour of port-wine or in the good looks of a lovely woman. On the contrary, he will say, port is just deep red and attractive to the eye (and to the palate), and the woman's features, so far from having anything divine about them, stimulate a man's sexual appetite. I accept his challenge. The colour of the wine does attract us physically, but that does not prevent its beauty, as such, from being divine in essence, any more than the sensuous attractiveness, to our ears, of the sounds produced by the four instruments in Beethoven's first Razoumovsky Quartet prevents its beauty from being essentially divine. The fact that the woman's beauty arouses sexual desires in a man is quite distinct from her beauty itself: the latter may be recognised equally by a man who is not attracted to her sexually at all or by another woman: its physical effect on certain men affords no reason why it should not in itself be divine. Moreover, a woman's beauty is affected by her character. Her features may be physically lovely—and to that extent a manifestation of divinity—but their loveliness may be impaired by a hardness of expression in the mouth or a cruel look in the eyes, which correspondingly indicates a falling-away from the divine nature. The most beautiful woman is one who combines loveliness of features with sweetness of expression, so that her outward beauty becomes a symbol of an inward and spiritual grace, and she is adored by her lover with body and soul. This kind of conception is to be found in two of Paul Heyse's poems in the *Italienisches Liederbuch*, which were set to music by Hugo Wolf. In "Ihr seid die Allerschönste" the lover compares his beloved's beauty to that of the cathedrals of Orvieto and Siena, and Wolf expresses this thought in solemn and noble music. In "Gesegnet sei, durch den die Welt entstund", the lover calls the Lord blessed for having created the world—the sea, the ships, Paradise, and the beauty of his beloved's face: Wolf makes a sudden "pianissimo" at the final words, with the voice nevertheless going up in the scale: it is a striking illustration of the divinity of a woman's loveliness.

The conception of the divinity of natural beauty recurs in literature from Biblical times to the present day.

The words of the psalmist: "The heavens declare the glory of God And the firmament showeth his handiwork" found later a counterpart in the Benedicite of the Prayer Book which calls on the heavens, the waters, the sun and moon, the stars, all the green things upon the earth, animals and birds, to bless the Lord, praise him and magnify him for ever. The beauty of these natural things is not expressly mentioned, but is implicit both here and in the psalm.

St. Augustine wrote:[1]

> "And what is this?" I asked the earth; and it answered "I am not He."
>
> I asked the sea and the deeps, and the creeping things that lived, and they replied "We are not thy God, seek higher than we." I asked the heavens, the sun, moon and stars: "Neither," say they, "are we the God whom thou seekest." And I answered unto all these things

[1] *Confessions*, X, vi, 9.

which stand about the door of my flesh, "Ye have told me concerning my God, that ye are not He; tell me something about Him." And with a loud voice they exclaimed, "He made us." My questioning was my observing of them; and their beauty was their reply.

It is significant that the great masters of Italian painting repeatedly introduced exquisite landscapes as a background for their pictures of religious subjects. Claude's *Rest on the Flight to Egypt* depicts the Holy Family reposing in a landscape of indescribable beauty—an idea which inspired Berlioz also in Part II of his sacred masterpiece *L'Enfance du Christ*.

Shakespeare puts these words into the mouth of the Duke living in banishment in the Forest of Arden:[1]

> Sweet are the uses of adversity,
> Which like the toad, ugly and venomous,
> Wears yet a precious jewel in his head;
> And this our life exempt from public haunt
> Finds tongues in trees, books in the running brooks,
> Sermons in stones, and good in everything.

Many examples might be given of Wordsworth's mystical visions of Nature. Let us turn to his *Voluntary composed upon an evening of extraordinary splendour and beauty*. I quote the first two stanzas:

I

> Had this effulgence disappeared
> With flying haste, I might have sent,
> Among the speechless clouds, a look
> Of blank astonishment;
> But 'tis endued with power to stay,
> And sanctify one closing day,
> That frail Mortality may see—
> What is?—ah no, but what *can* be!
> Time was when field and watery cove
> With modulated echoes rang,
> While choirs of fervent Angels sang
> Their vespers in the grove;
> Or, crowning, star-like, each some sovereign height,
> Warbled, for heaven above and earth below,
> Strains suitable to both.—Such holy rite,
> Methinks, if audibly repeated now
> From hill or valley, could not move
> Sublimer transport, purer love,
> Than doth this silent spectacle—the gleam—
> The shadow—and the peace supreme!

[1] *As You Like It*, Act II, scene 1, lines 12 ff.

II

No sound is uttered,—but a deep
And solemn harmony pervades
The hollow vale from steep to steep,
And penetrates the glades.
Far-distant images draw nigh,
Called forth by wondrous potency
Of beamy radiance, that imbues
Whate'er it strikes with gem-like hues!
In vision exquisitely clear,
Herds range along the mountain side;
And glistening antlers are descried;
And gilded flocks appear.
Thine is the tranquil hour, purpureal Eve!
But long as god-like wish, or hope divine,
Informs my spirit, ne'er can I believe
That this magnificence is wholly thine!
—From worlds not quickened by the sun
A portion of the gift is won;
An intermingling of Heaven's pomp is spread
On ground which British shepherds tread!

The magnificent lines entitled *The Simplon Pass*[1] voice a similar conception in a different setting:

.... Brook and road
Were fellow-travellers in this gloomy Pass,
And with them did we journey several hours,
At a slow step. The immeasurable height
Of woods decaying, never to be decayed,
The stationary blasts of waterfalls,
And in the narrow rent, at every turn,
Winds thwarting winds bewildered and forlorn,
The torrents shooting from the clear blue sky,
The rocks that muttered close upon our ears,
Black drizzling crags that spake by the wayside
As if a voice were in them, the sick sight
And giddy prospect of the raving stream,
The unfettered clouds and region of the heavens,
Tumult and peace, the darkness and the light—
Were all like workings of one mind, the features
Of the same face, blossoms upon one tree,
Characters of the great Apocalypse,
The types and symbols of Eternity,
Of first, and last, and midst, and without end.

[1] "Poems of the Imagination", VII—almost identical with *The Prelude*, vi, lines 621-640.

Just before the outbreak of the Second World War, George Villiers, with his wife, was driving his car towards London, to be interviewed for a post in the Censorship.[1] " Time, I thought, had entered the great golden afternoon, and somehow got suspended in it. Dash as we might down the grey road in front of us, we could never dash out of that golden afternoon. It was all around us, and about us, enveloping us, touching our hands and faces with glory. The sun was complete master of the situation. Everything was bathed equally and evenly in its superb, unhurried radiance. And my spirit rejoiced. This, I said to myself, will last for ever, this golden afternoon—not in time as splintered by man into hours and measured by clocks; but in eternity, as quality, a part of the everlasting background of things. For it signifies. It reveals to us an attribute of God—joy. Therefore it is an event; and Hitler and all his armies, and the embattled might of all the peoples in the world shall not prevail against it. War and peace have no meaning in relation to it. And it shall be for us forever as a covenant of the everlasting beauty." Then he describes the contrast of their entry into London—" Fear came out of the Capital towards us . . . ," but continues " Suddenly we sailed into Regent's Park, and there was the house, and the ducks on the lake, and the people lying in the shade, observing the people watching the ducks on the lake; and everything was in its right place . . . and we were caught up again into the golden afternoon, away from time—and there was happiness.

" And happiness, too, in arriving at the little house embowered in the trees at St. Andrew's Place, gazing out into the Park from its round Regency windows. And here was the first great surprise of these times (though it had nothing to do with the war and shouldn't have been a surprise), but I had never been in that house at that season before—I mean, the great dahlia border that swings round a curve in the Park in front of the windows. Now, this is an event. It signifies. It says something that really means something. It too proclaims an attribute of God—beauty. Oh, but you've never seen anything like it—hundreds and hundreds of huge, blazing, shock-headed flowers, each bigger than your two fists clasped together (as big as your heart, some of them), each a different shade within the same colour, each saying a different thing within the same meaning, each as important as the other, the whole chorus swaying and singing: 'Jubilate Deo'. At sight of them, Hitler seemed such an insignificant little fellow, and all the posturing of armies opposing each other of no consequence whatever. Which,

[1] *Noonday and Nocturne*, pp. 11-16.

amongst other things, was what they were saying, those flowers: 'Don't be frightened, don't look at the horror and disaster.... Behold the Everlasting Beauty and rejoice: for joy is of the Kingdom, and we are citizens of the Kingdom, and so are you. And the Prince of the Kingdom is the Word made Flesh, and we are His servants. Be ye also His servants. Jubilate Deo . . . Jubilate Deo.' The tide of colour is brimming still, these sixteen months after. They can never die, those flowers—not, at least, their deathless, vanquishing song. For that is an event which has happened, is happening, and will always happen. I share in this event, and wherever I go and whatever I do I partake of this proclamation of the Everlasting Beauty, and hear that syllable of the canticle of praise. The flowers have died to the sight of men, and their stalks have been thrown on the rubbish heap. I, too, shall die, and my body be thrown into the pit. But part of all my eternity will be the affirmation of those flowers still singing in the golden afternoon, and myself agape by the window watching them there . . . and echoing their song 'Jubilate Deo'."

Nearly all the manifestations of nature are beautiful. It is sometimes said that natural beauty has only been realised comparatively recently in human history. Yet there is ample evidence of an awareness of it in the Old Testament, and the notion that the ancient Greeks did not appreciate it does not hold water. Before man had learnt to conquer nature by scientific means it was natural for writers to voice the feelings of terror which wild seas and storms and savage beasts aroused in the minds of their contemporaries. Severely practical reasons prevented, or swamped, a sense of nature's beauty in her fiercer aspects. But Homer is full of the most detailed and lovely similes taken from nature—from animals, birds and insects, from sea and sky. Aeschylus' images of flowers, eagles and nightingales; Sophocles' description of Colonus, gleaming bright, where the nightingale sings, hidden by the ivy; where the narcissus blooms in clusters, and the golden-eyed crocus, and where the wandering streams of the Kephisus flow unsleeping; his pictures (in the *Antigone*) of the jutting peaks swept by the wind and lashed by the waves; or of the trees that bend before the storm, while those that resist are destroyed, root and branch; or of the stream of Castalia and the ivied slopes of the Nysaean hills and the vine-clad promontory; Euripides' constant allusions to rivers and birds, to mountain and valley, to the sea and the sun and the stars; all this is not the work of men insensitive to the beauties of nature. Aristophanes, too, intersperses his comic dialogue and situations with charming descriptions of birds and trees and flowers and bending dolphins, and watery clouds that climb the sky and throw a mantle over the tree-clad mountain tops.

Erasmus (1467–1536), describing his journey over the Alps *en route* to England, did not comment at all on the magnificence of the scenery. Mr. S. R. Hopper[1] suggests that this may have been because he was contemplating the writing of his *Praise of Folly*, or even more simply because he was rawboned and did not sit comfortably on his mule! He complained of other conditions of travel in those times. But Erasmus was an exception in not appreciating nature. A devout, tolerant, and attractive scholar, he was, nevertheless, as Dr. H. A. L. Fisher remarked,[2] "somewhat poor on the side of imagination". Natural beauty was recognised by his predecessors and contemporaries, by the earlier Italian painters, by poets such as Chaucer and Spencer. But it has been left to a more recent age to value the grandeur of nature in her more austere forms. Thomas Hardy; Gustav Holst (in his symphonic poem *Egdon Heath* inspired by Hardy's description of the place), Sibelius, when he depicted in the sombre magnificence of *Tapiola* the dark forest scenes of his native Finland; Vaughan Williams, when in the *Sinfonia Antarctica* he presents to us a conception of man confronted with nature in her bleakest aspect; show how the appreciation of the loveliness of nature has widened its scope as time went on. The recognition of beauty in severity is specially characteristic of the youth of the mid-twentieth century.

This all-pervading objective beauty of nature in its varied manifestations has thus been apprehended by men according to the degree of their enlightenment. It is evidence of design and therefore of creation by a Supreme Intelligence.

It might be asked: If beauty is divine, how do we account for the fact that nature is sometimes only pretty? According to those who believe in religion, nature is created by God; we can understand that there are degrees of beauty in artistic creations, because they, whilst divinely inspired, are the products of the imperfect human mind; but it may be contended that, logically, natural manifestations, in the production of which man has played no part, ought to be all equally beautiful if every form of natural beauty is divine. The answer, I believe, is that God reveals the Beauty of His Being in varying degrees in different manifestations of nature—I mean, literally in different

[1] *The Crisis of Faith*, p. 54.
[2] *A History of Europe*, first edition in one volume, p. 490.

landscapes and seascapes. The charming view of trees and grass and flowers and gentle little hills—for which " pretty " is the right word—affords us a more limited vision of the Divine beauty than the loveliness of Derwentwater ringed round by its mountains, on a bright day after rain, or a majestic waterfall, or a sublime range of snow-clad peaks gleaming in the sunlight beneath a brilliant blue sky.

Now, if natural beauty is divine and attests the existence of God, the same is true of artistic beauty. Fundamentally, the two are akin, the difference being that the beauty of nature owes nothing to man (except in so far as he may have contributed to it in the case of a garden, for example), whereas the beauty of art is created by man, albeit under divine inspiration. The true account, I believe, is that the human mind is, in varying degrees, itself divine. This theory conforms to the ancient Hebraic belief that God made man in His own image—a belief which was later absorbed by Christianity. It harmonises with the doctrine of the Holy Spirit dwelling in the souls of man, and is, of course, fully consistent with the conception of original sin. And in the single instance of Jesus himself, Christian believers find perfection, so that His mind was wholly divine. All other men partake of the divine nature, in infinite variety and in infinitely graduated proportions, ranging from the saintly character who approximates to Christ, to the appalling villain who has only a tiny spark of divinity in himself. We shall, of course, find many cases in the history of the arts, in which men whose character as revealed in their private lives leaves a good deal to be desired have produced art of great beauty; they rise above the worse side of their natures and put the best of themselves into their artistic creations. In music, the most conspicuous instance of this is Wagner.

Let us consider how this theory of the divinity of artistic beauty applies in the case of literature. In Chapter 1 it was pointed out that when we speak of certain literary works as being religious, we are referring to the fact that they deal unmistakably with sacred subjects. Specifically religious dramas such as the Miracle and Morality Plays, the Oberammergau Passion Play, Milton's *Samson Agonistes* and certain twentieth-century examples by Dorothy Sayers, T. S. Eliot, Emlyn Williams and Christopher Fry, might be said to correspond, in the dramatic sphere, to such epic poems as Dante's *Divine Comedy*, Milton's *Paradise Lost* and *Paradise Regained*, the Pope's monologue in Book X of Browning's *The Ring and the Book*, and various shorter religious poems both ancient and modern. But it is also possible for a play to have a spiritual quality, even though its subject is not religious.

One supreme instance of this is *King Lear*, and it is valuable to consider in this connection a play of Shakespeare, just because he has been accused of paganism and of showing in his works little regard for the life after death. *King Lear* is full of terrible cruelties, wickedness and tragedy, but the significant thing is that persons who are divinely good by Christian standards, such as Cordelia, Kent, Edgar—and we may even include Albany, Gloucester and the Fool—exist in that world of darkness, and that at the end all the evil characters perish and the realm of England is left in the hands of Kent and Edgar—even though Lear and Cordelia die as martyrs in the great sacrifice and the Fool is either dead or has disappeared from the story.[1] How different from the inspissated gloom of Eugene O'Neill's *Mourning becomes Electra*, and how widely the close of the latter play diverges from the serene ending of Aeschylus' Oresteian trilogy on which the whole drama (though cast in the American Civil War) is based! The spiritual quality of *King Lear* is not related directly to any religious association and the play is in fact set in a remote pre-Christian world, where even a good-hearted man such as Gloucester can cry:

> "As flies to wanton boys are we to the gods;
> They kill us for their sport."

There is no justification for suggesting that the thought here attributed to Gloucester reflected Shakespeare's own attitude of mind. The divine character of the drama as a whole, not explicitly displayed to us by the poet and yet evident to our apprehension, is akin to that present in those instrumental works which, without any verbal clue from the composer, we feel to be spiritual in quality. The instrumental masterpieces of Beethoven are as godlike as his *Missa Solemnis* or the sublime liturgical creations of Bach.

The divinity of beauty in painting is not confined to those pictures

[1] Albany leaves the rule of the realm to Kent and Edgar, though Kent replies:

> "I have a journey, sir, shortly to go;
> My master calls me, I must not say no."

The final speech, "The weight of this sad time we must obey . . ." is attributed by the Quarto to Albany and has thus been interpreted as meaning that he, after all, reluctantly accepts authority; but the Folio gives it to Edgar, and I agree with the editors of the Arden edition that Shakespeare probably meant it for Edgar, who was bound to answer Albany's speech abdicating the kingdom in favour of Kent and him, and that the words "We are young" fall more naturally from his mouth than from Albany's. In either case, the realm is left in the hands of a man of good character.

which have Biblical associations or even to portraits of men and women whose faces reveal a spiritual character. It extends, for example, to those Dutch interiors in which quite homely scenes of domestic life are illumined by the artist's genius and inspiration; and if the loveliness of nature is divine, the beauty of the landscape paintings of the great masters must be divine also.

So prevalent is this spiritual quality in beautiful works of art, that we can say that, as in the case of nature, the beauty is itself evidence of the existence of God. As we have seen,[1] this quality is revealed in music by a different method from that employed by other arts, because music does not necessarily rely on association and is not normally imitative. It translates. It is an independent language. It can convey anger, love, grief, joy, and the various types of religious or—in the wider sense, sacred—feelings and the most subtle shades of such universal emotions. But it does not individualise in the sense that a poet can write verses applicable to particular persons in a particular situation or a painter can portray individuals. It is, however, admirably adapted, for instance, to character-drawing in its own, more generalised way, and so it can express in a general form, peculiar to itself, prayers, religious calm and serenity, and also all the emotions which in themselves are consonant with the divine aspects of man's nature, even though they are not, in the ordinary and more restricted sense, religious. When it also conveys evil passions or voluptuous impulses for the purpose of contrasting them with the more spiritual qualities, the divinity of beauty dominates the composition as a whole, in the same way as it does in a Shakespearean tragedy.

C. E. M. Joad, in his last published work *The Recovery of Belief*—which I did not read until the present book was half written—expresses the divinity of beauty very well when he declares that goodness, beauty and truth are the three ways in which God reveals Himself to man, and he specifically includes the beauty of music as an example of this, with particular reference to Beethoven.

It is with these wide interpretations of the words "divine", "sacred" and "spiritual" that we are entitled to contemplate the beauty of music, whether evinced in secular or religious art. There is divinity to be found in the secular madrigals of the early Italian and English Tudor composers, in the instrumental art of all ages, in the German *Lieder*, in the music of the opera-house, and even in so-called "light" music, as well as in that which is set to religious texts.

[1] In Chapter I.

Alec Robertson, in his excellent book *Sacred Music*, makes the astonishing statement[1] "Music in itself cannot, of course, be religious", and according to John F. Runciman[2] there is no distinction between a sacred and profane style; no composer has had more than one style; there is no difference between the sacred motets and the secular madrigals of the early polyphonists, and the absence of dance measures from Bach's church music is the only distinction between his church and his secular compositions; the structure, manner and outline of his songs are precisely alike—"indeed, he dished up secular airs for sacred cantatas." Runciman similarly links Handel's *Semele* and *Samson* (conveniently ignoring *Messiah*!); Haydn's symphonies and *The Creation*; Mozart's symphonies and Masses; Schubert's symphonies or songs and his Masses or *The Song of Miriam*; Beethoven's Ninth Symphony and Mass in D.

A composer's style—his personal finger-prints—is common to most of his work. But the truth about Purcell cannot be summed up so easily as by calling all his music "secular". The question must always be, in the case of music intended to be devotional, is it appropriate to, and does it express, religious feeling? The fact that Bach used the same air for both a "secular" cantata and a "sacred" one or for the B minor Mass, does not settle the matter. Bach was a very religious man, and God is revealed in his secular cantatas and in his purely instrumental works, as well as in his avowedly devotional ones. Purcell's church music differs in style from the old plainchant and from that of the Elizabethan composers. He may not show, as a rule, the same religious ecstasy in his liturgical art as Byrd did, but nevertheless it is beautiful, sincere, and suited to the words, and it combines all these qualities with great technical mastery. In my sense of the term it is sacred—and so, too, is the great aria "When I am laid in earth" from *Dido and Aeneas*.

Sir Thomas Beecham was reported to have said that music is entertainment and nothing else—or words to that effect. This is a curious expression to use of such works as Beethoven's Ninth Symphony and his last quartets, Brahms' Fourth Symphony, and many other supreme masterpieces which will occur to the reader. It is obviously inappropriate to the religious music of the great composers, and though some music is simply entertaining, many of the finest compositions in the world are, to say the least, entertainment plus something else—unless we

[1] p. 10. [2] *Purcell*, p. 30.

are expected to understand the word in a very much wider sense than its ordinary one.

The music critic of *The Times*, in an interesting article on François Couperin[1] used these words: "Put crudely, the difference is that the French taste [in music] is for entertainment, ours and the German for edification, the Italian for passion."

Mr. Martin Cooper, in his valuable book *French Music from the death of Berlioz to the death of Fauré*, writes in a somewhat similar vein: "To seek in French music primarily for a revelation of the composer's soul or for marks of the sublime is to look for something which the French consider a by-product." It is rather "the art of arranging sounds in agreeable and intellectually satisfying patterns. Every composer worthy of his name will inevitably reveal himself, his character, in his music; but this revelation is a by-product to the French. . . . The qualities for which French art is famous—logic, clarity, moderation and balance—are the corollaries or the direct results of this deliberate restriction of field, this concentration on the data of the intelligence and the senses and this instinctive mistrust of the vague and large-sounding." He goes on to say that French exceptions to this rule among artists "show a bad head for heights. How uncertainly, for all their boldness and ardour, do Berlioz, Hugo and Balzac range among the peaks of the spirit! . . . César Franck, a Belgian by origin," was one "whose traditions were ecclesiastical rather than national, those of the Catholic church organist, rather than the French secular artist". This last statement seems to beg the question at issue, but the cases of Berlioz and Franck will be discussed more fully later in this book. Mr. Cooper admits that the unorthodoxy of Berlioz and Fauré in their settings of the *Requiem* "is not to be gathered from their music". "Piety", he says, "—i.e. 'pietas', meaning dutifulness—and resignation are the chief characteristics of Fauré's *Requiem;* but they are not his only response to death, and the unbiased listener will detect no false note in the specifically Christian devotion of the 'Pie Jesu', in the fear of the creature faced by his Creator expressed in the Offertory and the 'Libera me', or the anticipation of the Beatific Vision in the final 'In Paradisum'. The whole work is within the Christian framework and the absence of the 'Dies Irae' is as easily explained on aesthetic as on religious grounds. . . ." Gounod was "ardently pious" but turned to composing operas, yet after 1870 he wrote mostly oratorios—though we may well agree that they were "grandiose and blandly banal ones".

[1] January 12th, 1951.

Fauré and—as I shall hope to show—Berlioz and Franck, are sufficiently important exceptions to suggest that the notion that the French taste in music is mainly for entertainment is too sweeping. It may be granted that the French place more emphasis on " agreeable and intellectually satisfying patterns " in sound and " on the data of the intelligence and the senses " than other nations. But a people who have produced—apart from the creative artists already mentioned—great writers of tragic drama such as Corneille and Racine; Molière, who reveals such profound insight into the depths of human character beneath the surface of his brilliant comedies; the architects of some of the most sublime cathedrals in the world; and in François Couperin a great composer of religious music; who in our generation have shown so much enthusiasm for the art of Bach and Beethoven—to say nothing of Wagner—and have even presented the unique phenomenon of one of their greatest statesmen[1] writing a notable book on Beethoven—such a people cannot accurately be said to regard either music or any other art as little else than entertainment.

François Couperin (1668–1733) was not only the composer of exquisite pieces for clavecin and other instrumental works, but was equally great as a creator of liturgical art. He was organist of St. Gervais, in Paris, and one of the organists of the Chapelle Royale, for most of his life. In his youth he wrote two organ Masses, in which the instrument provides appropriate and beautiful music between the various parts of the service. Later, he produced a whole series of vocal compositions for the church, some of which unfortunately are lost. It is characteristic of the art of the *Grand Siècle* that his devotional work should combine sensuous harmonic beauty with a spiritual simplicity: this is nowhere more conspicuous than in the *Motet de Sainte Suzanne* and the three *Leçons des Ténèbres.* And the way in which the *brunettes*—the little French pastoral songs for one or more voices either unaccompanied or supported by the lute—show their influence not only in Couperin's instrumental creations but even in his church compositions too, is an example of the transformation of music of secular origin into art which is devotional not only in its purpose but in its actual character.

In our own day, the most conspicuous revolutionary French composer is Olivier Messiaen, and it is significant that he has sought to express the religious and mystical aspects of life, in such works as *Les Visions de l'Amen*, *Vingt Regards sur l'Enfant Jésus* and *Apparition de*

[1] M. Edouard Herriot.

l'Eglise Eternelle. His vast *Turangalila Symphonie*, though not religious, is certainly not mere " entertainment ": it is a work of elemental force and violent imagination.

Paul Hindemith, in his striking book *A Composer's World*, sets out an artistic creed which is opposed to the theory that music is simply entertainment. He sums up St. Augustine's doctrine contained in the sixth book of *De musica libri sex* as stating that "music has to be converted into moral power", though he is willing to modify it according to the conception of Boethius in the *De institutione musica*, written in the sixth century, that " music has the power either to improve or to debase our character". He admits that "music for all possible degrees of entertainment ought to be provided", but holds that moral effort is the hallmark of a work of art and that " other works, in which the composer's moral effort cannot be perceived . . . may evoke wonderful images in our mind; they may readily lead us to mentally reconstruct their forms; yet they may not impress us as works of art".

If we assume that Hindemith's theory represents the German attitude towards music generally, we may be able to understand the statement that the German taste is for edification—though we may feel that that particular word is an inaccurate description either of the Teutonic or of the British approach.

" Edifying " is not the right term to use about music from the standpoint of any nation. If it were, it would surely be enough to prejudice children, and any other potential lovers of the art, against music from the start. Music can have a moral effect, but this is not necessarily connected with its artistic value; for a military march which stimulates a soldier to feats of courage and endurance may be musically commonplace, and a hymn which makes a worshipper feel a better man may be banal. The religious appeal of music is, however, linked to its artistic merit. If a hymn is to be valuable as a piece of music, it must be devotional in character, and if a composition is really religious in feeling it is (apart from any technical or structural flaws) a work of art. If, however, a composer writes an aria which he intends to arouse a feeling of religious devotion but which does not do so, obviously this is an artistic failure on his part.

Most serious music-lovers, to whatever nation they belong, expect, not to be "edified", but to find, in the broadest sense of the term, a spiritual quality in that which they regard as the finest music. The reason why the art of Puccini, for instance, is below the supreme level is that, for all its expressiveness and consummate craftsmanship, it lacks the nobility which marks the work of greater men.

Vaughan Williams is reported to have said on the occasion of his eightieth birthday: "The honour and glory of our great art is that it is absolutely and entirely useless." At first sight this might seem to be directly opposite to Hindemith's former description of his own art as "Gebrauchsmusik", but Hindemith has since contended that what he meant was that music serves ends beyond itself, that it is an instrument in the larger purposes of life. If Vaughan Williams' meaning was that music is not—or should not be—utilitarian in the less exalted sense, many would agree with him. Whatever the theories of these two distinguished composers may be, their finest works have in common a spiritual value, corresponding to that which is present in varying degrees in all the most beautiful music of history.

The objection to the theory that music is, and should be, only entertainment, is that it relegates the art to a place of relative unimportance. The music that we value most is not a mere embellishment of life, but a spiritual enrichment of it.

6

THE CONTRAST OF BACH AND HANDEL

WE have seen[1] that at the time of the Reformation the relationship between music and religion shifted its ground. Thenceforward it was no longer to be largely internal to the Church, and thus the question of the sacred quality in music came to affect non-liturgical art to an increasing extent. It will now be my purpose to consider how the ideas about the divinity of beauty contained in the last chapter relate to various composers subsequent to Purcell and Couperin.

No truly religious work of art can be created without sincere faith, and a man's faith is largely shown in his conduct. (This remains true in spite of the extent to which some artists rise above themselves in their creative work.) Nobody is perfect, and even so good a man as Bach had his defects. He was often irritable and lost his temper. He had an obstinate belief that he was always right. He had a habit of being easy-going to start with, then remembering his " rights " too late, and finally, in his anger, making a mountain out of a molehill. These faults were shown in his relations with people whom he thought might be trying to interfere with his freedom.[2] As against all this, he was normally a most friendly and modest person; a man of great integrity, with a strong sense of fairness; kindly and always trying to help others; devoted to his family; economical but exceptionally hospitable; and deeply religious.

It is not surprising that such a man should have produced music which is imbued with a spiritual character from start to finish. No man has ever dedicated his art to God more completely and more consistently than Bach. And he had no conception of his own greatness as a creator—rather less, it would seem, even than Shakespeare. He was aware only of his eminence as a player upon the organ and the clavier and of his contrapuntal skill. How astonished he would have been had he known that the liturgical compositions which he wrote in such profusion for the church where he worked, or the instrumental pieces which he produced in the course of his duties, were

[1] At the end of Chapter 3.

[2] Albert Schweitzer, *J. S. Bach* (translation by Ernest Newman), Vol. I, p. 151.

to be acclaimed as masterpieces throughout the world in years to come!

So far as he was concerned, there was no conflict between his art and his religion—indeed, fundamentally there was no distinction between them. Music (whether liturgical or not) was, for him, a consecration, and combined with the orthodoxy of his Lutheranism was a strong vein of mysticism. He represented, in fact, the most complete embodiment of Christianity in music that the world has known hitherto. Byrd, a Roman Catholic, had written great music for the Church of England as well as noble settings of the Mass. Bach, a Lutheran, transcended the barriers dividing the sects of the Church by composing music of still greater richness and variety both for the Reformed Church and for the Latin words of the Mass, even though his mighty work in B minor is too vast for liturgical purposes.

There are many instances in Bach where music from his " secular " works was used by him in devotional compositions. Sceptics or atheists would have us believe that this goes to show that there is no such thing as intrinsically sacred music. Actually it proves nothing of the sort, if we look at the matter a little more closely.

The Osanna in the B minor Mass substantially reproduces the first chorus in the secular cantata, " Preise dein Glücke, gesegnetes Sachsen", which Bach at short notice wrote for the visit of the King and Queen of Saxony to Leipzig in 1734 and which was performed on an October evening in the market-place before their Majesties' windows. Even if the Osanna was composed first, as some authorities think probable, this would not affect the issue. The score is admirably suited to either setting.

Nearly all of the music in the cantata for St. John's Day, " Freue dich, erlöste Schaar", was taken from the secular cantata, "Angenehmes Wiederau", composed for the occasion when Count Johann Christian Von Hennicke rendered homage at the town of Widerau in 1737 on receiving possession of his land.

The music of three of the choruses in the Christmas Oratorio and of seven of its arias was transferred from two secular cantatas, " Tönet, ihr Pauken " (the " Dramma per musica " in honour of the Queen) and "Die Wahl des Herkules", and another aria came from the secular " Preise dein Glücke " cantata. The score of the choruses, so far from being inappropriate to the sacred texts, suits them even better than it does secular ones; and among the arias, " Schlafe, mein Liebster "—the song at the manger where the infant Jesus was sleeping—could fittingly be taken from a secular setting, because there too the exquisite music had typified the slumber song for any innocent child.

These examples show the broad scope of music as a means of expression and support the view that Bach's so-called " secular " art was, in the true and literal sense, sacred. That this was the attitude of Bach himself we know from his own words. In the rules of accompaniment which he gave to his pupils he says, " Like all music, the figured bass should have no other end and aim than the glory of God and the recreation of the soul." It is significant that he takes a technical device such as the figured bass to illustrate his conception, and that in the *Little Clavier Book* which had not, of course, any liturgical association but was composed for his eldest son Wilhelm Friedemann, as a boy, he wrote the words " In Nomine Jesu ".[1]

The consecration of Bach's ostensibly secular compositions is audible over and over again. The famous aria " Schafe können sicher weiden " (" Sheep may safely graze ") is one of the most beautiful melodies in the world and is as deeply spiritual intrinsically as any music can be, but it comes in a secular cantata, written for the birthday of Herzog Christian zu Sachsen-Weissenfels, entitled " Was mir behagt ist nur die muntre Jagd " (" My only delight is the merry chase "). The Air in the Third Orchestral Suite is popular for the very reason that its loveliness is literally sacred to all music-lovers. The Rondeau (Gavotte) in Suite No. 2 in B minor for flute and strings has a celestial character which would also seem strange, in a group of dances, if we did not remember that divinity can shine in light music of the finest quality. The E flat minor Prelude in Book I of the 48 is one of the most deeply felt of these instrumental expressions of faith, and the solo violin in the slow movement of the Violin Concerto in E seems to soar to heaven.

Most authorities—even the greatest Bach enthusiasts such as Parry and Schweitzer—have treated *The Art of Fugue* as technically marvellous and a supreme example of Bach's craftsmanship, and as little more, for the most part. It is certainly that, but, in my view, it is a great deal besides: I find that to listen to it is a great spiritual experience; it is a work of most moving beauty; much of it is definitely religious in quality and has that same profoundly devotional character that is present in the B minor Mass and the St. Matthew Passion: some of its phrases actually remind me of them.

The association in our minds between the organ and church worship does not wholly account for the intrinsically exalted character of

[1] See Schweitzer, *J. S. Bach*, Vol. I, p. 167.

Bach's organ compositions, which are a musical counterpart of great church architecture. This applies not only to the chorales which are based on old hymns or to such a work as the " St. Anne" Fugue, but also to the preludes and fugues, the toccatas and sonatas, which have no title to connect them with any devotional meaning.

Albert Schweitzer has shown how Bach, especially in his choral music, employs recurring " motives " which express all sorts of ideas suggested by the words that he sets, whether pictorial images such as waves, the motion of the clouds, the various steps of Jesus or of human beings, the devil (represented by a twisting motive to depict the serpent), or emotions such as tumult, exhaustion, terror, grief or joy. Where the words call for it, any of these may be combined together. Always they are enshrined in a setting of worship. There is no rigidity about their use. They appear in different works—cantatas, chorales, motets, the Mass, or the settings of the Passion—varied and adapted to suit the divergent purposes which the words or the situation require.

These motives enable Bach to impart to his music a dramatic character. The dramatic element in his deeply religious, liturgical works shows how fallacious it is to assume that music associated with the drama is secular as opposed to sacred, and that therefore anything " operatic " or " theatrical " is necessarily irreligious.

The drama in the music of the Passions according to St. John and St. Matthew is one of their most striking features. The Evangelist tells the great story in a series of recitatives as eloquent as the choruses, arias and concerted numbers themselves, and whenever the narrative introduces the words of a person speaking or the exclamations of a crowd, soloists or chorus give voice to these in short, vivid utterances. In the St. Matthew Passion, the sayings of Christ are accompanied, as it were, by a halo of softly playing strings.

In the B minor Mass, the mystery of the Incarnation is conveyed by very slow, chromatic music in the minor key, though closing on the tonic major; the "Crucifixus" is based on the motive of grief and dies away in profoundly moving accents, with the voices and instruments gradually sinking " pianissimo " to their deepest register as the body of Our Lord is lowered into the tomb. This is immediately followed by the blazing glory of " Et resurrexit " in D major. The "Sanctus", with its reverberating basses swinging to a majestic " step " motive, opens Heaven to our ears in music of the utmost sublimity.

In the church cantatas, Bach often dwells on the thought of death, but his music is never depressing. Death is looked forward to as a release—sometimes wearily, more often serenely or gladly, at other times even ecstatically.

In Cantata No. 82, "Ich habe genug", for bass solo and oboe obbligato, a longing for death is expressed in the first two numbers, both of which are yearning in character and extraordinarily eloquent and beautiful. The third number conveys the joy of the soul in attaining death—but does so in a minor key, albeit in a quick tempo.

The Cantata No. 21, "Ich hatte viel Bekümmernis", is a progression of the soul from affliction to comfort and joyful thanksgiving. The soprano solo "Seufzer, Tränen, Kummer, Not", is built from broken phrases of mournful beauty. The duet between the soul and the Comforter is dramatic in style and deeply moving. The final chorus is to the same text, though in German, as "Worthy is the Lamb" in Handel's *Messiah*, and includes three trumpets to add to its brilliant character.

Yet amid all these profound religious emotions, Bach can find room, even in a devotional work, for touches of humour. For instance, when in the "Magnificat" he is setting the Latin words of "He hath filled the hungry with good things; and the rich he hath sent empty away", he cannot resist depicting the word "inanes" (empty), by making the two flutes stop playing suddenly, with one note on the continuo left all alone to fill up the last bar! In the St. Matthew Passion, when the woman pours precious ointment on the head of Jesus, Bach depicts the indignation of the disciples at this "waste", and when he sets the words "For this ointment might have been sold for much and given to the poor" he does so by means of repeated notes in very rigid time, which deftly and humorously suggest the conventional comment (in the ensuing recitative, Bach sets Christ's memorable words, "Why trouble ye the woman? For she hath wrought a good work upon me. For ye have the poor always with you, but me ye have not always," to music of surpassing loveliness).

Bach does not descend from the sublime to the ridiculous, but admits humour even in the midst of sublimity. An elderly cousin of mine—a woman of great charm and wit—once remarked to me that she often thought that the Almighty "must hold his sides and laugh" at the variety of approaches to Him made by men's different religions. To a devoted believer his own faith seems the only true one, but whether or not we respond to my cousin's apparent impartiality, many of us can, I suggest, sympathise with her assumption of a Divine laughter. A God without a kindly sense of humour would, in my eyes, be no

God at all. Near one corner of Chartres Cathedral—that miracle of combined majesty and delicacy in which the most profound religious feeling is enshrined in noble architecture wedded to the exquisite loveliness of coloured windows—there stands on the side of the *clocher vieux* a statue of a donkey playing a hurdy-gurdy, which is said to symbolise in gentle irony the man who aspires to the music of the angels. Blessed thought! The sublime is not opposed to the ridiculous: it includes it. There is laughter in Heaven. It is characteristic of a French artist to express this truth in stone, and to associate it with music—and characteristic, too, of the old German cantor of Leipzig to reveal it in his art.

. . . . .

Handel, born in the same year as Bach, presents a great contrast to him as a personality. Bach's genius as a composer was not realised either by his contemporaries or by himself; he was a family man, twice married, spending his life in a succession of local official posts as organist and choirmaster, never leaving his native Germany, and quietly turning out a succession of supreme masterpieces which were not published in his lifetime and were only recognised as such long afterwards. Handel never married, travelled to Italy and England and became a naturalised Englishman, was acclaimed by kings and princes, by aristocrats and populace, a speculator, a *bon vivant*, ambitious, a lover of the applause of the multitude, albeit with a strong vein of romance in his nature. Yet in certain important ways these two men, who never met, were alike. Both were profoundly religious, immensely benevolent, hospitable, and blessed with a strong sense of humour. Thus it is not surprising that Handel should have produced, in *Messiah*, one of the most deeply devotional masterpieces of art ever created; that in the Chandos Anthems he should have expressed in grand and simple music the religious emotions of the various scriptural texts to which they are set; or that in the "Dettingen Te Deum" he should have uttered a magnificent paean of thanksgiving to God for victory. But it is also in keeping with his character that before he embarked on his great series of oratorios he composed a large number of operas, and that in the oratorios which followed, apart from *Messiah*, he set Old Testament stories in a dramatic and descriptive style which owed much to his operatic experience and are not what either Christians or modern Jews would call really religious in character, although their music is admirably suited to the words. *Israel in Egypt*, for instance, contains a magnificent series of choruses descriptive of the plagues, but with the exception of the setting of " But as for His people, He led them forth like sheep ", and the duet " Thou in Thy mercy ", both of which convey the Fatherly goodness of a loving God, the music, like the text of Exodus, rejoices that the Lord has thrown the horse and its rider into the sea and faithfully expresses the conception of God as " a man of war ".

When Handel had finished writing the " Hallelujah Chorus " in *Messiah*, his servant found him at his table in tears, and he said, " I did think I did see all Heaven before me, and the great God himself." And when Lord Kinnoul, after the first London performance of the work, complimented Handel on the noble " entertainment " which he had provided, the composer replied, " My lord, I should be sorry if I only entertained them; I wished to make them better."

The attitude both of Bach and of Handel to the problem of portraying evil in music was fundamentally the same. Mr. Arthur Little, in his book *The Nature of Art*, reached the conclusion that immoral art cannot be excused on the plea that it simply portrays the truth or that the impulse to produce it was spontaneous in the artist: to depict sin is only justified as a means of evincing the power of the soul and its natural reaction against evil, thus contributing to the further and greater experience of the nobility of man. It is in this way that we can understand the spiritual grandeur of a great dramatic or epic masterpiece which portrays bad characters as well as good; Bach's musical pictures of the devil; and the various examples, in Handel's works, of music which expresses moral evil. They are there for a dramatic purpose, for the specific object of pointing a contrast with the nobility or the spiritual quality of the remainder of the composition. " O ruddier than the cherry " from *Acis and Galatea* should not be sung just as a jolly tune: it is an apt expression of the greedy lasciviousness of the Cyclops Polyphemus gloating at the mere thought of clasping the fair form of the nymph, and should be interpreted accordingly: only thus do we get the full effect of her rejection of the giant and of her victory over grief when, though Acis has been slain, she transforms him by her divine power into a river, so that he may still rove through the plains, murmuring his gentle love for her.

There is not in Handel that strong vein of mysticism which we find in Bach. The chromatic idiom is used by Bach to express mysticism, sadness and suffering. Handel's style is mainly diatonic, simple and direct. The unexpected intervals—sometimes difficult for singers to execute—which occur in Bach's vocal works are not to be found in Handel, though both share that combination of robustness and delicacy (where appropriate) which is characteristic of German music as a whole.

Handel did not consciously dedicate all his art to God in the way that Bach did, or as he himself did in the case of *Messiah* and in his liturgical masterpieces; but in the widest sense that has been used elsewhere in this book, all his finest music is divine in a strong degree. Even the melodies in his secular works—" Ombra mai fu " from *Xerxes* (the famous Largo), the minuet in *Berenice*, " Non lo diro col labro " (" Silent worship ") from the opera *Ptolemy*, and movements in the *Concerti Grossi* and other instrumental compositions—are again and again, as in Bach's case, imbued with a deeply spiritual character.

7

THE DEDICATION OF HAYDN AND THE PROBLEM OF MOZART

JOSEPH HAYDN was born in 1732 at Rohrau, in Lower Austria, of humble parents who brought him up to be industrious, methodical, and above all religious. Towards the end of his life he said to his friend Griesinger (a Government official, who wrote some biographical notes about him), " Almighty God, to whom I render thanks for all his unnumbered mercies, gave me such facility in music that by the time I was six I stood up like a man and sang masses in the church choir, and could play a little on the clavier and violin." This refers to the time when he was at school at Hainburg, under the care of a distant relative, but at the age of eight, when an opportunity came, he was moved, with his parents' consent, to the Cantorei of St. Stephen's, Vienna. However, when his voice broke, he was of no further use there as a chorister; so advantage was taken of his having committed a practical joke on a school-fellow, and he was dismissed.

It is not necessary here to trace the various steps which led to his becoming Kapellmeister to Prince Paul Anton Esterházy at Eisenstadt and subsequently at the palace "Esterház", built as a summer residence in the country by Prince Nicolaus (who had succeeded his brother Paul on the latter's death). Most of the chapel staff were installed there for the greater part of the year, and Haydn composed, for local performance, operas, songs, music for marionettes, symphonies and chamber music, and works for church worship. Prince Nicolaus died in 1790, and though his successor continued, and even added to, Haydn's pension, he dismissed the whole chapel, whereupon the composer moved to Vienna. By that time he was famous, and his celebrated visits to England followed, under the auspices of Salomon. It is characteristic of him that during the first of these, when the honorary degree of Doctor of Music was conferred on him by Oxford University, he sent as his " exercise " a canon to the words " Thy voice, O Harmony, is divine ". After his second visit, he composed *The Creation*, and his own words were " Never was I so pious as when composing *The Creation*. I knelt down every day and prayed God to strengthen me for my work."

Before Haydn went to Eisenstadt, he had fallen in love with the younger daughter of a wig-maker in Vienna, to whose house he had been introduced by her brother who was violinist at St. Stephen's. He taught music to both daughters, but the younger one took the veil, and Haydn was persuaded by the father to marry the elder. Unhappily, she turned out to be a shrew, who (he said), " cared not a straw whether I was an artist or a shoemaker". She spent the last years of her life at Baden, near Vienna, and died in 1800.

It says much for Haydn's character that this miserable marriage did not embitter him. On the contrary, he was extremely benevolent, a generous and helpful friend, loved children, who called him " Papa Haydn", and was very fond of jokes. He was hard-working and methodical, and enjoyed honour and fame, but was not ambitious. He was a devoted and very observant Christian, and also became a Freemason. On all his scores he wrote " In nomine Domini " at the beginning and " Laus Deo " at the end—sometimes adding abbreviations to denote " Et Beatae Virgini Mariae et omnibus Sanctis " (" And to the Blessed Virgin Mary and all the Saints ").

Towards the end of his life he said: "I know that God has bestowed a talent upon me, and I thank Him for it: I think I have done my duty and been of use in my generation by my works: let others do the same."

Haydn consecrated the whole of his art to God, just as Bach had done before him. Yet it has been said that his Masses, of which he wrote twelve, are operatic in character and unfitted for church worship. I find this view unacceptable. " Operatic " does not necessarily mean irreligious, in any case, though if it were a true description of the style this might well make a work unsuited for the purposes of ritual. But Haydn's Masses are not operatic. It is true that, like *The Creation*, they contain a great deal of music which is charming; but the same can be said of much of the liturgical art of Bach, when we think of the graceful melodies that he associated with angels, the "Pastoral" Symphony in the Christmas Oratorio, and many other passages. God forbid that there should be no charm in our worship!

Haydn's church music is invariably apt for the words. It is worth while to consider this aspect in a little more detail.

The *Missa in honorem Beatissimae Virginis Mariae* (sometimes known as " The Great Organ Mass in E flat "—the second of his Masses), opens with a "Kyrie", which is a simple, devout prayer, in flowing phrases, partly contrapuntal, partly sung by voices answering one another in imitation. In the "Gloria", the words " Et in terra pax " are set to very slow, serene tones, followed by a quick and lively "Laudamus". The "Gratias" is slow and stately, with the lower strings moving in a steadily marching measure beneath the voices. The entreaties of the "Miserere", in a minor key, are followed by the cheerful strains of the "Quoniam".

The "Credo" opens with quick, confident music, continuing until we come to the "Incarnatus"; here the tenor solo is tender in character, though Haydn does not convey the mystery of the event. The "Crucifixus" is a chorus in slow, deeply felt, counterpoint. For "Et Resurrexit" Haydn composed an alto solo, happy and moderately fast in *tempo*; then the chorus take up the glad tidings. The "Et in spiritum sanctum" is marked by great scales in the lower strings, underneath the sustained notes of the chorus.

The "Sanctus" brings telling syncopated choral effects, and in the "Benedictus" there is serene music for organ and for the soprano and tenor soloists singing together. The "Agnus Dei", in very slow time, is an eloquent prayer sung by the choir, at first in the major, with some striking modulations, and later in the minor; it is perhaps the most beautiful and deeply religious part of the whole work. The Mass closes with an urgent plea for peace, to the words "Dona nobis pacem".

Haydn's Ninth Mass, in D minor, is the "Imperial" or "Coronation" or "Nelson" Mass,[1] composed in 1797, for soloists, chorus, trumpets, strings and drums. The "Kyrie" is a passionate entreaty for pity. The "Gloria" sounds a note of gaiety, but the "Qui tollis" for bass solo is a slow, solemn prayer for mercy. The "Quoniam" returns to a mood of cheerfulness.

The "Credo" again voices the composer's confident faith, and proceeds at a quick pace until the "Incarnatus", which is slow in *tempo*, meditative and idyllic in character, sung by the soprano solo. Mystery enters with the music of the "Crucifixus", portraying the deep, solemn tragedy of the event in a minor key, modulating to the major. Then the "Et Resurrexit" blazes triumphant and "forte", yet with a sudden hush at the words "Iterum Venturus". The music of "Et in spiritum sanctum" down to the end of the "Credo" expresses an eager faith and happiness, with an accompaniment of rushing violins.

The "Sanctus" returns to the mood of solemnity. The "Pleni sunt

[1] It was written for the Coronation of Francis II; Nelson heard it at Eisenstadt and exchanged his watch for the pen with which Haydn wrote it. The composer was very interested in the Battle of the Nile.

coeli " and the " Hosanna " together form a hymn of praise, in fairly quick *tempo*. The " Benedictus " begins with an orchestral introduction in slow, stately measure and a minor key, followed by a soprano solo and chorus imbued with grandeur of spirit. The key changes to major, and back to minor. The music rises to sublimity, with Beethovenish hammerings on drums and trumpets supporting the chorus. After this, the " Hosanna " is briefly recapitulated.

The way in which the solo voices, in the "Agnus Dei", enter one by one with their slow, tender music in the major, is extremely beautiful. Finally the chorus sing " Dona nobis pacem " to joyful strains in quick time.

The " Maria Theresa " Mass in B flat (1799) starts its " Kyrie " in stately fashion, followed by a quick contrapuntal movement.

The " Gloria " has an exultant opening, but at the words " Et in terra pax " the music becomes quiet and mysterious. " Gratias " is set to a flowing melody, for solo voices, in slow time: it may be contended that this does not differ in style from Haydn's instrumental slow movements, but they, after all, are so often spiritual in character.

The " Credo " of this Mass is remarkable for the omission of the words " Et in Unum Dominum Jesum Christum Dei unigenitum "—apparently owing to the haste of composition. The " Incarnatus " is again tender, rather than mysterious, the " Crucifixus " a solemn movement in a minor key and the " Resurrexit " is remarkable because it starts also in the minor, and is not markedly quick in *tempo*, but dignified: the latter part is in the major.

The " Sanctus " is slow moving, very " legato "—with a characteristic counterpoint in the lower strings; while the " Benedictus " is a tender, lyrical " andante " for solo voices, with a quicker accompaniment.

" Agnus Dei " is an urgent plea for mercy, by the chorus, which at the outset sings in unison: it is in slow time, in the minor, and the quick, happy music of the " Dona nobis pacem " provides a final contrast.

Haydn's " Creation " Mass (No. 11 in B flat), is so-called because the " Qui tollis " reproduces the melody of Adam's and Eve's duet " The dew-dropping morn " in *The Creation*. Its " Kyrie " starts with the orchestra alone, followed by a short soprano solo, leading to a stately chorus; this becomes cheerful and quicker in *tempo*, but later the music sounds a deeper note of entreaty, more in keeping with the words.

The " Gloria " is a song of praise in a major key, the " Et in terra pax " quiet and in the minor. " Laudamus te " and " Gratias " form a flowing, contrapuntal chorus, and " Qui tollis " is a duet, meditative in character, afterwards taken up by the chorus. " Quoniam " is again cheerful. The " Cum sancto spiritu " contains a rich fugue to the words " in gloria Dei Patris. Amen."

The " Credo " is yet another illustration of this composer's supremely confident faith, as far as the words " descendit de coelis ". The " Et incarnatus " gives us quiet, tender, celestial strains on the strings and the flute stop of the organ, taken up by the solo tenor. The " Crucifixus " opens in quiet pathos, but the chorus come in " fortissimo " at the words " Sub Pontio Pilato " and then the movement ends softly. " Et Resurrexit " provides a joyful contrast, for chorus followed by soprano solo: there is a quiet mystery in the setting of " judicare vivos et mortuos " and of " vitam venturi saeculi ".

The " Sanctus " is a serene meditation, first with the instruments, then with the voices entering one after another. The " Pleni sunt coeli " is a quick chorus of praise, the " Hosanna " an acclamation by solo soprano and chorus. The " Benedictus " is a quartet for the soloists, of the utmost serenity, with its extremely simple, gently flowing phrases.

" Agnus Dei " is also a quartet, followed by the chorus, uttering a prayer in slow time. The contrapuntal " Dona " is a resolute call for peace.

Haydn's " Te Deum " in C (No. 2, written in 1800) is entirely choral—a triptych comprising two joyful songs of praise, with a devout prayer offered between them. Here is another example of a liturgical work which is completely devotional in its nature.

These ritualistic compositions of Haydn are no more operatic or secular in character than *The Creation* or than the great religious masterpieces of his predecessors or of certain of those who followed him. He does not convey the mystery of the Incarnation in musical terms, in the way that, for instance, Bach, Beethoven and Vaughan Williams have done, for the simple reason that there was not in him the strong vein of mysticism that is to be found in them. The cheerfulness which, so to speak, keeps on breaking in, during the course of Haydn's Masses, is in conformity with the happy character of so much of *The Creation* and of his instrumental art. Haydn clearly regarded a cheerful spirit as being completely in keeping with a religious attitude of mind, and there are many devout people who will heartily agree with him.

Among Haydn's compositions the supreme example of grave solemnity in a religious work is his setting of *The Seven Words of our Saviour on the Cross*, commissioned by the Cathedral at Cadiz for use on Good Friday. He described it as " seven sonatas, with an introduction, and at the end an earthquake", and no fewer than three instrumental versions of it were produced, one for orchestra, one for strings (hence its performance sometimes as a string quartet), and one for pianoforte; later, either Haydn himself or his brother Michael or someone else transformed it all into a cantata, in two parts divided by a Largo for wind instruments. The seven " sonatas " are really seven slow movements, each of such heavenly beauty that we are not conscious of monotony even if they are performed in one of the instrumental forms without intervals. Actually, each of the seven " words " of our Lord, set by Haydn to a bass recitative, was followed by the Bishop's exhortation; then, while he knelt at the altar, the appropriate " sonata " was played.

There are other sublime movements among Haydn's instrumental works, but the quality which is perhaps most characteristic of him—apart from his delightful gift of arousing surprise by his unexpected modulations and turns of phrase—is the springlike freshness of his music, the natural product of his early childhood in a small village and the many years which he spent at the Esterházy palace in the depths of the country. Thus the divinity of the beauty of nature finds a musical counterpart in the God-like art of this simple-hearted man. It was fitting that his last work should have been *The Seasons*, in which he depicts so many outdoor scenes in graphic, fragrant tones. *The Creation* combines musical pictures of nature with songs of praise to the Almighty Father of Heaven and Earth and Sea so that the whole composition is a conscious act of worship. *The Seasons* is not, for the most part, expressly devotional, but is no less divine, as a spontaneous portrayal of natural beauty.

. . . . .

From the aspect with which this book is concerned, Haydn's case is a relatively simple one, if the views which I have expressed above are accepted. He consciously dedicated the whole of his art to God, and his works, for all their variety, were consistent with that dedication. Mozart presents a more complex problem. As a man, he was a less perfect character than Haydn, though the faults which we can now see in him, and which the nineteenth century had not discovered, still leave him as a person in whom the good preponderates. When a boy, he was impudent and mischievous, but solemn and thoughtful where music was concerned. He wrote obscene letters to his young girl cousin " Bäsle " (Maria Anna Thekla Mozart). He was brought up to be so dependent on his parents that on maturity he lacked worldly wisdom, and was, as Melchior Grimm, the journalist and encyclopaedist, remarked, "too good-natured". His father, Leopold, described him as hot-tempered and impulsive; when not actually in want, lazy; when he had to bestir himself, impatient and hasty. His consciousness of his own musical genius prevented him from being discreet enough to avoid incurring the dislike of mediocre people. He tended to pick on the laughable or faulty side of a man rather than on his good qualities. Yet when he married Constanze Weber he was a sympathetic husband who did his best to make life easy for her, though she was a bad and thoughtless housewife who never looked ahead, uneducated and lacking in *savoir faire*. Mozart was not even sure of her faithfulness, but she had no real reason to suspect him of infidelity, though he undoubtedly had an idyllic friendship with the beautiful and accomplished singer Anna Selina Storace, the first Susanna in *Figaro*, to whom he dedicated a love scena and aria " Ch'io mi scordi di te".

Mozart was a patriot, but sufficiently international minded to write Italian operas (thank goodness!) and to be fond of England and the English, though he did not appreciate the French.

In his youth, the Mozart family were devout Roman Catholics, but they had no illusions about individual members of the priesthood—or, for that matter, about any important people. Mozart, who was insensitive to the beauty of nature, hated even so lovely a place as Salzburg, largely because he was working there for Archbishop Colloredo whom he disliked. Doubtless the Archbishop was at fault for not appreciating him, but Mozart was difficult. Colloredo wanted a conscientious Court musician, and a temperamental artist like Mozart was ill-fitted for the post. The composer was treated as a servant, but at that time (1781) he was twenty-five and the Archbishop could not foresee that he was to be recognised as one of the most universal geniuses that the world has ever known. A series of incidents led to the final parting. Mozart asked the Archbishop for leave to appear at the Tonkünstler-Societät, which was at first refused and only later reluctantly granted. The composer wrote contemptuously about Colloredo in letters to his father, which the Archbishop probably read. Eventually, when Mozart gave a false excuse for not coming back from

Vienna to Salzburg, on a particular day, Colloredo told him to go to the devil. The composer took this as an invitation to ask for dismissal. He did so, and on his third attempt to get his request accepted, Count Arco, the son of the Court Chamberlain, kicked him out of the door.

At the end of 1784 Mozart, and in the spring of 1785 his father, became Freemasons. Thereafter the composer remained a sincere Catholic, but discovered in Freemasonry something wider still, with its striving for the good of humanity, its search for moral purity, its attitude of treating death as something to be welcomed, at any rate for the person dying—" soothing and consoling ", rather than " terrifying ", he wrote to Leopold on August 4th, 1787.

In contrast with his experiences at the hands of the Archbishop, Mozart found himself treated as a " brother " in his Lodge, on an equality with representatives of the aristocracy. He wrote music for the funeral of two brother members and for other Masonic ceremonies; and in the last year of his life, at about the same time as his *Requiem*, he composed *Die Zauberflöte*—strongly associated with Freemasonry—and the Masonic cantata "Die ihr des unermesslichen Weltalls" (K. 619) which calls on all who worship a Divine Creator—whether as Christ, Jehovah, or Brahma—to love one another as brothers. The Roman Catholic Church and Freemasonry remained with him side by side to the end.

Now, the external events of a creative artist's life are often quite unrelated to the nature of the art which he is producing at the time. We see this, for instance, in Mozart, whose worldly fortunes were at a low ebb when he composed some of his most joyous works such as *Così fan tutte* and the E flat and C major Symphonies (K. 543 and 551). But the personal character of the artist certainly has a bearing on his creations, though even here we have to remember that in some cases the finest aspect of the man is revealed in his art rather than in his private life.

There is, I suggest, an important contrast between Haydn and Mozart. Haydn avowedly consecrated his art, because he was an extremely religious man, and though he, too, became a Freemason, he was a very unobservant one. His church music is intrinsically devotional, because it was part of his simple faith that it should be so. Mozart, a lovable but somewhat less unblemished character, was an orthodox Catholic for the first twenty-eight years of his life, with an attitude towards his religion, however, that was essentially gay, and not merely cheerful like Haydn's; and from the time that he became a

Freemason he was no longer what the strict authorities of the Church would call a good Catholic. But throughout his life, the creation of operas was his ideal: the human voice was for him the most beautiful instrument, and he hankered after the large orchestra and the opportunity of expressing dramatic emotions. That is why in his church music—unlike that of Haydn—there is a remarkable combination of operatic and devotional styles.

For instance, the second of Mozart's two settings of " Litaniae de venerabili altaris sacramento " (K. 243) shows how he could incorporate the most varied musical conceptions of the words " Miserere nobis " in the course of one work. At one point they are sung by the tenor solo to a cheerful, operatic strain which might have come out of *Figaro*; at another, by the choir, in slow, chromatic tones, expressing a real prayer of entreaty, followed, however, by music again in the style of opera; the words recur in a serene, seraphic chorus for women's voices, truly religious in character; in a quick chorus of a liturgical nature, containing syncopated effects; and in the final melodious and beautiful chorus in slow *tempo*, which is more devotional in quality than some of the previous numbers. The soprano's first solo has a lovely melody—divine in a wide sense, but not specifically religious: it does not differ in style from the more serious arias in the great Mozart operas. The " Agnus Dei " is a simple soprano song, beautiful but entirely operatic, with coloratura passages and ornamental trills.

Mozart's Mass in C minor (K. 427) was left unfinished, and the only complete sections are the "Kyrie", "Gloria" and "Sanctus", though the first two numbers of the " Credo " are almost complete. Various reasons for this have been given: that having vowed to have a new Mass performed in Salzburg if he married Constanze, in celebration of her recovery from an illness, he simply could not finish it in time for the first performance on August 25th, 1783, at St. Peter's Church, when the missing parts are said to have been supplied from earlier Masses of his; that he wrote it when he was starting to become interested in Freemasonry; that a good many fragments of compositions date from that time particularly—an anxious period of his life when he had no settled appointment after the termination of his service with the Archbishop. In any case, Alois Schmitt, a Dresden conductor and composer, deserved the gratitude of posterity when in 1901 he completed the work by the addition of movements from other church compositions by Mozart, though this naturally involved some fresh endings and filling-in of parts. In the original portions of the Mass we find, though to a smaller extent than in the "Litaniae", an admixture of secular or operatic style with music which is supremely religious. The " Christe Eleison " was taken from one of the " solfeggi " written for Constanze and in its later part becomes operatic in character. The " Et Incarnatus " conveys a feeling of charming, serene domesticity, in contrast to the profound mysticism of Bach's setting of the same words to express the greatest mystery of the spiritual world. Elsewhere in the work Mozart has written music of a deeply devotional kind, rising at times to sublime heights which he never surpassed. It is unfortunate that he left it unfinished, but Schmitt filled the gaps from other compositions of his with consummate taste. It has been said that it was a mistake for him to set the " Agnus Dei " to the music of the opening "Kyrie", on the ground that this makes too sombre an ending for an ordinary Mass: but the Latin words of the " Agnus Dei " are a prayer for mercy and " miserere " means the same as the " eleison " of the " Kyrie "; and Mozart's music of the part of the " Christe Eleison " in the major key is peaceful and well suited to the spirit of the final " Dona Nobis Pacem ".

Mozart's *Requiem*—the only other of his liturgical compositions which is on the same level of tragic grandeur as the Mass in C minor—was also left unfinished, but this was due to his having to complete *La Clemenza di Tito* and *Die Zauberflöte* and to his death soon afterwards when he was not quite thirty-six. It was commissioned by a certain Count whose identity Mozart is said not to have known, but who had lost his wife some years earlier, wished to have a Requiem for her, and sent his steward to Mozart with an order for its composition. Mozart finished only the initial " Requiem and Kyrie " and sketched the various sections of the " Dies Irae " and the "Offertorio". After his death his pupil Süssmayr undertook to complete the work at Constanze's request: he filled in the sketches, composed music of his own for the " Sanctus ", " Benedictus " and "Agnus Dei " and repeated Mozart's " Kyrie " fugue to the words "Cum Sanctis tuis". Although at the end of Mozart's life Freemasonry meant more to the great composer than Roman Catholicism, the worship of God and the thoughts aroused by death are common to both and inspired him to the creation of some of his most wonderful music—for example, the resignation of the opening " Requiem aeternam ", the sublimity of the first section of the " Dies Irae " and the deeply felt prayer at the words " Recordare, Jesu pie . . . "

Both in the C minor Mass and the *Requiem* we find a deepening and enrichment of the spiritual character of his art, which is attributable to the influence of Handel and especially of Bach. His move to Vienna in 1781 brought him into contact with Baron Gottfried van Swieten, at whose house a group of musicians used to meet on Sundays and perform music for their own delight. It was by this means that Mozart became acquainted with the art of Bach and Handel, and it is interesting to remember that van Swieten (who was Imperial chargé d'affaires at the Prussian Court from 1770–1777) in turn had come to know Bach's music through King Frederick the Great. Mozart's music does not at all resemble the work of either of the other two great masters—he was far too individual a genius for that—but his introduction to it had a vital effect upon his artistic soul.

Alfred Einstein[1] suggests that the liturgical works of Mozart are the musical counterparts of the eighteenth-century churches of south Germany and Austria which in place of austerity or mystic quality are full of festive gaiety. " The columns rise in serpentine spirals, the altars gleam in purple and gold, and in the bright ceiling paintings the Holy Trinity is surrounded by throngs of saints and cherubs." Those churches are, he adds, not " secular ", but " of a childlike piety that is no less truly devout than the purest Gothic ". We may agree with this view in general, yet still feel that there are some parts of Mozart's church compositions which by reason of their operatic style do not wholly succeed in expressing a mood of prayer or devotion to God, however sincerely the composer may have intended them to do so, and that in this respect they differ from the Masses of Haydn. Both for Haydn and Mozart religious art must be warm and human: God is the creator of secular things, and music which ignored them would not have expressed the characteristic attitude of these two masters towards divine worship. Nevertheless we do not find in Haydn's liturgical compositions the occasional incongruities which appear in those of Mozart, with his operatic ideals. When we come to trace the finger of God in the history of opera,[2] we shall realise that in Mozart's case there could not be a sharp dividing line between " sacred " and " secular " art. He was concerned with the music of humanity. For him music aspired to the condition of opera (if I may adapt Walter Pater's phrase).[3] But whereas other great composers have been pre-eminent

[1] *Mozart, His Character, His Work* (English translation), p. 80.

[2] Chapter 17, infra.

[3] " All art constantly aspires to the condition of music."

in certain fields, Mozart had as great a genius for instrumental music as for opera, and he shone in liturgical art, too: the Mass in C minor and the *Requiem*, although unfinished, are among the greatest pieces of church music between Bach and Beethoven, and these were not his only devotional masterpieces.

The *daimôn* in Mozart's music, about which much has been written, was no demonic power, but a flashing insight into the depths of human nature, revealed thereby as partly divine. It is to be found often in his instrumental works, particularly in profound passages or movements written in the minor, whilst a spiritual or definitely religious quality sometimes also takes the form of tranquil or ethereal music in a major key.

G minor is associated in Mozart with resignation in the face of the menaces and problems of existence—an essentially religious attitude. This appears in the first movement of the Quartet for pianoforte and strings in that key (K. 478), though the Andante (in B flat) seeks, as it were, to calm us down, and the final Rondo in G major is brave and cheerful. The opening movement of the String Quintet in G minor (K. 516) expresses a noble sorrow, the Minuet strikes a note of resignation, with an intervening touch of comfort from above in the Trio, and the Adagio non troppo has a profound, forlorn, yet devotional character. In the Allegro molto of the G minor Symphony (K. 550) there is again a deep undercurrent of sadness and resignation; the Andante is full of mystery and pathos, expressed by chromatic passages and unusual intervals, even though the main key is E flat major; the anxiety of the Minuet is relieved for a brief while in the Trio, where Mozart's muse seems almost to be trying to reassure him, but the anxiety returns, just as nature and the structure of the movement alike would lead us to expect; and the symphony ends with a Finale which is still troubled in spirit. G minor has remained true to its character.

C minor also is a sad, even a tragic, key for Mozart; but like all great tragedies, the finest music that he wrote in this key has a spiritual quality. The *Sinfonia Concertante* for violin, viola and orchestra in E flat (K. 364) opens with an Allegro maestoso which is profoundly serious though in a major key; but its Andante in C minor is deeply sorrowful, and though this movement ends on a more peaceful note of resignation, all the buoyancy of the final Presto is needed to restore our spirits. In the Fantasia in C minor for pianoforte (K. 475) deep undertones of sorrow and resignation alternate with messages of divine comfort in a major key. It is one of Mozart's most sublime works, and another is the Pianoforte Concerto in C minor (K. 491): the first movement of this is imbued with tragic grandeur, the Larghetto (in E flat) is peaceful and utterly simple; but in the theme and variations of the Allegretto (again in C minor) there is a supernatural quality, with intervening periods of relief but no final reconciliation such as we get in the D minor Concerto (K. 466).

In this D minor work, the first movement is a contest between the supernatural menace of the orchestra and the human pathos of the solo pianoforte; the first and last parts of the Romanza (in B flat) are full of celestial peace, but the middle section is again menacing, as might be expected from the key of G minor; the drama is resumed in the Finale, but in the coda it is resolved in radiant sunshine.

Another work in a minor key which exhibits that restrained but profound emotion so typical of Mozart, is the Sonata for violin and piano in E minor (K. 304). It is, I suggest, this very restraint of grief which imparts so spiritual a character to some of his finest compositions.

But he by no means depended on the minor key for the revelation of the divinity within him. Apart from the particular movements in major keys in the works which I have mentioned, we find many instances of a religious, or at least a spiritual, quality in music written in the major. His last Wind Serenade in C minor (K. 388) has an Andante in E flat which is a heartfelt prayer in happy mood. The Andante (in A flat) of the E flat String Quartet (K. 428) is a mystical dream. The Adagio (in E flat) of the "Hunt" Quartet in B flat (K. 458)[1] is a lovely dialogue between the four voices, ending in ethereal calm.

There is a strength and divinity in the "Linz" (C major) and "Prague" (D major) Symphonies (K. 425 and 504) such as we do not find in the same degree in any of Mozart's earlier, more light-hearted, symphonies. His last three compositions in this genre were all written in the summer of 1788, and the two in major keys present a strong contrast to the divine sadness of the one in G minor. The Symphony in E flat (K. 543) opens with a mysterious introduction, but there is a blessed happiness in the ensuing Allegro; the Andante voices an inward peace; the Minuet is festive, with an almost unbelievably simple Trio; and the work ends with a buoyant Allegro. The final Symphony in C

[1] So-called, because of the resemblance of the opening theme of the first movement to the sound of the hunting horn.

(K. 551) certainly does not owe its divinity to any association with Jupiter, and it was singularly inept for anyone to call it by the name of the supreme god of Roman theology. There is nothing pagan about Mozart, but Greek poise and grace would seem to be more characteristic of him than anything redolent of ancient Rome. Bravery is the chief quality of the first movement; the Andante cantabile is almost a prayer of submission to God's will, with many touches of wistfulness; the Minuet is a miracle of grace; the divine joy of the Finale ends in contrapuntal glory.

The Piano Concerto in B flat major (K. 595), completed in January 1791—the year of Mozart's death—has a first movement expressive of controlled resignation, with moments of grief; the Larghetto (in E flat) is calm and devotional; there is restraint in the contentment of the Finale, and indeed the whole work conveys restrained happiness rather than heartfelt joy.

The Quintet for clarinet and strings (K. 581), is not actually religious in quality, but it is idyllically beautiful and seraphic, even when, as in some places in the Finale, it is humorous. It is significant that another of Mozart's three great works for clarinet solo,[1] the Concerto (K. 622), is also in A major: it is his farewell to the concerto form, written in the last year of his life, and if we are to judge by the serenity of this lovely music we might infer that Mozart was reconciled to life in spite of the troubles and disappointments through which he had passed, were it not for our knowledge of the circumstances surrounding the composition of the *Requiem*.

Tovey,[2] in discussing the G minor Symphony, wrote that " Mozart's whole musical language is, and remains throughout, the language of comic opera." This is a strange saying, and seems difficult to reconcile with his description of the slow movement of the Pianoforte Concerto in G (K. 453) as " one of those profound utterances of Mozart in terms which are almost confined to formulas; the language of the ' Zauberflöte,' the last (so-called 'Jupiter') Symphony, and the 'Requiem' ";[3] or with his statement apropos the C minor Concerto (K. 491): "Tell me that a mature but unknown large work of Mozart is in a minor key, and I will confidently assert that while it may have humorous passages it will certainly have both passion and pathos, and that while

[1] The third was the Trio for pianoforte, viola and clarinet in E flat (K. 498), a composition of intimate beauty.

[2] *Essays in Musical Analysis*, Vol. I, p. 192.

[3] Ibid., Vol. III, p. 35.

the pathos will almost certainly not amount to tragedy, it is very likely that much of the work will border on the sublime."[1]

With the later instrumental compositions of Mozart, there is little or none of the " galant " or comic-opera style which is often to be found in his earlier works, and the depth of character and emotion free from all dross, which they express in music of transcendent beauty, reveal in a pronounced degree the divine side of human nature.

[1] *Essays in Musical Analysis*, Vol. III, p. 44.

8

THE MIRACLE OF BEETHOVEN

IN Beethoven, the paradox of the relationship between God and music reaches its climax. It is true that he composed certain works which were avowedly devotional—*The Mount of Olives*; the six *Geistliche Lieder* (op. 48), to Gellert's words, of which *Die Ehre Gottes* (*Creation's Hymn*) is today the best known; and the two Masses. True also, that here and there we have clues, outside the music itself, to the ideas which inspired it—the title "Eroica" and the earlier association of that symphony with Napoleon; the programme of the "Pastoral" Symphony; the words of songs and of Beethoven's only opera, and the connection between the overtures and the dramatic works for which they were written; the title of the sonata *Les Adieux, L'Absence et le Retour*; an occasional verbal indication given by the composer as to the "meaning" of an instrumental movement; the vocal Finale of the Ninth Symphony, and so on. But the bulk of his work is for instruments alone, unaccompanied by any such clues as these, and yet, though it bears no resemblance to music previously associated with divine worship, we recognise it as profoundly spiritual in character.

The other aspect of the Beethovenian paradox is that the Mass in C and the *Missa Solemnis*, one of the supreme expressions of Christian faith in the history of art, were created by a man who was not a regular churchman and who has even been alleged—wrongly, in my view—to have been a deist rather than a Christian.

The spiritual element in his music—even more than his stupendous imagination, his unsurpassed mastery of technical resource and his astonishing power of construction—is Beethoven's essential glory. He was not only the greatest musical genius that the world has yet seen. He is also, in a special sense, a tremendous benefactor of humanity, by reason of the particular quality of his art.

If we were to try to form an idea of Beethoven's personal character from his music alone, we should judge him to have been, as a man, almost entirely noble. In fact, he was an extraordinary mixture: he was arrogant, ill-mannered, at times inconsiderate of other people's feelings, contemptuous of many of his less gifted acquaintances, yet eager to help the needy and imbued with a longing for the brotherhood of humanity; unselfishly devoted to the welfare of his nephew, yet tragically unsuited by reason of his temperament and his deafness to act as his guardian; in an age when artists had no such bodies as a Performing Rights Society to fight their battles and had not acquired the protection of our modern copyright laws, not always over-scrupulous in his dealings with his publishers, but indignant in his refusal to lower his artistic ideals for the sake of monetary gain; a man of sublime courage, whose life was a conflict and who expressed that conflict in music of incomparable grandeur and nobility. As a person, his faults were far outweighed by his qualities.

A friend of mine once said that in the art of Beethoven the whole of human nature is mirrored; it is truer to say that it is transfigured. For, with one exception, there is a singular absence of the portrayal of evil in Beethoven's music, and in it the emotions, thoughts and aspirations of men are idealised.

The exception is the music for Pizarro in *Fidelio*. Beethoven's imagination was too intense for him to fail to get inside the skin of the character, and the wickedness of this governor of the prison is vividly portrayed in the menacing key of D minor, with a chromatic figure "allegro agitato" on the violins at the beginning of the Aria, violent thrusting rhythms for the bass voice, and diminished sevenths leading to villainously triumphant major chords at the close. But Pizarro is an isolated case, and it is significant that *Fidelio* was Beethoven's only opera. His genius did not, in the main, lie in that direction, and there is nothing surprising in his difficulty in finding an operatic subject suited to his artistic bent or in his inability to discover another.

The varied emotions of mankind—joy, sorrow, melancholy, gaiety, love, occasionally anger, and so on—are portrayed even in Beethoven's early works, but even in these they are infused with a spiritual quality, which deepened with the years and ultimately took on a mystical character. It is present, for instance, in the very first Sonata for pianoforte, op. No. 2, No. 1 in F minor, with its opening Allegro, which is resolute yet has a touch of wistfulness, and its serene Adagio in the major. Through all these first period compositions of Beethoven we can discern, in the light of our knowledge of the greater music to come, the early signs of that idealisation of human emotions which was to form so marked a characteristic of his later works. But there was, as yet, little or no conflict. As a result, however, of his mother's death and his father's habitual drunkenness and death when Beethoven was just twenty-two, the composer had already incurred the responsibility of his brother's education and had experienced suffering and poverty. And when in his late twenties the first symptoms of deafness appeared, which were to increase steadily and eventually to become almost total, all his heroism was needed to face the anguish of soul that sprang from an affliction so terrible for a musician.

The " Eroica " Symphony, though associated with Napoleon before he assumed the title of Emperor, is Beethoven's musical conception of the heroic character, rendered possible only as a result of his own experiences. He presents the portrait in various aspects, and does not seek to describe events in chronological order. Thus the opening Allegro seems to give a picture of strength and nobility, of tenderness and anguish, of mystery, of hope, and of ultimate triumph. The second movement is the most tremendous funeral music in existence. The whole world seems to be paying its last homage to the great man whose glorious career has been cut short so tragically; and though the composer more than once lifts the veil of mourning and vouchsafes to us a voice of comfort, sweet beyond compare and assuring us of the hero's immortality in Heaven, yet at the end the solemn dirge returns, until the sad procession, with faltering steps and slow, gradually moves out of sight.

The Scherzo shows the lighter side of the hero's nature. It is instinct with the spirit of youth—youth in its most buoyant, vivacious and sprightly form. To Beethoven, who—as we know from the story of his life and from innumerable passages in his works—was gifted with a strong sense of humour, it would have been inconceivable that the ideal man who formed the subject of his symphony should constantly have been serious and dignified. The hero could not always be heroic. But the movement is not light-hearted throughout: in the Trio the music assumes for a while a graver tone, and we are afforded a glimpse into that eternal mystery which lies, potent and incomprehensible, behind and beyond the sparkling gaiety of youthful enthusiasm.

The Finale leaves on our minds an impression of growth. After a loud preliminary flourish, the strings give out in soft " pizzicato " notes the bass alone of the melody on which the rest of the movement is built. This curious beginning strikes us at first as being anything but heroic: on the contrary, it is almost insignificant, and its continuation is no more dignified. Even the theme itself, charming though it is, seems scarcely to be of the stuff of which heroes are made. It is as if Beethoven is showing us how even the greatest of mankind begins by being quite undistinguished, and yet may become a mighty leader and benefactor of men. Gradually the music becomes with successive variations more and more complex, as though it is reaching maturity. In the vigorous G minor episode, which alone interrupts the course of the variations, we seem to see the hero bracing his determination to accomplish his purpose. Throughout his career we watch that same simple nature of his, ever developing, until at last the composer in the Poco Andante section unfolds the wondrous tableau of the hero's ascent to the abode of the blessed.[1] The original air, once so delicate and childlike, is now transfigured by a vast change of *tempo* and instrumentation, and then thundered out in all its beauty and strength by the brass. The hero's life-task has been accomplished. He has entered the Kingdom of Heaven. And at the end of the symphony the orchestra seems to lift the melody shoulder high and, personifying all humanity, to proclaim the hero's glory.

The C minor Symphony was not completed until 1807. As early as November, 1801, when Beethoven's deafness was growing worse, he wrote to Wegeler: "I will seize Fate by the throat." He himself said of the main theme of the symphony's first movement: "Thus fate knocks at the door." Throughout this period of his life he conceived Fate as a stern, supernatural, external force, and the symphony is an idealisation of man's struggle and ultimate triumph over it. The Andante is a point of repose, in which his hopes and prayers for victory are expressed. The third movement, which is certainly no "scherzo", no "joke", again reveals the supernatural influence which dominated the opening Allegro: there is a return to its ominous rhythm of three short notes followed by a longer one—a rhythm which we find elsewhere in Beethoven's compositions, when he seems to portray some fateful agency that stands in man's path and challenges him in the struggles of life, for instance, in the first movement of the so-called *Sonata Appassionata* (op. 57 in F minor) and in the "Egmont" Overture; the motif recurs in the midst of the victorious Finale of this symphony, a reminder that a relentless, superhuman force is still at work, though the music of spiritual triumph soon rings again in our ears.

The Fourth and Sixth Symphonies are gentler and more restful in character. The Fourth, after a cloudy and anxious introduction, radiates pure happiness, and its slow movement portrays the idyllic

[1] It was Sir George Grove who first suggested that this section represents the apotheosis of the hero (*Beethoven and his Nine Symphonies*, p. 80).

love of man and woman. The "Pastoral" (Sixth) Symphony does not merely reflect joy in the countryside but in its freshness and fragrance brings man into closer communion with God through nature: and after the raging of the storm music it ends in a tranquil hymn of thanksgiving. The radiant beauty of the Fourth Piano Concerto, the confidence and the ethereal calm which inspire the Violin Concerto and the Fifth Concerto for piano in E flat, are characteristic of the same aspect of Beethoven's art at this period, when he felt, anyhow temporarily, at peace with the world.

Beethoven naturally falls below his own tremendously high level sometimes—for example, in the "Battle" Symphony, the *Ruins of Athens* music and the "King Stephen" Overture; but apart from such instances as these, he ennobles every emotion which he expresses. In the slow movement of the first Razoumovsky Quartet (op. 59, No. 1) he transfigures grief in music of sublime beauty; the Adagio of the next quartet opens up a vision of serene loveliness; in the "Andante con moto quasi Allegretto" of the last of these three quartets the composer reveals his soul's loneliness and despair, yet there is no trace of morbidity or self-pity in it. All the Razoumovsky Quartets show a conflict of the soul, but all of them end in triumph. The F minor Quartet (op. 95) anticipates Beethoven's third period in the intensity and mystery of its first movement, the profound calm of the "Allegretto ma non troppo", the sombre passion of the "Allegro assai vivace ma serioso" and the restless, yet noble, yearning character of the Finale; relief only comes near the close, with a "ppp" major chord followed by a short, happy Allegro.

The middle period of the composer's creative activity ends in a blaze of glory with the Seventh and Eighth Symphonies and the Trio for piano, violin and 'cello in B flat (op. 97). In these works the composer has, for the time being, put his sorrows and struggles behind him. He exults in his newly-found strength of spirit. In the Seventh Symphony, the spacious grandeur of the Introduction leads to a Vivace pulsing with joyous, rhythmic vigour. The Allegretto is a reflection, not of sadness, but of majestic melancholy with a religious strain in it, and even this is relieved by the voice of comfort in the serene middle section. The third movement bubbles over with exuberant vitality; the essentially spiritual quality, even in such vivacious music of Beethoven's as this, accounts for the fact that it leads perfectly naturally and without the slightest incongruity into a stately alternating section which is based on a pilgrim's hymn of

Lower Austria. The Finale is still more ecstatic: yet even amidst its unflagging rhythm, its violent explosions, its bursts of boisterous humour, we are conscious of the guiding hand of a master spirit; and when towards the close of the movement the lower strings gradually make their way downward by semitones, until they settle on the low E, while the violins still play reminiscences of the original whirling theme, against long notes sounded on the wind instruments, the music takes on a character of spiritual calm and nobility; but the change of mood is not for long: the whirlwind returns, and the symphony ends in a vast climax of joyous freedom.

The Eighth Symphony is lighter-hearted. It contains more pure laughter and high spirits than any other work of Beethoven's maturity. All traces of the old conflicts have temporarily disappeared. And even in the more intimate, more tranquil pages of the glorious B flat Trio there is no sadness, no pang of regret: the first movement is noble and serene, the Scherzo humorous but at times imbued with mystery, the Andante a set of lovely variations on one of Beethoven's most sublime melodies, the Finale gay from start to finish. But Beethoven's happiness was not destined to last. We should judge from the character of his music at this stage that he believed that he had conquered Fate; but his terrible malady grew worse, his loneliness increased, his anxieties over his nephew and his own poverty had still to be faced. He had to learn even to welcome suffering, because only by endurance could he survive and produce the still greater masterpieces which God's inspiration, his own genius and his prodigious efforts enabled him to bestow upon mankind.

At the entrance to Beethoven's third period stand the Pianoforte Sonata in A (op. 101) and the gigantic " Hammerklavier ", Sonata in B flat (op. 106). The former is even more profound than its predecessors in its tenderness, its pathos and its determination. And the " Hammerklavier " contains all the depth of his suffering, the splendour of his bravery and resolution. But it is not illumined by hope from above. There is sublimity in the courage with which he faces life, alone, cut off from the world; but fortunately for humanity, this mighty outpouring of his soul, expressed in some of the most tremendous music ever conceived, was to be followed by a spiritual awakening. It was in the light of this that he created his last three pianoforte sonatas, the overture *Die Weihe des Hauses*, the *Missa Solemnis*, the Ninth Symphony and the final quartets.

The E major Sonata (op. 109) shows that Beethoven had recovered his faith. Its first movement reflects happy tranquillity; the impetuous Prestissimo in the minor key is scarcely more than an interlude leading to the sublime serenity of the final variations. The Sonata in A flat (op. 110) has greater variety of moods—the calm and grace of the Moderato cantabile, the resolute vigour of the Molto Allegro, the majestic sadness of the slow movement, and the reassuring confidence of the final fugue, which, beginning quietly, increases in faith and hope and, though interrupted by a return of the sorrowful melody of the Adagio, ends in thankfulness and spiritual victory. Beethoven's last Sonata, in C minor (op. 111), consisting only of two movements, is perhaps the greatest of all. Its first movement is a stormy combat, but the slow Arietta with variations, which follows, is a song of profound, celestial happiness.

Before we approach Beethoven's remaining masterpieces, we must consider the question of his religion. He was brought up in the Roman Catholic faith. In each of his three periods he composed works which *prima facie* indicate belief in the basic doctrines of Christianity: the oratorio *Christus am Ölberg* (*The Mount of Olives*) about which in later years he said that it had been a mistake to treat the part of Christ in the modern, vocal style; the Mass in C; and the *Missa Solemnis*. His nephew, testifying in the guardianship proceedings in 1818, said that Beethoven had arranged for him to be instructed in religion by the former priest of Mödling, had admonished him to pray, and prayed with him every morning and evening. Beethoven's brother, Johann, tells how on his death-bed he decided " with the greatest readiness " to make his peace with God. Dr. Wawruch, who in his youth had thoughts of entering the priesthood, states in his report that he told Beethoven that his death was near, " so that he might do his duty as a citizen and to religion." " With the greatest delicacy," he says, " I wrote the words of admonition on a sheet of paper. . . . Beethoven read the writing with unexampled composure, slowly and thoughtfully, his countenance like that of one transfigured: cordially and solemnly he held out his hand to me and said ' Have the priest called '. . . . The sacrament was then administered and was received by Beethoven with edification."

Schindler, in a letter dated April 12th, 1827, to the *Cäcilia* magazine founded by B. Schott & Söhne, the music publishers, wrote: " On the day before (the 23rd March) there remained with us only one ardent wish—to reconcile him with heaven and to show the world at the same time that he had ended his life a true Christian. The Professor in

Ordinary [Wawruch] therefore wrote and begged him in the name of all his friends to receive the holy sacrament; to which he replied quietly and firmly, 'I wish it.' The physician went away and left us to care for it."[1]

In spite of all this evidence, it is customary to say that Beethoven's religious beliefs were not orthodox, and Thayer[2] goes so far as to declare that there is not the remotest indication that he believed in the necessity of any mediator between the soul of man and the Divine Father. His deep faith in God is shown by his constant invocations of Him in letters, in short prayers which he wrote down, and in records of conversations. But it has been suggested that the transcriptions which he made from Oriental writings probably express his own beliefs more truthfully than the words of the Catholic Mass. Let us consider this theory.

Thayer[3] quotes the following, which he describes as "perhaps the finest of all his [Beethoven's] transcriptions from Hindu literature":

> God is immaterial; since he is invisible he can have no form, but from what we observe in his works we may conclude that he is eternal, omnipotent, omniscient and omnipresent—The mighty one is he who is free from all desire; he alone; there is no greater than he.
>
> Brahma; his spirit is enwrapped in himself. He, the mighty one, is present in every part of space—his omniscience is in spirit by himself and the conception of him comprehends every other one; of all comprehensive attributes that of omniscience is the greatest. For it there is no threefold existence. It is independent of everything. O God, thou art the true, eternal, blessed, immutable light of all times and all spaces. Thy wisdom embraces thousands upon thousands of laws, and yet thou dost always act freely and for thy honor. Thou wert before all that we revere. To thee be praise and adoration. Thou alone art the truly blessed one (Bhagavan); thou, the essence of all laws, the image of all wisdom, present throughout the universe, thou upholdest all things.

Thayer also refers to Beethoven's enjoyment of Persian literature and quotes the following extracts from Schiller's account, in his essay *Die*

[1] Thayer, *The Life of Ludwig van Beethoven* (edited by H. E. Krehbiel), Vol. III, pp. 305 ff.

[2] Ibid., Vol. II, p. 169.

[3] Ibid., Vol. II, p. 167.

Sendung Moses, of the wisdom of the Egyptians in which the great Hebrew law-giver was learned:

> The epoptae (Egyptian priests) recognised a single, highest cause of all things, a primeval force, natural force, the essence of all essences, which was the same as the demiurgos of the Greek philosophers. There is nothing more elevated than the simple grandeur with which they spoke of the creator of the universe. In order to distinguish him the more emphatically they gave him no name. A name, said they, is only a need for pointing a difference; he who is only, has no need of a name, for there is no one with whom he could be confounded. Under an ancient monument of Isis were to be read the words: "I AM THAT WHICH IS", and upon a pyramid at Sais the strange primeval inscription: "I AM ALL, WHAT IS, WHAT WAS, WHAT WILL BE; NO MORTAL MAN HAS EVER LIFTED MY VEIL". No one was permitted to enter the temple of Serapis who did not bear upon his breast or forehead the name Iao, or I-ha-ho—a name similar in sound to the Hebrew Jehovah and in all likelihood of the same meaning; and no name was uttered with greater reverence in Egypt than this name Iao. In the hymn which the hierophant, or guardian of the sanctuary, sang to the candidate for initiation, this was the first division in the instruction concerning the nature of the divinity: "HE IS ONLY AND SOLELY OF HIMSELF, AND TO THIS ONLY ONE ALL THINGS OWE THEIR EXISTENCE".

Schindler tells us that the sentences in capital letters were copied by Beethoven "and kept, framed and under glass, always before him on his writing table."[1]

We have also to recall the references which Beethoven made to the great figures of Greek and Roman mythology—Bacchus, Hercules and others—in his letters, and to reflect how vividly they seem to have symbolised in his conception certain basic influences in life.

But to argue from all this that Beethoven was not a believing Christian, but only a deist, is quite inconclusive. The fact that he was absorbed in Eastern literature and even had certain sentences from it constantly before him, indicates simply that he had a wide outlook in these profound matters. So does his interest in classical mythology. In spite of the lack of culture in the education which he received at Bonn, he managed to acquire it by his friendship with the cultured von

[1] Thayer, *The Life of Ludwig van Beethoven*, Vol. II, p. 168.

Breuning family and from other sources. Christianity is strengthened, not weakened, by insight into other religions, and it is noticeable that the particular aspects of Oriental beliefs which Beethoven emphasised, show points of contact with, not departure from, the fundamental tenets of the Christian faith.

It is true that outside his music he speaks of God, but not of Christ. Arguments from silence, however, are of exceedingly doubtful validity; and they are particularly so in the case of Beethoven, who was by no means a master of language and was articulate in music to an infinitely greater extent than in words. As against the theory, which rests on the flimsiest foundation, that Beethoven did not believe in Christian doctrine, we have, in addition to the biographical facts already quoted, the overwhelming evidence of his music, and especially of his two great settings of the Mass.

The Mass in C (op. 86) is a very beautiful work of his middle period. It used to be performed more frequently than the later *Missa Solemnis*, but has recently been so much overshadowed by this that it has been unduly neglected. There is really no more reason to displace it in favour of the *Missa Solemnis* than to overlook the C minor Symphony because we rightly regard the Ninth as an even greater masterpiece. The Mass in C is in each of its sections a deeply-felt and imaginative revelation in sound of the thoughts underlying the liturgical text. It startled Beethoven's contemporaries by its originality, in the same sort of way as the " Eroica " and the C minor Symphonies did, in contrast with the music of his predecessors, though to us nowadays it naturally seems quite simple. The fact that the words of the Mass inspired him to such freshly thought-out musical ideas, shows how strong a hold upon him they had. In particular, the lovely "Kyrie", with its novel three-part plan, has an original, " pianissimo " close; the " Sanctus " has most striking harmonies; the " Agnus Dei " is deeply expressive; and the beautiful " Benedictus " is unusually elaborate. The music everywhere seems to express an implicit belief in the main Christian doctrines, though delving rather more profoundly into the heart of them than some of his predecessors had done. He wrote to Breitkopf and Härtel on June 8th, 1808: " I do not like to speak about my Mass, and least of all about myself; I, however, believe that I have treated the text as it has hitherto been seldom treated."[1]

While the Mass in C penetrates with deep feeling into the significance

[1] *The Letters of Ludwig van Beethoven* (translated by J. S. Shedlock, J. M. Dent & Son, 1909), Vol. I, p. 140.

of the words, its mighty successor, the *Missa Solemnis*, towers to Heaven in music of sublime grandeur and mystic vision. The " Kyrie " is a glorious, soaring prayer to God; the " Christe Eleison " is more restless, conveying the thought of Christ as mediator. In the "Gloria" Beethoven calls upon all humanity to sing the praise of God in the highest. When he comes to the "Credo", he thunders out his declaration of faith in a tremendous motto theme which forms the foundation on which all the wonderful fabric of his expression of the tenets of Christian belief is to be built. Everyone agrees that Beethoven devoutly believed in a Divine Father, and when he is presenting the idea of the " Maker of all things, visible and invisible " his music suddenly softens to a quiet reverence at the words "et invisibilium". The notion that he did not believe in the Divinity of Christ is set at nought by the ensuing asseveration that he believes " in one Lord Jesus Christ, son of God . . .", with the same musical motto for " Credo " and with no change of mood until he reaches the words "et incarnatus", when the mystery of the Incarnation is set forth in " adagio " time and with modal harmonies which go back to the days of the sixteenth century and a crescendo and trill on the flute are heard at the reference to the Holy Ghost. The joy inhabiting the music for the words which tell that Christ was made man is followed by the anguish and mystery of Beethoven's setting of the Passion and Crucifixion. The Resurrection is told in a single line of unaccompanied, triumphant chorus, and the remaining parts of the Creed in eloquent music always bound together by the great motto theme.

The " Sanctus " is a devout act of worship, in slow *tempo*, with a vivid fugue for the words "Heaven and earth are full of Thy glory". Then follows the miraculous setting of the " Benedictus "—the solo violin descending from Heaven with a divine melody and intertwining with the voices and the other instruments. The noble " Osanna " is a fugal crescendo of praise within the framework of the "Benedictus". The " Agnus Dei " is a prayer in sorrowful mood in the key of B minor, but eventually gives place to the sublime "Dona nobis pacem", which Beethoven calls " prayer for inward and outward peace ": twice the victorious tranquillity of the music is interrupted by the terror of warlike sounds on the trumpets and drums, first softly as though at a distance and then nearer at hand "fortissimo". But the Mass ends with peace, proclaimed by the chorus, and the notes of victory on the orchestra.

I suggested in another context[1] that it is not within the scope of music to argue or theorise; but that it may express conceptions so sublime or so far-reaching as to reveal a glimpse, or more than a glimpse, of the infinite. This is what Beethoven has accomplished in the *Missa Solemnis*. Bach has, of course, done the same thing, but the attitude of the two men towards religion and devotional music presents a strong contrast. Bach's life was, relatively speaking, unruffled and happy; he held a succession of appointments as organist, Kapellmeister and cantor of a church school, his Christian faith was devout and unquestioning, and his genius enabled him to express it in serene and majestical music; the depth of his belief and the vividness of his imagination also fired him to portray in eloquent tones the drama of the Passion story and the multifarious religious emotions contained in the many liturgical texts which he set. But to Beethoven life presented a challenge from his youth onwards. He, too, could compose serene music even in the middle period of his life, but it was a serenity won only as a result of a struggle either with superhuman forces or with the effects of his own tempestuous nature. The conflicts of his later years meant that he again had to struggle for the attainment of serenity in religious faith; but that he did attain it is shown in the *Missa Solemnis*, and in parts of the Ninth Symphony and of the works that followed. He was not normally a church-goer. Yet, paradoxically, his *Missa* is a liturgy, actually intended for use at the installation of his great friend and patron, the Archduke Rudolf, at Cologne, as Archbishop of Olmütz, and though it was finished too late for the ceremony, Beethoven was inspired by the words of the Mass to compose music of the utmost sublimity, and by the magnificence of so unique an occasion to summon up all the resources at his command; whereas Bach, who unlike Beethoven was normally ecclesiastical in his outlook, created in his B minor Mass a work which was set to the Latin words of the Roman Catholic ritual, though he was himself a Lutheran, but which because of its length and complexity could not be used for liturgical purposes, although it is intrinsically suitable for performance in a church.

Beethoven was an artist of the most profound sincerity; the notion that he could have asserted in music expressive of fervent religious emotions and deep conviction his belief in a creed which in fact he did not accept, is to me incredible. There are degrees of orthodoxy. Beethoven was not a strict Catholic; but his faith and his art were those of a Christian, though wide enough in outlook to embrace the beliefs

[1] *The Soul of Music*, p. 60.

and conceptions of other religions which were not in conflict with those of Christianity.

The great overture of Beethoven's third period is *Die Weihe des Hauses* (" The Consecration of the House "), which far transcends the occasion for which it was written, the opening of the Joseph Theatre in Vienna in 1822. It is as though Beethoven intended not merely to celebrate the event, but to consecrate the building. The majestic opening chords, the exalted melody that follows, first softly on the wind instruments and then " fortissimo " on the full orchestra, and the magnificent double fugue, combine to make the work a creation of noble solemnity and spiritual grandeur.

The first movement of the Ninth Symphony is a gigantic spiritual struggle—a conflict not between head and heart as Beethoven said of the opening movement of his Pianoforte Sonata in E minor (op. 90) nor between man and an external Fate as in the first Allegro of the C minor Symphony, but between heroic endurance and the forces of anxiety and grief that might have dragged a less courageous soul than his into the pit of despair. And in spite of the comfort and hope voiced in the second subject in B flat major, the movement threatens to end in the anguish, desperate, yet not morbid, of the Coda—that sublimation of tragic grandeur—but at the last moment closes by reaffirming his resolution with a restatement of the main theme in its most emphatic form. This movement is universal because generation after generation of men recognise that Beethoven's inward conflict represents a spiritual struggle common to mankind, albeit glorified here into art of sublime beauty.

In the second movement, Beethoven's unconquerable vitality asserts itself in music of boundless energy, pulsing with vigorous rhythms; yet the minor key prevails, until it is interrupted by the happy song of the middle section in D major; but this happiness is short-lived, and the movement closes with a " reprise " of its first part: in Beethoven, the sonata form is never a structure imposed on the thought or emotion of a movement; the spirit of the music assumes that form as its natural embodiment, varied or extended according to the composer's wisdom.

The Adagio is the greatest slow music ever composed for orchestra. Both its main themes are in the major, the first, in B flat, a melody of exalted serenity and tenderness, the second (in D at the outset) a tune of gracious beauty, which, after a subsequent reappearance in G, withdraws from the scene and leaves the opening melody to unfold itself in a chain of indescribably beautiful variations. But this is not the music of escapism: it expresses the inward peace of mind which has accepted suffering. Never has the soul of a creative artist been nearer to Heaven while dwelling on earth. But at its close, the Finale bursts in abruptly with a harsh dissonance, which is stilled by a dignified recitative on the lower strings. Then, reminding us of the opening themes of the preceding movements, the composer tells us, in eloquent orchestral tones, that none of them expresses the aspirations which are now filling his soul. There follows the great melody of transcendent joy, upon which the rest of the Finale is built.

Verdi declared that the first three movements of the Ninth Symphony are magnificent, but that the last is much inferior. Great composers are, however, not always good critics: they are sometimes too deeply absorbed in their own creative art to be able to enter completely into the spirit of another composer whose outlook is different from theirs. And if the vocal Finale of the Ninth Symphony seems below the level of its glorious other movements, this has been, I suggest, due to the inferiority of the performance, not of the music itself. The Finale is a series of sublime variations on a sublime theme. The grandeur of the conception can only be realised if the performance rises to the height of the great argument. It is vital to an understanding of the whole symphony to recognise that the last movement is essentially religious. Beethoven selected certain verses from Schiller's *Ode to Joy*, and to him, as to Schiller, Joy was " Götterfunken " (God-descended) and " Tochter aus Elysium " (daughter of Elysium): Beethoven's range was far too wide and profound for him to fail to know that though Elysium was originally a pagan name for Heaven, Christianity does touch other religions at many points. The Seraph that stands before God evokes the most wondrous music from him; and in contrast to the terror of war which he depicted so vividly in the midst of the " Dona nobis pacem " of the *Missa Solemnis*, here he writes military music for Schiller's stanza in which heroes are compared to suns coursing through the heavens. The mighty orchestral fugue which follows, leads to the sublime hymn of the universal brotherhood of mankind, " Seid umschlungen, millionen " (" Be embraced, O ye millions "); and this in turn to the transcendent and mystical music in the upper registers of voices and instruments, expressing the thought that from man's prostrate awe he feels the presence of God dwelling above the stars. After this, religious joy fills the music until the end of the symphony, always in quick *tempi* with the exception of a moving passage " poco adagio " for solo voices and a final impressive drop into

" maestoso " as the chorus affirms " Freude, schöner Götterfunken " before the last, excited surge of melody on the orchestra.

At the present stage of our knowledge and civilisation it is impossible to conceive greater music than the tremendous works of Beethoven's third period which we have just been considering. Yet in his last string quartets he penetrated even further into the mystery of things. It is as though at the end of his life, driven inward upon his own spiritual resources, he was vouchsafed a vision of the infinite which required for its interpretation not the vast panoply of orchestra and chorus nor even the harmonic richness of the pianoforte, but only the unaided sounds of two violins, a viola and a 'cello. Through this simple medium, and this alone, he could communicate to humanity a mystical experience to which no creative artist in any sphere has hitherto attained.

In discussing these quartets I shall take them in the order of their composition, which does not entirely correspond to the sequence of their opus numbers. In the first of them, op. 127 in E flat, the four-movement structure which had become the normal form used by Haydn and Mozart for sonatas, quartets and symphonies, and, more often than not, by Beethoven himself, still sufficed for his purpose. It responded to a basic spiritual process, consisting, for instance, of conflict, meditation, awakening and resolution: this is, of course, not the psychological succession followed in all, or even in most, cases, but is simply taken as an example to show that the four-movement structure is not something adopted arbitrarily, but is the musical reflection of a perfectly natural order of soul-states. The first movement of this quartet is, indeed, not a conflict at all, but suggests rather the triumph of the spirit after many struggles. The Adagio, in the form of a melody of supreme beauty with wonderful variations, is a serene revelation from Heaven. The rugged vigour of the Scherzando vivace alternates with a sense of mystery in the Presto section. In the Finale Beethoven seems to find happiness again, even though it is short-lived.

In the ensuing quartets, except the last of all, Beethoven increased the number of movements beyond four, as his inspiration bade him. The A minor Quartet (op. 132), which is the next one chronologically, opens in suffering, alleviated by a lovely theme of comfort in F major, and eventually abated by courage and resolution. The Allegro ma non tanto strikes a note of resignation, but in the alternating section there is a vision of celestial happiness. Then comes the profoundly beautiful slow movement, a prayer of " devout thanksgiving to God for recovery, in the Lydian mode", with its vigorous counterpart in D major "regaining vitality", but otherwise maintaining its deeply-felt absorption in prayer (" mit innigster Empfindung ") until it ends in complete serenity. The Alla Marcia in A major, which follows, is a brief, gallant effort to face the world again, but there is pathos beneath its show of bravery, and after a shuddering piece of recitative we are caught up in the surge and struggle of the Allegro appassionato, in A minor once more; at times it seems as though the soul must be overwhelmed; but at the end, in the Prestissimo in the major key, it reaches the haven of victory.

The B flat Quartet (op. 130) is in six movements. The first is characteristic of Beethoven's third period in which so often the emotions are complex: here, for all the zest and energy of the music, there is an undertone of wistfulness, as though the memory of previous suffering arouses misgiving. The ensuing Presto in B flat minor is as light as a feather, yet profound in its mystery. The Andante con moto is almost domestic in its quality of intimate contentment. The Alla danza tedesca is another example of music which is not so happy as it appears on the surface—a charming, gently-swaying waltz with an undercurrent of sadness. Concerning the sublime Cavatina, which is in E flat major except for a brief passage in the minor, Beethoven said to Karl Holz " Never did music of mine make so deep an impression on me; even the remembrance of the emotions it aroused always costs me a tear."[1] In this movement he poured out his soul to his Maker in yearning for that ideal serenity to which he had never attained. The original Finale of this quartet was the " Grosse Fuge ", which, because of its length and difficulty, Beethoven was induced by the publisher Artaria to replace by a new movement. It later appeared separately as op. 133, and for many generations was regarded as incomprehensible. Only in our own day has it won recognition. It has been transferred to the strings of the orchestra; in this form the greater richness of tone softens its asperities; it remains great music, but the arrangement is, in my view, justified solely as a means of sending us back to the original. We need not doubt that Beethoven intended the Fugue to be harsh and difficult in parts. He was here expressing the power of the will in a grim struggle, though strengthened by the spiritual tenderness of the intervening passages " meno mosso e moderato " and culminating in triumph. Our generation, which has lived through the terrors of two world wars and has learnt that agony must be endured and that

[1] Paul J. Bekker, *Beethoven* (translated by M. M. Bozman), p. 332.

ideals must be fought for even from the depths of despair, has also come to see the beauty of nature in her most austere forms—in the bleakest hills of Scotland when no heather or any gentle flowers are in bloom, in the forbidding precipices of vast mountains. To us, then, it has been given to scale the giddy heights of the "Grosse Fuge", provided that there are quartet players great enough to surmount the task of interpretation. Nevertheless, though the Fugue is the ideal conclusion of the B flat Quartet, we can be grateful that Beethoven composed another Finale: it is his last creation, and seems to show by its joyous character that at the end he was, after all, at peace with the world.

There are seven numbered movements in the C sharp minor Quartet (op. 131), with no breaks, but those marked 3 and 6 are short introductions to the movements which follow them. The work is an organic whole—a profound mystical experience unfolded in five main stages. The slow opening fugue is a sublime vision of the infinite. It leads to an Allegro molto vivace in D, in which we seem to enter this world again, but to find it a world full of hope and promise, purified by the ethereal experience of the preceding vision. "No. 3" is an expectant recitative introducing the variations of the Andante, ma non troppo e molto cantabile, with its warm, human happiness, which seems at the end to soar to Heaven. The ensuing Presto is the apotheosis of radiant joy and humour. But the sadness of "No. 6", the "adagio" introduction to the Finale, warns us that we have to face the realities of life's struggles, and in the last "allegro" we find the courage that acknowledges pathos and strives on its way through suffering; towards the end the *tempo* slows down to "poco adagio": the music is still in the minor key, marked "semplice, espressivo"; but with the return of quick time, "crescendo", it suddenly changes to the major and ends "fortissimo" in victory.

The last Quartet, in F (op. 135), reverts to the four-movement structure and shows us that at the end of his creative activity Beethoven had won serenity of mind at last. The opening Allegretto is in cheerful mood, though it is the cheerfulness of a man who has experienced life deeply, and has its moments of light and shade. The Vivace is a humorous frolic, with syncopated rhythms and a light-hearted alternating section; the fun reaches its climax when the three lower strings vociferously shout the same five notes over and over again while the first violin leaps up and down with excitement. The Lento assai, cantabile e tranquillo, is a set of variations, brief but profound, based on a melody of sublime simplicity. Beethoven entitled his Finale

"Der schwer gefasste Entschluss" ("the difficult resolution") and wrote mottos "Muss es sein? Es muss sein!" ("Must it be? It must be!") for the "Grave" introduction and the Allegro which follows. But there is no tension in the movement, which runs its course in happy vein and ends blissfully.

The spiritual quality in Beethoven's art is a particular manifestation of the divinity, which, as we saw in Chapter 5, is present in all forms of musical beauty. With Beethoven, it springs either from a conflict of the soul, or from the tranquillity which arises after or in consequence of that conflict, or from the prayers and efforts of man, his joys, sorrows and triumphs, his reconciliation with the world around him.

Beethoven's life was one of struggle, joy, suffering and resignation, in the service of mankind. Thus in his own person and in spite of his faults, consciously or unconsciously he embodied the Christian spirit. His faith in an Eternal God of Love, his matchless genius and unconquerable will, enabled him to give to the world music so exalted, so wide in its range of idealised human emotions, thoughts and aspirations, that nothing comparable to it has been known before or since. In the art of Beethoven, humanity is glorified.

9

THE INSPIRATION OF SCHUBERT

IT has often been said that Beethoven and Schubert stand on the threshold of the Romantic era in music. The truth of this depends on the meaning of "romanticism". Elsewhere[1] I have suggested that it is a real quality in music, and indeed a fundamental attribute of human nature, but that its musical embodiment is to be found much earlier than has sometimes been assumed. Any music which faithfully expresses the passion of love, or is dreamy in character, or tells a fairy tale, or sings of the deeds of a hero, may appropriately be called romantic. For reasons which it would be outside the scope of this book to discuss, the nineteenth century produced a great deal of music of that kind (in addition to some that was not romantic at all); and if we believe that divinity, in varying degrees, exists in all musical beauty, we shall find it in full measure in that "romantic" age. But religious emotion is not romantic; and when a composer who is steeped in romanticism creates music which is either set to sacred words or purports to have a devotional significance, the question arises in each case whether the work is intrinsically religious or only divine, in the wider sense, on account of its beauty.

Now, Beethoven's art contains romantic qualities, though the fairy element is not among them; but he was much more than a romantic composer. To some extent, the same is true of Schubert. In Beethoven, spiritual glory predominates over romanticism. Schubert expresses the basic simplicities of human nature in an unsurpassed wealth of lovely melodies, modulated and varied by the imagination of genius. As with Beethoven, the greater part of his output was in the forms which are commonly called "secular", but he also composed six Masses and many other liturgical works. He was, in the opinion of many, the greatest of song-writers; and in his songs we often meet with Schubert the romantic, but occasionally, too, we find in them a religious element.

He was a true Bohemian, easy-going, good-tempered, affectionate, fond of the society of his friends and deeply loved by them; a shy, modest, guileless creature. Music literally poured out of him in an effortless stream, presenting a strong contrast to the labour with which

[1] *The Soul of Music*, Chapter 15.

Beethoven hewed his mighty creations out of (sometimes) unpromising material.

The home in which Schubert was brought up in Vienna was a very devout one. His mother died when he was a boy of fifteen. His father, a schoolmaster of peasant stock, remarried about a year later a woman only fourteen years older than Franz, who proved to be a good wife, mother and step-mother. The Schubert household combined intense loyalty to the Imperial House of Austria with an almost bigoted reverence for the Church. Fortunately, the atmosphere of the home was very musical: an Austrian schoolmaster in those days had to be a musican and to teach music as well as other things. So Franz had music lessons in his father's school, and at the age of seven was apprenticed to the choirmaster of the Liechtental parish church and learnt singing, organ-playing and counterpoint. As a chorister he took part in the singing of liturgical music, which (Alfred Einstein[1] thinks) was almost certainly not the *a capella* compositions of the time of Palestrina, but the works of the great and lesser Austrian composers, many of which tended to be similar in style to operatic music; so that when he came to compose music for the Church, he quite naturally followed that tradition, because no other was known to him. He was educated at the Royal Imperial Municipal Convict, which was run by monks of the Order of Piarists and was a place of preparation for University students and of training for choristers of the Chapel Royal.

Schubert was far too sweet-natured a person to be rebellious against the strict orthodox régime in which he was brought up; but as he matured, whilst remaining a Catholic, he became an unorthodox one.

Among his six Masses, the great Schubert appears in the last two. The Mass in A flat seems to express, in its variety of keys and in the warmth of its emotion, that brightness of colour which characterised the Austrian eighteenth-century churches and of which mention has been made in discussing Mozart's liturgical compositions.[2] The Mass in E flat is simpler in its key relationships, largely choral, and deeply spiritual in character. In neither of these two works, nor in any of the church music, shall we find the mystical quality that is present in the devotional art of Beethoven and Bach; but in both of them and in the fragment of *Lazarus*, which is entitled a " religious drama " but was described by Schubert as an "Easter cantata ", there is religious feeling.

He was a child of nature, and both in nature and in music he felt the presence of God. The divinity of beauty is in no composer more

[1] *Schubert*, p. 12. [2] Supra, Chapter 7, p. 75.

completely and simply revealed than in Schubert. He expresses it, for instance, in his songs: in the grandeur and sublimity of *Die Allmacht*, in the humility of *Grenzen der Menschheit*, in the loving thankfulness of *In Abendroth*, in Ellen's hymn to the Virgin, *Ave Maria*, which is unliturgical but essentially sacred; in the abiding faith which inspires the Nun in *Die junge Nonne* to pass from the terror of the storm into the morning of peace; in the sorrow and sympathy of *Vom Mitleiden Mariae*; in the *Litaney auf das Fest Aller Seelen*, which is a hymn of rest for the souls of the departed and of comfort for the mourners. These are all directly religious songs. But God inspired Schubert also in the spring-like fragrance of his countless nature pictures—the babbling brook, the gentle movement of trees, the loveliness of flowers, the stress of thunder; and in the infinite variety of his simple portrayal of the emotions of men and women. *An die Musik* is really a prayer, an apotheosis of the art of music itself. *Du bist die Ruh* idealises love with such tranquil adoration as almost to deify it: if Christianity says that God is Love, Schubert seems to answer, reverently, " Yes, and Love is God."

The beauty, and therefore the divinity, of human nature, shine brightly, too, in the spiritual quality which inhabits the greatest of Schubert's instrumental works: in the anguish, consoled by sweetness, present in the first movement of the " Unfinished " Symphony in B minor, and the eternal peace of its Andante; in the serene loveliness of the Impromptu in A flat for pianoforte (op. 142, No. 2); in the idyllic happiness of the B flat Trio (op. 99); in the romantic reflections on life and death which fill the pages of his three finest quartets, in A minor, D minor (*Der Tod und das Mädchen*) and G major. In the great C major Symphony Schubert transcends romanticism. If in his songs his vivid imagination enabled him to embody in music the emotions and thoughts of the persons portrayed or of the poet himself, and if in most of his instrumental works he was expressing his own feelings and conceptions, in this symphony there is a more impersonal note: the music seems to hold the mirror up to nature and mankind—humanity living its life in a world of natural beauty; in the Andante there is wistful melancholy, but the Scherzo is imbued with glorious vigour, and the Finale courses on its way like a great river, which is also the river of life, full, exuberant, exultant even at moments of terror. The joy of composition and the faith, not of an orthodox churchman, but of a firm believer in a loving God, inspired Schubert to create this sublime, exhilarating symphony.

The crowning glory of his chamber music is the Quintet in C for strings (op. 163). There is a note of resignation in the opening theme of the first movement, but this is offset by the celestial loveliness of the second subject, which enters on the two 'celli and is then taken up by the first and second violins. The Adagio is an idyllic dream; an interlude full of stress and anguish breaks in upon it, but the vision of peace returns. The Scherzo abounds in vigorous life, but the Trio is solemn and mysterious, though the return of the Scherzo brushes this mood aside, and the Finale, though it begins in the minor, dances with joy. It is delightful to think that Schubert, though he suffered abject poverty, disease and discouragement, showed no trace of bitterness and found such happiness in the creation of beautiful music. This was his offering to God. Within a few months of the completion of the C major Quintet he contracted enteric fever, and in a fortnight he was dead.

10

WAS BERLIOZ AN ATHEIST?

LAURENCE HOUSMAN, in *What Next? Provocative Tales of Faith and Morals* (1938, reprinted in *Back Words and Fore Words* 1945) tells the story of "The man who did not pray." Nahti-poo refrained from praying in the temple as a boy, because he noticed that so many of the prayers of others were not answered: "God has not time to answer them," he thought. "If fewer prayed, more prayers would be answered." He waited, because it was not his turn or because there were others in greater need. Later on, just for the fun of it, he started answering their prayers himself, if he could—that is, if they were asking for quite simple things, but he left off playing this game when he found that people quarrelled over what they got: perhaps God knew better than he did. When he grew up, neither the people nor the priest could understand Nahti-poo, who went to the temple regularly and listened to the prayers of others (in order to get to know them) but never prayed himself. When his father was in his last illness, Nahti-poo did not pray for him, but tended him constantly "with a woman's care". Afterwards he married a beautiful maiden; he did not pray for her when she was in labour, but bade her submit to the will of God, and she died, leaving a baby son for him to care for; but greatly though he loved the child, it also died, from an illness, and Nahti-poo lived out his life alone, and still he did not pray: "I have everything that I need; why should I trouble God by praying to him? Does He not know better than I what is good for me?" Eventually Nahti-poo died and passed to the world of spirits; and the voice of the Beloved said to him: "O Nahti-poo, all thy life has been a prayer. Enter thou into the joy of thy Lord."

The true atheist is unlike Nahti-poo, who believed in God and had implicit faith in Him. But is it, perhaps, possible for one who thinks himself to be an unbeliever to have an unconscious faith, just as Nahti-poo had been praying all his life without realising it? Berlioz (1803–69) pronounced himself an unbeliever, yet of his major works two are settings of the liturgy, one is a sacred oratorio and several others[1] have

[1] Two of these are the operas *Benvenuto Cellini* and *Les Troyens*, which are discussed in Chapter 18.

religious associations in varying degrees. Both as man and artist he was of the utmost integrity. What is the explanation of the apparent inconsistency?

Berlioz's own *Memoirs* and Professor Jacques Barzun's brilliant book, *Berlioz and the Romantic Century*,[1] give a picture of a most attractive personality, marred by few blemishes. He was passionate, daring, impetuous, sensitive, impressionable, susceptible to despair, but with a strong will and lucid mind; modest and shy, yet conscious of his superiority, so that he did not suffer fools gladly; gay and humorous, grateful and tender-hearted, and a good friend; an exceptionally fair-minded critic; devoted to his affectionate, unorthodox father, and only prevented from being attached to his harsh, devout mother by her denial of love for him. He made a mistake in marrying Harriet Smithson, the Irish actress, but he deeply loved their son Louis. His one great fault was in his neglect of Louis in early boyhood during the long agony when his marriage to Harriet was breaking up, and he paid grievously for it by his own anguish when he came to realise the unhappy effect on Louis' character.

One could hardly expect a man of Berlioz's temperament to be a strict churchman in his maturity, but writing in March 1848, when he was forty-four, he gives a graphic account of what his youthful attitude towards religion had been. (I quote from Chapter i of the *Memoirs*, translated by Rachel (Scott Russell) Holmes and Eleanor Holmes, annotated, and the translation revised, by Ernest Newman):

" I need scarcely state that I was brought up as a member of the Holy Catholic and Apostolic Church of Rome. Since she has ceased to inculcate the burning of heretics, her creeds are charming. I held them happily for seven years; and though we quarrelled long ago, I still retain the tenderest recollections of that form of religious belief. Indeed, I feel such sympathy for it that had I had the misfortune to be born in the midst of one of those ponderous schisms evolved by Luther or Calvin, my first rush of poetical enthusiasm would have driven me straight into the arms of the beautiful Roman faith. I made my first communion on the same day as my eldest sister, and in the Convent of the Ursulines, where she was being brought up. It is probably owing to this curious circumstance that I retain so tender a recollection of that religious ceremony. The almoner came to fetch me at six o'clock, and I felt deeply stirred as we crossed the threshold of the church. It was a bright spring morning, the wind was murmuring softly in

[1] See, especially, Chapter 20, in Vol. II.

the poplars, and the air was full of a subtle fragrance. Kneeling in the midst of a multitude of white-robed maidens we awaited the solemn moment, and, when the priest advanced and began to intone the service, all our thoughts were fixed on God. I was rudely awakened by the priest summoning me to take precedence of all those fair young girls, and go up to the altar first. Blushing at this act of discourtesy, I went up to receive the sacrament. As I did so the choir burst forth into the eucharistic hymn. At the sound of those virginal voices I was overwhelmed with a sudden rush of mystic passionate emotion. A new world of love and feeling was revealed to me, more glorious by far than the heaven of which I had heard so much; and, strange proof of the power of true expression and the magical influence of real feeling, I found out ten years afterwards that the melody which had been so naïvely adapted to sacred words and introduced into a religious ceremony was Nina's song, 'Quand le bien-aimé reviendra!' What joy filled my young soul, dear Dalayrac! And yet your ungrateful country has almost forgotten your name.

" This was my first musical experience, and in this manner I suddenly became religious; so religious that I attended mass every day and the communion every Sunday; and my weekly confession to the director of my conscience was, 'My father, I have done nothing'; to which the worthy man always replied, 'Go on, my child, as you have begun'; and so I did for several years."

Berlioz, from his youth onwards, had "a natural bent for religious subjects"[1] which he shared with his teacher Lesueur, who was an eminent church musician as well as a composer of operas. One of his very early works was an oratorio on a Biblical theme, for which he wrote the words himself, *The Crossing of the Red Sea*, completed when he was twenty. Another was the Mass of 1825, which prepared the way for later, liturgical compositions.

Religion even figures in the *Symphonie Fantastique* (op. 14, composed when he was twenty-six). Berlioz wrote a detailed "programme" of it, but his words that he "aimed at developing from certain scenes what they contain that is musical" should warn us against treating the symphony as merely descriptive. Nevertheless, when in revising the work about a year afterwards he added twenty-four bars marked "religioso" at the end of the first movement, the adjective is fully justified by the consoling nature of the music. The Finale—the "Witches' Sabbath"—in which the shapely melody of the *idée fixe*

[1] Jacques Barzun, *Berlioz and the Romantic Century*, Vol. I, p. 54.

is transformed (in his words) into a "trivial, ignoble, drunkard's song", typifying the appearance of the beloved at the weird, supernatural orgies in the guise of a courtesan—contains a parody of the "Dies Irae", which according to Berlioz's "programme" is here being burlesqued by the choirs of evil creatures in their infernal revelry.

The second symphony, *Harold in Italy*, has a religious slow movement, which is one of Berlioz's most beautiful creations—"March of Pilgrims singing the Evening Hymn". After each of the four appearances of the lovely march phrase (which modulates into different keys) a prolonged C and B played on the woodwind and strings produce an other-worldly effect. The slow, meditative main theme of the symphony shows us Harold watching the devout procession. A "canto religioso" is heard in the higher registers. The double basses keep up the march tread, "pizzicato", and at the end the music dies away as the pilgrims gradually pass into the distance.

Berlioz's *Messe des Morts* (*Requiem*) was originally intended for the annual service to commemorate the heroic victims of the 1830 Revolution on the seventh anniversary of their death, July 28th, 1837; but the intrigues and delays which obstructed its performance resulted in its not being produced until December 5th, when it was associated with the news, received in Paris in October, that Constantine in Algeria had been taken by the French and that the Commander, General Damrémont, was among those who had been killed in the battle. The composer records in his *Memoirs*[1] that in 1836, when he received his commission for the work, "For a long time the text of the *Requiem* had been to me an object of envy, on which I flung myself with a kind of fury when it was put within my grasp. My head seemed ready to burst with the pressure of my seething thoughts. . . ." But though he was thus filled with the inspiration of setting the sacred text, he had to adapt his ideas to the practical needs of the occasion. The body of the General was to be brought into the huge chapel of Saint Louis at the Invalides, which would be crowded with a large congregation, and he had to consider the acoustics of the place. Therefore he called for an orchestra of 190 instruments, 210 voices, additional tympani, and four brass choirs (consisting of trombone, cornet, tuba and trumpet) to sound fanfares in the "Tuba Mirum" from the four corners of the chapel—north, south, east and west of the other performers (he modified these directions later to meet the conditions of different places,

[1] Ernest Newman edition, p. 206.

and was satisfied if the brass choirs were situated away from the rest). It must not be imagined that these extra resources were the sign of an inflated conception. The additional tympani were partly required in order to produce a novel and beautiful sound by playing soft chords near the end of the work: drums were less resonant in those days, and we no longer need sixteen of them with ten players. The effect of the four brass choirs is sonorous and impressive: there is nothing extravagant or gargantuan about it.

In the "Dies Irae", Berlioz vividly portrays the Day of Wrath, in accordance with the traditional, Catholic, medieval conception of it, but in his characteristic Berliozian, nineteenth-century colours. It is this number and the thunder of " Rex tremendae " which have prompted some critics to complain that Berlioz is too vociferous for a composer of liturgical music, and, indeed, to deny that the *Requiem* is truly religious at all. Even Hamilton Harty, who knew more about Berlioz than most people and conducted his music superbly, said in the programme notes of a symphony concert given by the Hallé Orchestra on November 14th, 1930, that " Berlioz was less concerned to give his work a religious character than a dramatic one." Bach's settings of the Passion, as I have pointed out, are full of drama; and as we shall see, opera and music drama throughout their history have contained a good deal of religious music. The opening " Requiem aeternam " in Berlioz's work is serene and solemn, the " Quid sum miser " is marked to be sung by tenors only with an expression of humility and fear and is accompanied by cor anglais and bassoons in moving tones; the " Rex tremendae " itself has a contrasting section of a peaceful nature at the words " Qui salvandos . . ."; the " Quaerens me " is an unaccompanied chorus of infinite purity; the " Offertorium" is a quiet, sorrowful meditation; the " Sanctus "—in which section alone the solo tenor voice enters—is ethereal in quality, with the instruments confined to the upper registers; and the concluding " Agnus Dei " is solemn and restful. Thus it is misleading to speak of the composition in general as though it were a noisy work, pagan in character. Berlioz's music is tremendous and awe-inspiring where the text makes it appropriate that it should be so. A great deal of it is peaceful and gentle.

The composer himself said two years before his death that if all his works were to be ordered to be burnt, he would ask that the *Requiem* might be spared.[1] We can well understand his feeling like that about

[1] Jacques Barzun, *Berlioz and the Romantic Century*, Vol. I, p. 289.

this great creation which expresses religious emotions in an idiom different from that employed by any of those who went before or came after him.

Some parts of the eight-movement Dramatic Symphony, *Romeo and Juliet*, show Berlioz at the height of his powers—particularly "Romeo's reverie and the Capulets' ball", the "Love Scene", and the "Queen Mab Scherzo"; but the work is unequal, and the Finale, with Friar Laurence's recitative and air and the reconciliation between the two houses after the deaths of the lovers, which alone gave the composer an opportunity for introducing a religious element, does not, in my view, represent him at his best, and so has little bearing upon the subject of this chapter.

Berlioz's musical preoccupation with the theme of death was a reflection of part of his spiritual outlook. In addition to the "Marche au Supplice" in the *Symphonie Fantastique*, and the great *Requiem*, he wrote two funeral marches on Shakespearean themes—for Juliet and Hamlet—and a ballad on the death of Ophelia. And the *Grande Symphonie Funèbre et Triomphale* was a "military symphony composed . . . for the funeral ceremony of July 28th," in 1840, to commemorate the tenth anniversary of the 1830 Revolution. As the performance was to take place in the open air, in the Place de la Bastille, the work was scored for large resources, which can be adapted to suit the acoustics of a concert hall. The first two sections are entirely orchestral, the opening one being a magnificent funeral march and the second an impressive "funeral oration" with a solo trombone representing the orator; the third section is entitled "Apotheosis": it is brilliant, thrilling music, with the chorus joining in triumphantly towards the end, singing of the heroes still victorious in death and calling on all to join with the angels in proclaiming their glory.

After Goethe by his great poetic drama had renewed interest in the old legend of Faust, composers started turning their attention to it. With its many supernatural ingredients it naturally appealed to creative artists of the romantic nineteenth century; and the story, whether in Goethe's version or earlier ones, has a strong religious connotation, if only through the person of Mephistopheles as an emissary of the infernal regions which had always formed part of the Christian belief, and the manner in which the tale is made to end. The events of Berlioz's "Dramatic Legend", *La Damnation de Faust*, correspond roughly to the First Part of Goethe's drama. Let us consider those passages which have a religious significance.

In scene 4, Faust is alone in his study, meditating on life and death; just as he is about to poison himself, he is interrupted—and saved—by a heavenly chorus singing an Easter Hymn of great beauty; he joins in it, but at the end Mephistopheles appears, heralded by devilish chords on the trombones, and after a brief colloquy sweeps Faust off to Auerbach's cellar. The burlesque " Amen " chorus sung by the revellers there is very far from being a sign that Berlioz was contemptuous of religion. On the contrary, the whole point of it is that he regarded rapid choral fugues on the word " Amen " as being blasphemous and therefore allotted one to be sung by a crowd of drinkers. He wrote to the Abbé Girod: " All the fugues on the word ' amen ' are fast, violent, noisy; they resemble nothing so much as a chorus of drinkers interspersed with bursts of laughter, for each part is vocalised on the first syllable of the word: A——a—a—a—men, which produces an effect at once grotesque and indecent. These traditional fugues are nothing but senseless blasphemy. . . . A beautiful fugue of a truly religious character to express the pious wish ' amen ' . . . would have to be a slow fugue, full of humility and quite short. For however well one renders it musically, the repetition of a word cannot be protracted without becoming ridiculous."[1]

Berlioz's Mephistopheles is a strongly drawn character: even the tune of his serenade in scene 12 has a biting gaiety about it, with a furious, wicked accompaniment on the strings.

In scene 16 Faust invokes Nature and in a pantheistic utterance of great power prays to winds and forests, rocks and torrents, to assuage the longings of his soul. But in scene 17 Mephisto climbs the rocks and tells him that Marguerite is in prison, having unintentionally poisoned her mother through giving her a sleeping draught too often, to make her slumber during Faust's and Marguerite's amours. Faust agrees to make a bond with him if he will save Marguerite. The game is up. In the next scene Mephisto and Faust gallop " on black horses " in a " Ride to the Abyss", with the strings portraying the rhythm of the horses, the plaintive notes of the oboe accompanying Faust's cries of terror, and the brass instruments sounding fantastic, supernatural discords. " Pandemonium "—the following scene in Hell—alternates between horror and desolation, and in the " Epilogue on Earth " the chorus tells us that Faust's punishment has been accomplished. The work ends with the apotheosis of Marguerite in Heaven, set to music of celestial beauty: the angelic choir tells us that God pardons her, and that

[1] Jacques Barzun, *Berlioz and the Romantic Century*, Vol. I, pp. 569 f.

His great mercy will, perhaps, extend one day also to Faust. Eternal perdition, though the Middle Ages believed in it, is repugnant to modern minds. The possible forgiveness of Faust in the future, indicated in Berlioz's French text, accords with the culmination of the Second Part of Goethe's masterpiece; unfortunately it does not appear in the translation customarily used in England. It has a bearing on the subject of Berlioz's religious outlook.

Berlioz composed his *Te Deum* in 1849, hoping that it would be heard at some public ceremonial, but the first performance did not take place until April 30th, 1855 at the Church of St. Eustache. He wrote to Liszt: " The ' Te Deum ' was performed today with magnificent precision. It was colossal, Babylonian, Ninivite. . . ." Jacques Barzun suggests[1] that he probably got this image from Sir Henry Layard's *Nineveh and its Remains*, published in 1848–9 with illustrations, or from *Discoveries in the Ruins of Nineveh and Babylon*, which appeared in 1855, the year of that letter. It may well be, however, that Berlioz was simply comparing the tremendous effect of the music in general to that of the monuments of Babylon and Nineveh. To take his words out of their context and allege that he himself meant that the music was " Oriental in its splendour "[2] is inappropriate, for there is nothing Oriental whatever in the idiom or character of the score, which belongs essentially to Europe and the nineteenth century. Berlioz in the same letter went on: " This time it isn't a matter of ' piccoli paesi ', but of a scene from the Apocalypse "—which is an apt description of the " Judex crederis ".

In this work it was Berlioz's intention that the organ at one end of the church should answer the orchestra and two choirs at the other, with a third large choir, representing the mass of the people, taking part from time to time in a vast sacred concert.[3] This arrangement is not always practicable, but if it can be carried out, the separation of the organ from the rest of the performers corresponds to the four choirs of brass instruments in the *Requiem*.

The opening " Te Deum laudamus " is a solid double fugue, leading to the "Tibi omnes", which begins with a melodious organ prelude: this section is an eloquent hymn to God, the first " Sanctus " being accompanied by arpeggios on the flutes and woodwind, and the organ solo returning near the end. Then comes an orchestral prelude, which

[1] Jacques Barzun, *Berlioz and the Romantic Century*, Vol. I, p. 565.
[2] *The Times*, February 9th, 1953.
[3] *Memoirs* (Ernest Newman edition), p. 489.

Berlioz said was to be played only if the *Te Deum* is being performed at a thanksgiving for victory or other ceremony linking itself to military ideas; it is based on the opening fugue theme. The "Dignare" is a tranquil prayer for peace and mercy; the "Christe Rex gloriae", a tremendous outburst of exultant adoration. Again we have a contrast, with the quiet supplication of "Te ergo quaesumus" sung by tenor solo and chorus; and the climax comes in the monumental, apocalyptic strains of the "Judex crederis". The work ends in a march of triumph.

L'Enfance du Christ is a religious triptych, with *The Flight into Egypt* as the central panel and *Herod's Dream* and *The Arrival at Sais* flanking it on either side. In *Herod's Dream*, after the Narrator has set the scene, we have a graphic, mysterious march in quiet orchestral colours as the Roman soldiers patrol on night duty in a street at Jerusalem, and a brief colloquy between two officers. Herod, alone in his palace, sings, in simple moving tones, of the vision of the "Wondrous Child" that threatens his throne, and of his yearning for rest. The soothsayers foretell his future, employing a weird rhythm of seven beats, with unusual orchestration. In the scene of the stable at Bethlehem, there is exquisitely beautiful music, as the Virgin sings to the Infant Jesus while feeding her lambs, which are charmingly portrayed by a skittish accompaniment. A chorus of unseen angels warns her and Joseph of the danger menacing the Child: a lovely effect is created by their distant voices.

The Flight into Egypt opens with a delicate little prelude as the shepherds gather in the stable at Bethlehem. Their chorus of farewell to the Holy Family is set to a fine melody, with beautiful part-writing; there is a noble and striking change of key at the fifth line of each verse on its repetition. Then the Narrator and orchestra, in pastoral strains of idyllic loveliness, tell of the repose of the Holy Family in the desert; at the end, we hear the angels again, quietly singing their Halleluias.

At the beginning of *The Arrival at Sais*, the Narrator tells how the Family made their way through burning sands: there is the feeling of a weary journey in the marching tread of the music. He describes their arrival, and then we hear how they are rejected by all until at last the father of a family of Ishmaelites offers them hospitality: like Joseph, he, too, is a carpenter. A charming trio for two flutes and harp is played by three of the Ishmaelite children, to welcome them.

In the Epilogue, the Narrator tells how "Our Saviour", after being sustained by the hand of strangers and of Gentiles, was eventually to win us eternal life through sacrificing His own life on the Cross. Then,

Narrator and chorus sing the soft, unaccompanied, unearthly music, "O my soul, bow down in awful contemplation", which brings this deeply devotional work to a sublime and tranquil end.

In addition to the major compositions which I have discussed, Berlioz wrote various minor works on sacred themes, and a beautiful *Méditation religieuse* based on Moore's poem "This world is all a fleeting show".

What are we to make of this "unbeliever" who constantly worshipped God in his music? Berlioz was scarcely an atheist, though in one place he uses that word about himself[1] and though he had ceased to be a Roman Catholic. Some years after writing the first chapter of his *Memoirs* from which I have already quoted an extract, he wrote to his friend Richard Pohl (in 1861) "Liszt told me that you would like to have a triangle: here is one from Sax's which has just served in the 'Harold' 1st movement. Its shape is in the image of God, like all triangles, but more than other triangles, and more than God in particular, you will find it plays true."[2] But we must not pin Berlioz down to such passages. He was both a wit and a romantic to the core. And perhaps he was what one might expect as the offspring of an agnostic father and a pious mother—something of a mixture. He frequently invokes God in his literary writings. In his *Lettres Intimes*[3] he wrote "in that vocal peroration [of '*L'Enfance du Christ*] the whole work is summed up, for it seems to me that the feeling of the infinite, of divine love, is in that passage." It would scarcely be too much to say that "divine love" is one of the dominant motives in Berlioz.

The composer summed up the general characteristics of his art in the postscript to his *Memoirs*: "The prevailing characteristics of my music are passionate expression, intense ardour, rhythmical animation, and unexpected turns. When I say passionate expression, I mean an expression determined on enforcing the inner meaning of its subject, even when that subject is the contrary of passion, and when the feeling to be expressed is gentle and tender, or even profoundly calm. This is the sort of expression which has been discovered in the 'Enfance du Christ', the 'Ciel' scene in the 'Damnation de Faust', and the 'Sanctus' of the 'Requiem'."[4] It is significant that he selects examples of his music

[1] In his copy of *Paul et Virginie* (a work on natural philosophy) he wrote "This book would make one an atheist were one not so already". (Translated by Jacques Barzun, *Berlioz and the Romantic Century*, Vol. II, p. 100, from Adolphe Jullien's *Hector Berlioz: La Vie et le Combat; les Oeuvres.*)

[2] Jacques Barzun, ibid., Vol. II, p. 94 n. (translated from Louise Pohl, *Hector Berlioz' Leben und Werke*).

[3] p. 219.

[4] *Memoirs* (Ernest Newman edition), p. 488.

associated with religion. If we were seeking to describe the main aspects of Berlioz's art, we should include in addition to " intense ardour " and " passionate expression "—even in the wide sense in which he uses it—many other non-religious emotions and scenes which he depicts, and the delicate fancies contained in such things as the " Danse des Sylphes " and the " Queen Mab Scherzo ". But we should have to assign an important—perhaps the most important—place to religion in the broadest sense of the term, seeing that in work after work he turned to sacred subjects and expressed them in deeply felt music. In *Euphonia*, his plan for a Utopian city of music, religious music occupies a central position. His Faust apostrophises Nature pantheistically, but we cannot be sure that a character envisaged by so imaginative a creator as Berlioz was voicing the composer's own beliefs. Berlioz literally idolised Shakespeare, Virgil and Beethoven. That was part of his particular brand of romantic divinity. It was not inconsistent with belief in an Almighty, loving God. He may not consciously have been a follower of the Christian faith (any more than Nahti-poo was conscious that he had been praying all his life). But he was always expressing " sympathy " for it, and in any case God found in him an eloquent musical messenger.

II

THE GOD OF MENDELSSOHN, CHOPIN AND SCHUMANN

IT has been said—for instance, by Professor Paul H. Lang[1]—that the romanticists of the nineteenth century returned to Catholicism; that they had found that the worship of the classic world of antiquity had already passed its peak and was not mystical enough; and that therefore they tried to evolve a new mythology from forces that could still be made living and universal. "Catholicism seemed to offer fulfilment to romanticism's longing for the infinite." Nevertheless, Professor Lang finds that the romanticists were too subjectively human in their idealism really to abide by the unilateral requirements of the Church. "They Catholicized, but they were not Catholics; what they desired was merely a union of all faiths, a totalization of love and friendship. What they expected from religion was the elevation of man from finite to infinite life; religion was to them nothing but a segment of the romantic cult of the infinite."

This may help to explain how it is that Beethoven, the unorthodox Catholic, fits into the picture of romanticism, though he transcended it; how Schubert, who offered his art to God without devoting most of it to religion, stood on the threshold of romanticism; and how Berlioz, a romantic through and through, could not keep away for long from Christian subjects, though he had ceased to be a Roman Catholic.

I have earlier[2] expressed the view that religious emotion itself is not romantic. And Mendelssohn, who was not a Catholic but a devout Protestant, lived in the nineteenth-century romantic era and had many of the qualities of romanticism, but expressed Christian piety by virtue of the religious element in himself which was apart from his romantic side. There was something Hellenic in the formal perfection of his structures and the exquisite chiselling of his workmanship that made him in this respect a kind of nineteenth-century counterpart of Mozart. His romanticism came out in his gift for opening the magic casement to the world of fairies; in his response to the beauties of nature, which he evinced pre-eminently in the "Hebrides" Overture; in the reminiscences of Scottish scenery and legend which found expression in his

[1] *Music in Western Civilisation*, p. 738. [2] p. 98.

Third Symphony; and in the tender, sometimes sentimental, strains of the *Songs without Words*. The religious aspect of his art is quite distinct and is manifested in several branches of his creative activity.

Too much has perhaps been made of the fact that Mendelssohn was a Jew. He was of Jewish blood, but for anyone who did not know this it would be hard to detect it in his music—in the way, for instance, that Jewish aspirations are present in the music of Ernest Bloch. In his private life Mendelssohn had a strong sense of family affection, which is indeed a Jewish characteristic but is, after all, to be found in other races as well. Both his aunts became Roman Catholics, and his father had him and his brother and sisters baptised and brought up as Protestants.

Mendelssohn's sweetness of disposition, manliness, charm, and good looks, made him a favourite wherever he went, whether at the English Court, in the company of distinguished men, or in the society of women. Sir George Grove[1] records that Thackeray told Richard Doyle (who told Grove), "His face is the most beautiful face I ever saw, like what I imagine our Saviour's to have been". He came of a prosperous banking family, and from the material standpoint life dealt easily with him. He suffered the sorrow of family bereavements, but not to a greater extent than most other men, and there was none of the struggle with adverse circumstances, poverty or intrigue which tested the endurance and strengthened the characters of some other great composers. The result was that the emotions expressed in his music, genuine as they are, do not sound the depths to be found in the compositions of Beethoven, Chopin or Wagner; nor did his creative imagination glimpse the sublime visions of the supreme masters of the art.

The religious note in Mendelssohn's music is not limited to his Biblical choral works. It is present, for instance, at some points of his setting of Goethe's ballad *The First Walpurgis Night*, though here the devotional feeling is conveyed not by the Christians in the story, but by the Druids. According to old legend, the eve of May 1st was consecrated to St. Walpurgis, who converted the Saxons from Druidism to Christianity, and on that night evil spirits were abroad. In Goethe's poem, the Druids perform their rites in the mountains to avoid interference from the Christians; they disguised their sentinels as devils, who frightened the approaching Christians away with torches, pronged forks and noisy, rattling instruments. The subject not only gave Mendelssohn the opportunity of describing the fantastic scene in music of

[1] *Grove's Dictionary of Music and Musicians* (3rd edition), Vol. III, p. 418.

vivid imagery, but of conveying the religious emotions of the Druids in their prayer to the " Father of all " at the beginning of the work and in their final hymn of praise.

Again, the Andante of the " Italian " Symphony has not without reason been called a " Pilgrims' march ", though without the composer's authority: it certainly has a religious character. The " Reformation " Symphony was intended for the Tercentenary Festival of the Augsburg Confession on June 25th, 1830, in celebration of the anniversary of the confession of faith presented by Luther and Melanchthon to the Emperor Charles V at the Diet of Augsburg in 1530; but opponents of the celebration prevented the performance. Mendelssohn produced it in December 1832, after which it was neglected for many years. The contest between the old and the new faiths is represented in the first movement—the old faith being typified by the "Dresden Amen". The Lutheran hymn " Ein' feste Burg ist unser Gott " is the theme of the Andante con moto which forms an introduction to the Finale, and is blazed out in all its glory by the full orchestra at the close of the work.

Like other great Christian composers, Mendelssohn did not confine his sacred music to his own branch of the Christian religion. He wrote for the Roman Catholic service three motets (op. 39) for women's voices and organ and the *Lauda Sion* for chorus and orchestra. But most of his devotional work was naturally that of a keen Protestant, and was based directly or mainly on Biblical texts. He composed several fine settings of Psalms—" Why fiercely rage the heathen? " (Psalm ii), " Judge me, O God " (Psalm xliii), " My God, why hast thou forsaken me? " (Psalm xxii), " Come, let us sing " (Psalm xcv), " As the hart pants " (Psalm xlii), " Not unto us, O Lord " (Psalm cxv) and " When Israel out of Egypt came " (Psalm cxiv). Nevertheless, he felt—somewhat oddly—that music was really out of place in the Lutheran service: he could not see how artistic music could be fitted into it without appearing (as he wrote in one of his letters) " a mere concert with a more or less devotional effect". Fortunately for the world this did not deter him from reviving the " St. Matthew Passion " of Bach for the first time since its composer's death, and thus starting the great recognition of the glories of Bach's liturgical masterpieces which has grown and continued thenceforward. But he intended his own settings of the Psalms, the *Hymn of Praise*, and his two oratorios *St. Paul* and *Elijah*, to be performed at festivals or in concert rooms.

This does not in the least prevent them from being definitely religious in character. The *Hymn of Praise* is a unique composition; for although its outward form resembles that of Beethoven's Ninth Symphony in consisting of three orchestral movements followed by a choral section, it differs radically from it not only in its intrinsic nature but in the sense that the instrumental movements are by way of being only a fairly lengthy introduction to the vocal part, which is the Hymn of Praise proper and is the most important part of the whole. The strength of the opening Allegro, the meditative quality of the Allegretto and the devotional mood of the Adagio religioso attune the mind for the beautiful choruses and solo numbers which follow.

St. Paul (written when Mendelssohn was only twenty-five) deals with the martyrdom of St. Stephen, the conversion of St. Paul and the remainder of the Apostle's life, by means of expressive recitatives, arias which vividly portray the emotions of the words, and choruses which are masterly in their skill and richly varied according to the moods and characters of those who are represented as uttering them.

Elijah, however, marks the climax of Mendelssohn's career as a religious composer. The dramatic element is stronger, the pictorial aspect more life-like, and the devotional feeling deeper in quality, than in any other of his sacred vocal works. It begins with Elijah's prophecy of drought, voiced in a solemn and impressive recitative, and then proceeds through a series of widely contrasted choruses—some dramatic, some descriptive, others reflective or exhortatory—and arias which are either simple expressions of prayer or comfort or are full of power and energy, until the chorus paints the scene of the prophet's ascent to Heaven in fiery colours. The ensuing music and words which conclude the oratorio, anticipate the coming of Christ. Mendelssohn began another oratorio on the subject of *Christus*, but did not live to finish it.

In recent times there has been a tendency to concentrate on the instrumental side of Mendelssohn's genius, as exemplified particularly in the exquisitely beautiful Violin Concerto in E minor, the "Midsummer Night's Dream" and "Hebrides" Overtures, the Octet, and the "Italian" Symphony; or even to depreciate his value altogether. Both of these attitudes I believe to be short-sighted. For our purposes I have naturally dwelt more on his sacred works than on others, but even apart from this I see no grounds for regarding them as below the level of his non-devotional and more romantic compositions.

Chopin and Schumann are not composers whom we ordinarily

associate with religion. Yet in the art and character of both of them there is a religious element and a strong degree of the divinity of beauty.

. . . . .

Chopin was not religious in the normal sense of the term, but he was a most lovable person: utterly sincere, a man of very deep feelings, which he voiced in his eloquent music. If we may, without irreverence, apply to so human an individual of the nineteenth century A.D. Isaiah's famous prophetic description of the Messiah which later ages have associated with Christ Himself, we can say that Chopin was "a man of sorrows, acquainted with grief". He led a most tragic life, in spite of contemporary recognition of his genius. He was devoted to his family, to his native Poland, to France, and to his friends. In his early manhood he loved Marie Wodzinska idyllically and asked her to marry him; she consented, but changed her mind, and Chopin never truly recovered: he put her notes, with the rose of Dresden, in an envelope marked "my grief"; the packet was tied with a ribbon, and was found after his death.[1] After Marie had rejected him, his acquaintance with Aurore Dudevant (George Sand, the celebrated authoress) ripened into friendship, and the friendship developed into passionate attachment.

Guy de Pourtalès speaks of "Mr." Sand and "Miss" Chopin.[2] It may be that as a human personality Chopin had in him more of the woman than the man. But every human being is a compound of the characteristics of the two sexes in infinitely varying degrees. If it be held that in Chopin's music, as in his character, the female element preponderates, perhaps this would be a compensation for the fact that hitherto there have been so few distinguished women-composers. Guy de Pourtalès, on the other hand, holds that Chopin's "musical travail was always virile".[3]

Apart from the irregularity of Chopin's liaison with George Sand there was no trace of evil in his nature; and even in that affair she was the dominant—or rather, domineering!—and, at the outset, quasi-maternal, partner. The liaison eventually broke up sadly. Chopin became worn out with tuberculosis, which caused his death in 1847 at the age of thirty-nine.

[1] Guy de Pourtalès, *Chopin, a Man of Solitude* (translated by Charles Bayly, Jnr.), p. 93.
[2] Ibid., p. 102. [3] Ibid., p. 74.

It is interesting to recall the religious moments in his life. We read how on Christmas Eve, 1830, in Vienna he heard of the revolution in Warsaw and went to the Church of St. Etienne, where, " standing in the darkest corner under the dome, he leaned against a Gothic pillar and dreamed of the family Christmas tree, lighted with candles, of the modest presents he and his sisters gave each other, of the traditional supper where the whole family gathered about the table and broke the holy bread that the lay brothers of the convents had distributed during Advent."[1] In his letters to his family from abroad he constantly invoked God. He was devoted to Bach's music and always practised it before his concert appearances. At his last concert on February 16th, 1848, he played, among other things, his *Barcarolle*, of which Ravel has said " one dreams of a mysterious apotheosis ".

In his last illness, from his bed he wrote that a Scotch friend, Mrs. Erskine, who was a very good Protestant, possibly wanted to make a Protestant out of him, because she was always bringing him the Bible, talking to him of the soul, and marking Psalms for him to read: " She is religious and good, but she is very much worried about my soul. She *saws* away all the time at me, telling me that the other world is better than this, and I know that by heart. I reply by citations from Scripture and tell her that I know all about it."[2]

On his death-bed, a childhood friend, Abbé Alexandre Jelowiçki, visited him. " I would not like to die ", he said, " without having received the sacraments, lest I should pain my mother; but I do not understand them as you wish. I can see nothing in confession beyond the relief of a burdened heart on the heart of a friend."[3] On October 13th, 1849, the Abbé asked Chopin to give him something for the birthday of his (the Abbé's) dead brother, and said that he wanted Chopin's soul: Chopin answered " I understand; here it is. Take it." The Abbé presented the crucifix to Chopin, who began to weep. He at once confessed, made his Communion, received extreme unction, and said, " Thank you, dear friend. Thanks to you I shan't die like a pig." A few days later he said to the doctor, " It is a rare favour that God gives to a man in revealing the moment when his agony begins; this grace He has given to me. Do not disturb me."[4]

Chopin poured out his griefs to the pianoforte, sometimes with infinite pathos, sometimes in turmoil or despair, sometimes in resignation or even in defiance. He expresses also gaiety and serenity, but in

[1] Guy de Pourtalès, *Chopin, A Man of Solitude* (translated by Charles Bayly, Jnr.), pp. 46 f. [2] Ibid., p. 241. [3] Ibid., p. 253. [4] Ibid., pp. 253 f.

his music there is never anything savouring of evil, and no trace of morbidity or of sentimentality. It is romantic, but pure-hearted music. He speaks to us by means of lovely melodies and a peculiarly varied range of melting harmonies, and also even in his ornaments, which are not mere accessories but seem to grow like leaves or blossoms upon a graceful tree and to form a natural part of the design. There is nothing superficial or artificial in Chopin's music, but only genuine emotions and none of the ugly ones, except an occasional burst of anger. That is why it contains so great a measure of divinity. And there are also passages which seem to express religious feelings: the sublime C sharp minor section of the Prelude in D flat (op. 28, No. 15); the Funeral March which forms the slow movement of the Sonata in B flat minor—with its noble grief in the presence of death, alternating with a message of comfort; the stately second section of the first of the two G minor Nocturnes (op. 15, No. 3), and the hymn-like central part of the other one in the same key (op. 37, No. 1); the majestic grandeur of the E major Prelude (op. 28, No. 9); the solemn, measured tread of the one in C minor (No. 20), with its deeply felt, changing harmonics; the serene loveliness of the opening melody of the Etude in E (op. 10, No. 3) and of the central section of the G major Nocturne (op. 37, No. 2). Serenity—internal peace of mind, whatever the man's outward circumstances may be—is, fundamentally, religious, and we may be thankful that Chopin sometimes experienced it, even though it may have been interrupted by more disquieting emotions (as in the E major Etude).

. . . . .

Schumann had one of the noblest characters of the great composers. His was a tender-hearted, rapturous, deeply sympathetic nature. His artistic idealism prompted him to start in 1834, with certain friends, a magazine called *Neue Zeitschrift für Musik*, in order to combat superficiality, vulgarity and mediocrity in music. His articles in it were written under pseudonyms, the chief of which were Florestan and Eusebius: these represented the two contrasted sides of his character, Florestan the vigorous, stormy element, and Eusebius the gentler, more poetic. The "Davidsbündler", which figures in his writings, purported to be a company of artists or art-lovers who were leagued together to fight Philistinism, but was really fictitious and merely enabled him to present his own opinions from different points of view, though sometimes he fathered his own sentiments on real persons whom he knew—or could assume—to be sympathetic to them. The activity involved in editing and contributing to the magazine helped to counteract his shyness and tendency to concentrate too much on himself. He formed several castles in the air about this time: to write books about the lives and works of Bach and Beethoven, and a dictionary on similar lines dealing with living musicians; to promote the regulation by law of the relations between operatic composers and managers; to set up an agency for the publication of musical works, in order to benefit composers; and a musical union for Saxony. All these ideas show his interest in the welfare of his fellow-artists and in music other than his own. Indeed, his enthusiasm and admiration for Mendelssohn and other great contemporaries, such as Berlioz and Chopin, illustrate his complete freedom from envy; and in his middle age his sympathy for the younger generation of composers was a marked characteristic: his remarkable prophecy of the future greatness of Brahms, made when the latter was only twenty, indicated also the soundness of his judgment.

From his youth onwards he was greatly influenced by the poetry of Jean Paul, with its tenderness, its vivid imagination and its exuberant feeling. His own romantic marriage to Clara Wieck, despite her father's opposition, proved idyllically happy, and he remained devoted to her and to their eight children until his death after a tragic period of mental derangement.

Schumann was nominally a Protestant, but his attitude towards religion can be gathered from the following extract from his words on the last page of a note-book called " Hottentotiana " (probably written in 1832) quoted by Mr. Willi Reich in his chapter on " Schumann the man " in *Schumann, a Symposium* edited by Professor Gerald Abraham; as Mr. Reich says, the " Sch." described is certainly either Schumann himself or a character embodying himself in one of his writings: " He loves purely and holily, he has loved much, nobly and divinely. . . . The earth is no pleasure garden for him, rather a holy temple of Nature. He is religious without religion. . . ."

Schumann's genius did not lie in the direction of church music. The springlike freshness and fragrance of his earlier pianoforte compositions are the flowers of his romantic divinity. Weaknesses of orchestration and even of structure do not prevent his symphonies from containing some of his most inspired music. The noble manliness of his outlook is revealed in such things as the " Manfred " Overture, the " March of the Davidsbündler " at the end of *Carnaval*, the Finale of the *Etudes Symphoniques* and the last movement of the great Pianoforte Concerto; but his humanity was so wide, deep and true, that he also showed a remarkable insight into a woman's mind in his song-cycle *Frauenliebe und Leben*, even though Chamisso's poems seem old-fashioned in their outlook nowadays.

In the greatest of his songs he expressed love in its purest, most idyllic and most fervent forms, with never a trace of sentimentality or voluptuousness, and a deep sense of the beauties of nature. Here and there, both in his songs and elsewhere, religious emotion is conveyed. In the majestic and solemn tones of " Im Rhein, im heiligen Strome " (the sixth song in the *Dichterliebe* cycle) he was inspired by the beauty of Cologne Cathedral, as he was also in the slow movement preceding the Finale of the " Rhenish " Symphony in E flat; this movement was originally conceived as " an accompaniment to the solemn ceremony " of the appointment of Archbishop Geissel of Cologne as Cardinal on September 30th, 1850, at which Schumann was present, and is imbued with spiritual grandeur and religious fervour. *Talismane* (the eighth song in the "Myrthen" Liederkreis (op. 25)) is a moving prayer for God's guidance. In *Widmung* (the first of the op. 25 songs) both Rückert (the poet) and Schumann idealise the beloved in such exalted fashion as to identify her with Heaven, and at the end of the song the voice soars from A flat to F as she is proclaimed to be " mein besseres ich " (my better self). The Requiem at the close of the *Manfred* music suffuses the whole imaginary scene with a gentle glow.

Although he composed a Mass and a Requiem at the end of his life, his finest choral works are the secular cantata *Paradies und die Peri* and his setting of scenes from *Faust*. Most composers who have turned their attention to Goethe's great drama have concentrated on the First Part, but two-thirds of Schumann's work are drawn from Part Two. In the three scenes which are derived from Goethe's First Part, Mephistopheles only appears in the Garden scene; both the other two scenes are religious in character—Margaret before the shrine of the " Mater Dolorosa " and the episode in the Cathedral. Schumann's remaining sections, based on Goethe's Second Part, are even finer musically, and his last scene, which closely follows the final scene of Goethe's poem, is the greatest of all. In exalted and eloquent tones it expresses the transfiguration of Faust and his ascent to Heaven, as revealed in Goethe's mystic vision.

In 1851 Schumann was planning to compose an oratorio: he hesitated between a Biblical and a historical theme, and eventually decided on Luther as his subject, but he could not agree with Richard Pohl, the poet, on the length and form of the work, and the project failed to materialise before Schumann's mental health began to give way.

In January 1851 he wrote to a friend: " It must always be the artist's highest aim to apply his powers to sacred music. But in youth we are firmly rooted to the earth by all our joys and sorrows; it is only with advancing age that the branches stretch higher, and so I hope that the period of my higher efforts is no longer distant."[1]

By " sacred music " we are entitled to assume that Schumann here meant music which is sacred to God in the wide sense, not liturgical music. Throughout his life he had composed music of such nobility, fragrance, purity and idyllic fervour, that he can truly be said to have consecrated his art to God subconsciously where he did not do so deliberately as in the examples which I have mentioned. The words just quoted indicate that if it had not been for the tragic and premature collapse of his powers, he would have ventured still further into the realms of celestial art.

[1] Quoted in Philip Spitta's article on Schumann in *Grove's Dictionary of Music and Musicians* (3rd edition), Vol. IV, p. 684.

12

LISZT BECAME AN ABBÉ

LISZT presents a vivid contrast to those of his contemporaries whom we have been considering in the last two chapters. Unlike them, he was a fervent, if somewhat intermittent, Roman Catholic all his life. He was at least as ardent a lover as Schumann, but never regularised his passions by marriage, though this was partly owing to circumstances outside his control. He was as romantic in his outlook as Berlioz, Chopin or Schumann, and more so than Mendelssohn. He surpassed all musicians who ever lived in his prodigal generosity. Love and religion were the two dominant influences in his life, and indeed in his nature they were mystically intertwined. A far greater proportion of his music was avowedly religious than was the case either with Chopin or even Schumann; and in creating these works he was as devout as Mendelssohn. Berlioz composed sacred music, but called himself an unbeliever; Liszt's devotional compositions—whether vocal or purely instrumental—were the intensely felt outpourings of a simple worshipper of God in Christ, but have been found hollow by some music-lovers, though appreciated by others: in recent years, they have been unduly neglected.

As a boy, he was taught various subjects by the priest of Raiding, in Hungary, where he was born in 1811, and loved most of all the stories from the Bible and from the Fathers of the Church. His parents, religious though they were themselves, even found it necessary to curb what Guy de Pourtalès[1] calls his "tendency towards mystical exaltation", which was showing signs of becoming too strong for his health. His father, and, later, his confessor, the Abbé Bardin, felt bound to restrain him from taking Holy Orders, persuading him that his art would be a medium better suited to his temperament for serving God and the Church.

Liszt was always in love, either on a grand scale or on a small one. In Paris, his youthful idyllic attachment to his young pupil, Caroline de Saint Cricq, ended unhappily: her father, the Count, a Cabinet Minister, put a stop to the music lessons when he saw the direction in which they were leading. One religious crisis followed another.

[1] *Franz Liszt: the man of love* (translated by Eleanor Stimson Brooks), p. 17.

Ultimately Liszt reappeared before the public as the brilliant pianist that he was. Then one day, through a friend, he met the revolutionary Abbé de Lamennais, who invited him to stay at his château and taught him how art is united to God through love.

He was only twenty-one when he met the Countess Marie d'Agoult and found " redemption " for his soul in a liaison which tempted her away from a marriage of convenience to a man much older than herself and from her three young children. She bore to Liszt also three children, the second of whom, Cosima, was to become the wife of Hans von Bülow and later of Wagner. Religion mingled with passion in the love of Liszt and Marie. When they visited Lamartine at Saint-Point, the poet read to them his *Bénédiction de Dieu dans la solitude*, which inspired Liszt to compose his beautiful piece of that name for the piano (one of the *Harmonies Poétiques et Religieuses*). At Bellagio, on the Lake of Como, they read the *Divine Comedy* together, and his piece " After a reading of Dante " in the *Années de pèlerinage* (*Deuxième Année*) was the outcome. He was thrilled by Raphael's picture of St. Cecilia at Bologna, with the figures of St. John and Mary Magdalene and St. Augustine accompanying her; and at Rome by Michelangelo's paintings in the Sistine Chapel and the music there. The ardour of his love affairs constantly alternated with his addiction to mystical theology and periods of attending mass every morning. As time went on, Marie came to realise that he no longer burnt with the same passion for her, though she herself still loved him, and she did not understand that his love of freedom included a desire for freedom even in love! Liszt, the now famous master of the pianoforte, went back in triumph to Hungary, without her, and after revisiting the house where he was born at Raiding, prayed in the church in the company of the villagers. And he spent that night with a beautiful gypsy girl.

Ultimately he and Marie parted company, after ten years together. Three years later, he met and fell in love with the Polish Princess Carolyne of Sayn-Wittgenstein, who was separated from her Russian husband. Their love for one another was enhanced by their piety, and she, like Marie, adored Dante, and was deeply absorbed in theology and philosophy as well as art. For many years they made their house at Weimar an artistic centre, encouraging fresh developments in music.

Liszt was a true Christian in his conduct towards his fellow-men and in regard to causes which lay near to his heart. He largely paid for the Beethoven memorial at Bonn. He earned huge sums in Russia and gave them away in charity. He befriended Berlioz by producing his works. His constant friendship for Wagner, which included financial support and survived breaches caused not by him but by Wagner, received its final acknowledgment when, at a banquet after the last performance of *The Ring* at its first production at Bayreuth in August 1876, in the presence of 700 guests including Liszt, Wagner said "There is the man who believed in me first of all, when no one as yet knew anything about me, the one without whom you might never have heard one note of my music, my very dear friend Franz Liszt."[1]

Liszt had shown his characteristic kindness to Hans von Bülow many years before, when Wagner introduced Bülow to him, by not merely taking him as a pupil for the piano but installing him as a guest in his house. When Wagner fell in love with Cosima, Liszt tried to comfort Bülow. In 1877, when Bülow, who had somewhat unaccountably turned against him and apparently thought it necessary to decry his works in order to praise those of Brahms, Liszt's reaction was to visit Bülow, who was resting in a sanatorium after overwork, and to forgive him completely.

All through Liszt's association with the Princess, they had tried to arrange for her divorce from her husband to whom she had been wedded as a minor, so that she and Liszt could marry. But the Tsar, at the instance of her husband's family and anxious to keep a vast estate for an officer of his, had stood in the way. And when in March 1860 the divorce was eventually agreed, the Bishop of Fulda refused to recognise the validity of the decree. Liszt was miserable, but the undaunted Princess went to Rome and had an audience of the Pope, who was overwhelmed by her entreaties and later granted her request for the marriage. Liszt joined her in Rome, and everything was set for the wedding to take place on his fiftieth birthday, but on the very evening before it, after they had taken Communion together, a message came from the Pope reversing his decision: the Wittgenstein family had pointed out that she had not been forced to marry her husband and would therefore be committing perjury if she were to take a fresh oath, and this plea proved too strong for the Pope's scruples.

The Princess had become increasingly jealous of the Liszt-Wagner friendship and during her recent one and a half years in Rome, separated from Liszt, he had found, though he still loved her, that it was possible to live without her, and she had been devoting herself to

[1] Guy de Pourtalès, *Franz Liszt: the man of love*, p. 262.

theology. As Guy de Pourtalès puts it,[1] "Finding in her very sacrifice the means of saving her love, she conceived from this moment the thought of dedicating Liszt to God." So it was that they ceased to live together, and he entered upon the final, dedicated stage of his life. He became an Abbé, and, later, Canon of Albano. He completed his *Legend of Saint Elizabeth*, composed his oratorio *Christus*, a Mass for the Coronation of Francis Joseph in Hungary, and other sacred works, and began *Saint Stanislas* which he did not live to finish. In spite of advancing age and failing health he continued to travel to the Continental cities that he had loved in the course of his life. He died at Bayreuth in 1886, from congestion of the lungs. The Princess did not survive him for as much as a year. He was a deeply and widely loved man, and had been so lavish in his generosity throughout his career that he had sacrificed all his worldly goods and had come to welcome poverty. He left nothing but his cassock, a little linen, and seven handkerchiefs.[2]

Nothing else, that is, except the memory of him, the tradition of his piano playing, and his compositions. How ironical it is that the art of a man to whom religion meant so much should have been accused by his critics of being showy, flamboyant and even meretricious! As a pianist, Liszt was one of the greatest performers that the world has ever known. He hated mere virtuosity, and though his technique was unsurpassed in its brilliance he did not use it as a vehicle for display, but for the profound interpretation of the music of Beethoven and other masters. Some of Liszt's own piano compositions are conspicuous for their embellishments, and the *Campanella*, the *Liebestraum*, the *Hungarian Rhapsodies* and the E flat Concerto are not among his greatest works. Even here, however, we should be careful in our judgment. The *Rhapsodies* are full of colour and cheerful (for the most part), rather than showy. The E flat Concerto, if performed as it should be, is a work of genuine charm; if it seems to be only an affair of glitter and tinsel, that is the fault of the pianist, who is using it as a means of displaying his executive skill and is insensitive to its true delicacy and sweetness.

Sometimes in Liszt's music we meet a strain of bombast, where the rhetoric seems empty and the passion overdone. This is the case at times even in so great a work as the Sonata in B minor, which in the main is a masterly creation imbued with genuine emotion, and in some of the symphonic poems. But in Liszt at his best we find a

[1] Guy de Pourtalès, *Franz Liszt: the man of love*, p. 216. [2] Ibid., pp. 283 f.

convincing portrayal of authentic feelings, a faithful response to the suggestiveness of nature, brilliance in character drawing (in the generalised sense in which music achieves this), and, in other places, the expression of religious emotion.

The *Années de pèlerinage* contain charming impressions of natural scenes and personal reflections, but among them and still more among the *Harmonies poétiques et religieuses* there are several instances of devout music in a gentle mood, far removed from the excitement and occasional rhetoric of some of his more grandiose achievements.

The symphonic poem *The Battle of the Huns* embodies the legend of a war between the spirits of the Huns and of the Roman soldiers who had been killed before the walls of their city, as depicted in a cartoon by Kaulbach. The tempestuous music ends in the victory of the Christian faith, with the hymn " Crux fidelis, inter omnes " finely scored and a culminating orchestral paean of triumph. The first movement of the " Dante " Symphony paints the picture of the Inferno in wild, barbaric music, with a mournful, gentle interlude expressing the fate of Paolo and Francesca da Rimini; the Purgatorio is represented by a restful strain which seems to look forward to the bliss of Paradise, and then by a fugue, sad but resigned in character; this movement leads to a Magnificat which takes the place of Dante's Paradiso and in which a solo soprano and a chorus of altos join the orchestra: in his setting of " Hosanna, Halleluja! " he creates beautiful " pianissimo " effects.[1] The *Faust* Symphony shows Liszt at the height of his powers, the characters of Faust, Gretchen and Mephistopheles being conveyed with great mastery and subtlety in three successive movements: his method of representing Mephistopheles is to parody and pervert the Faust themes of the first movement, thus suggesting that the devil makes use of Faust's own evil desires and does not rely only, or even mainly, on supernatural influence. After this powerful music it is unfortunately an anti-climax to come finally to a setting of Goethe's " Chorus Mysticus " for tenor solo and male choir, which is somewhat dull by comparison.

Liszt's sacred choral works are unequal. They contain fine things, usually combined with other numbers which seem to miss the mark or are secular or operatic in style (perhaps as a result of the influence of Wagner) rather than suitable either for oratorio or liturgy. The *Missa Solemnis*, known as the *Graner Festmesse* because it was first performed at the consecration of the Basilica at Gran, in Hungary, in

[1] Liszt also composed an alternative, " fortissimo ", ending.

1856, is very dramatic and picturesque and has a striking "Kyrie", "Christe" and "Gloria", but its quality is not always consistently maintained. It is remarkable for introducing leitmotives into a religious choral work, an example later followed by Elgar. Thus, the arresting motive of the "Gloria" reappears as that of the "Resurrexit"—a happy stroke—and again in the "Hosanna"; the motive of the "Christe" recurs in slightly altered form in the "Benedictus"—appropriately enough, as Christ was the Blessed One who came in the name of the Lord; and in the final "Dona" the chief themes of the work are recapitulated, culminating in the emphatic motive of the Credo.

The *Legend of Saint Elizabeth* also contains leitmotives; the scene of "The miracle of the roses" combines charm and a kind of saintly innocence in its graceful phrases, and the orchestral Interlude at the beginning of the sixth scene, in which the leading themes are recapitulated, is impressive music.

Liszt's *Requiem*, composed at Rome in 1867–8 for the unusual combination of men's chorus, two trumpets, two trombones, timpani and organ, a few years after the deaths of his son and elder daughter, is completely free from the ornament and profuseness of some of his earlier compositions: terseness of utterance and economy of means are its characteristics. Just because it is exceptional among Liszt's works, it is interesting to remember its main features. The "Requiem aeternam" begins very quietly, with unaccompanied chorus. In the "Dies Irae" there is stern, chromatic music; its "Recordare" strikes a note of earnest entreaty; the "Qui Mariam" expresses gentle sweetness and the "Dona eis requiem" complete tranquillity. The "Offertorio" opens with a simple dialogue between the solo voices and the chorus and anticipates the whole-tone music of a future age in the setting of the words "ne absorbeat eas Tartarus"; whilst the "Tu suscipe" is a devout prayer. The "Sanctus" proclaims the holiness of God in stately tones; in the Hosannas the brass enters with splendid effect; the "Benedictus" is quiet music for solo tenor and chorus; the second Hosanna fades away in the distance. The "Agnus Dei" begins with a chromatic solo for baritone voice, and the "Lux aeterna" is another profound prayer, for eternal light. In the sixth and last section, "Libera me", chromatic intervals and quick rhythms depict the terrors of the Day of Wrath, but the subsequent "Requiem aeternam" brings utter peace at the end.

This moving and beautiful work possesses an intrinsically religious quality which is not consistently present throughout all Liszt's devotional compositions: I am unable to find it in his setting of the Thirteenth Psalm (1855–65), though his sincerity there is unquestionable: the particular chromatic flavour of the music does not strike a note of real devotion, and the closing section is somewhat tawdry.

On the other hand, the oratorio *Christus* (1863–73) which dates from Liszt's last period of creative activity, contains much beautiful music. First performed in May 1873 at Weimar, it is set to a Latin text selected by Liszt from the Bible and the Roman Catholic liturgy, and is in three parts—"Christmas Oratorio", "After Epiphany", and "Passion and Resurrection", each being sub-divided into several sections. Again Liszt uses leitmotives, some of them being adaptations of liturgical chants; in two numbers he follows a Gregorian chant closely. In the "Christmas Oratorio", the "Stabat Mater speciosa" is very simple, but moving in its effect; there is a great deal of charm in the instrumental "Pastorale", though it is rather lengthy; the "March of the Three Kings" is effective and popular in style—its most impressive section is the "Adagio sostenuto assai", depicting the adoration of the magi. In the second part, "After Epiphany", the setting of the Beatitudes is the most convincing: without being based on any liturgical or Gregorian originals, it is simple music, intrinsically sacred in feeling. In the third part, Christ's Passion is portrayed by repeated chromatic effects; the "Stabat Mater dolorosa", in which a mezzo-soprano solo is supported by the choir and the other soloists, has at times a noble pathos; the Easter Hymn, "O filii et filiae", in its peaceful simplicity provides welcome relief after the agony depicted in the preceding music; the final "Resurrexit", though it starts quietly on the violins and woodwind and has its tranquil moments, ends in "fortissimo" exuberance for chorus and orchestra, as the voices proclaim their Hallelujas, Hosannas and Amens.

Liszt is sometimes so lavish in his use of musical notes as to seem prolix, at any rate to some listeners. There is no prolixity in the *Gran Mass*, and neither prolixity nor lavishness in the *Requiem*. If at times we find exuberance and excessive ecstasy in his music, we have to remember that he was an exuberant and ecstatic person; if we do not like these qualities, then in those passages he is no composer for us. And if elsewhere he is also lavish, that is the musical expression of his lavishly generous disposition. He poured out his emotions; some may say that he wore them on his sleeve. His art is sometimes ornate; but then he was, in the best sense of the term, an ornate personality. That does not mean that he, or his music, was not genuine, any more than the ornateness of some Roman Catholic churches is a reflection of any insincerity in those who created them or their decorations. No one would contend that Liszt's sacred choral works are in a class with the greatest religious music; but they have their place in musical history, and it is a pity that they are performed so rarely.

13

VERDI'S RELIGION, FRANCK'S CHRISTIANITY, AND THE ORTHODOXY OF BRUCKNER

THE contrast intended in the title of this chapter should not be misunderstood as implying either that Verdi's religion was unique or that the faith of Franck and Bruckner was merely conventional. Verdi was an anti-clerical Christian, whose religious conviction is evident from his vocal works outside the opera house. Both Franck and Bruckner, on the other hand, were churchmen, whose religious music was inspired by a profound belief in the faith in which they were brought up, though even they differed in their attitude towards it.

Verdi, the son of an innkeeper, born at the little village of Le Roncole in Northern Italy, was in his childhood associated with ecclesiastical music, but from his early days he developed a dislike of priests and priesthood which persisted throughout his life. At the age of seven he heard the organ in church for the first time, while he was serving the priest as acolyte during mass; he was so absorbed in the music, that, when the priest asked him three times for water, he took no notice; eventually the priest pushed him, in order to arouse his attention, and he fell down the three altar steps and fainted. On recovering, however, he merely repeated his previous request to his father that he should be allowed to study music. While still a boy, he became the village organist, and when there was talk of replacing him by a protégé of the bishop, the villagers protested. Later, at Busseto, whither his father had sent him to give him the chance of a better education, he wrote a motet and a Te Deum for the Cathedral, in addition to other music, and deputised at the cathedral organ.

After his transfer to Milan, he was recalled to Busseto by the administrators of the charitable institution known as the Monte di Pietà e d'Abbondanza (which had given him a grant when he went to Milan), with a view to succeeding his old master Provesi, who had died, as organist of the Cathedral; but the ecclesiastical authorities objected and appointed Ferrari, who had the support of two bishops.

These instances of clerical opposition to his prospects probably influenced Verdi at an impressionable time of his life. In his maturity, he was never a churchman. Far the largest part of his artistic output consisted, of course, in his operas, and the occasional part which religion plays in these is mentioned in a later chapter. But though he was anti-clerical, his wife's statement that he believed nothing need not be taken too literally. Sincerity and simplicity were the keynotes of his character and of his art, and the best of Verdi's religious compositions could not have been written by a man who had no faith. He was not an observant Catholic, and doubtless he objected to the temporal and political influence of the Church, but the evidence of his sacred music is the best proof of his religious convictions.

Apart from the earlier of the two settings of " Ave Maria " and the "Pater Noster", produced in 1880, which are not of any great consequence, Verdi's mature devotional works consist of the great *Requiem Mass* composed on the occasion of the death of Alessandro Manzoni (1873), whom he admired tremendously both as poet and man, and the *Quattro Pezzi Sacri* (Four Sacred Pieces) which were his last compositions.

The *Requiem* has been criticised as "theatrical", but the comment at least needs qualification, when we reflect that drama is largely ritualistic in origin, that religious plays continue to be written, and that religion often finds a place in opera. Naturally Verdi, who had devoted his art almost entirely to the creation of operas, was so steeped in his operatic idiom that he could scarcely be expected to change it completely when he was moved to set the words of the Requiem Mass to music as a tribute to Manzoni. And those who complain at finding parts of the work " theatrical " or " operatic " are perhaps too prone to think only in terms of Palestrina on the one hand and of the liturgical art of Northern Europe on the other. To appreciate Verdi's masterpiece, it is necessary to transport ourselves in imagination south of the Alps to sun-kissed Italy and to bear in mind also the political, social and artistic atmosphere of nineteenth-century Europe, when the romantic spirit, never wholly absent from the hearts and minds of men, was predominant.

Moreover, the element of drama in the Manzoni *Requiem* marks a further development in the dramatic treatment of devotional music. As I have pointed out in Chapter 6, in Bach's settings of the Passion according to St. John and St. Matthew, and even in parts of the B minor Mass, we find this quality, which is certainly present also in the *Requiems* of Cherubini and Berlioz and in Beethoven's *Missa Solemnis.* Verdi's score is intensely pictorial, but so was Bach's church music, as Schweitzer has demonstrated. It is largely a matter of degree.

Verdi's setting of the "Dies Irae" with its thrilling choral effects, mighty chords, sweeping passages on the strings, beats on the big drum, and trills in the woodwind, has a Dantesque vividness and terror. The keynote of the *Requiem* is, however, a prayer for peace—the peace of the "Lux aeterna" and the soft entreaty for deliverance from everlasting death with which the work ends. This music, coming from so genuine an artist as Verdi, could not have been composed by a man who was not fundamentally a believer in the Christian faith.

The *Quattro Pezzi Sacri* consist of "Ave Maria", "Stabat Mater", "Laudi alla Vergine Maria" and "Te Deum". None of them shows that theatrical quality which has been attributed to parts of the *Requiem*, and indeed the unaccompanied "Ave Maria" and "Laudi" possess a spiritual kinship with the liturgical music of Palestrina, which Verdi always loved so deeply. The "Laudi" is set to words from the last canto of Dante's *Paradiso*. The "Stabat Mater" directly portrays, in graphic, simple, eloquent tones, the scene of the Virgin contemplating her Son's agony on the Cross. The "Te Deum" ranges from the solemn glory of the opening and the "Sanctus" to the sombre character of "Dignare, Domine, die isto", the moving prayer "Salvum fac populum" and the climax of faith in "Te, Domine, speravi".

Verdi's wife had died less than a year before the production of these works. He was now a lonely old man in the middle eighties, and his physique was beginning to fail. It is fitting that his long, active life, spent largely in the creation of a sequence of operas which embodied faithfully the varied emotions of humanity, should have been rounded off by these four pieces which express religious feeling with so much art and authenticity.

. . . . .

César Franck has been called a Belgian by origin (see Chapter 5) but at the time of his birth at Liège in 1822 Belgium had not yet acquired independence. He subsequently obtained French nationality, and the French have always taken him to their hearts and treated him as one of their great representatives. From the standpoint of this book, the point is relevant as showing how important in French eyes the spiritual element in music can be (in view of the character of Franck's art) and as regards one aspect of his nature, namely his deep loyalty to France: he was settled in Paris by his commercially-minded, authoritarian father as a boy, and remained devoted to his adopted country throughout his life.[1] In Paris, in his early twenties, he fell in love with a French pupil of his, but in those days under French practice a father's consent to marriage was required up to the age of twenty-five, and this was not forthcoming. In 1846 César at last decided to leave home and to live independently, turning his back on his father's ambition to make him a virtuoso pianist to the exclusion of everything else, and devoting himself to the life of organist, teacher and composer. Even then, such was his filial sense of duty that he made an undertaking to pay off all his father's debts alleged to have been incurred in educating him. He married in 1848, after reaching twenty-five, and his father, realising that further objections were useless, was present at the wedding, together with his mother and the bride's parents. Franck seems to have inherited his sweetness of disposition chiefly from his mother. As time went on, he was to find that by marriage he had escaped from the commercial tyranny of a father, to fall under a wife's benevolent, but sometimes unreasonable, dominion.

Franck was a church organist all his life, but in the decade before he was appointed in 1859 to Sainte-Clotilde he composed very little, being too much obsessed in maintaining his wife and children, his promise to pay his father's debts, and his wish to help his own and his wife's brother, both of whom were extravagant. Because he always held a church appointment, was a Christian, kindly, modest and dutiful, and the creator of music which is often religious in character, his pupil and biographer Vincent d'Indy, the composer, pictured him as a kind of mystical saint, producing holy music. Even Mr. Norman Demuth, in his book on Franck, called him "an ardent Roman Catholic". But, as M. Léon Vallas has shown, his own children and grandchildren described him as a believing, but not a practising member of the Church; and Charles Bordes, also a pupil, in reviewing d'Indy's book in *La Tribune de Saint Gervais*, November 1906, wrote that "Franck

[1] M. Léon Vallas, in his admirable book *César Franck* (translated by Hubert Foss) states that on his father's side there was probably in Franck some distant Austrian ancestry rather than Walloon; in the mid-sixteenth century, the family settled in the Liège province at Völkerich, near Gemmenich which is quite close to Aix-la-Chapelle (Aachen) and only just within the Belgian border. Franck's mother was German. In 1837, the father, whose great object was to exploit the musical gifts of both his sons, became a naturalised Frenchman, chiefly in order to get them into the Paris Conservatoire. It was only in 1873 that César, having been nominated for the organ professorship at the Conservatoire, discovered that he himself had not thereby acquired French nationality and took steps to rectify the matter.

was indeed a Christian artist, but more evangelical than really Catholic. . . . The Jesus who sang to him was rather the Jesus of the first centuries of the Christian Church than the Christ of Catholic doctrine. His nature overflowed with charity and altruism, but had nothing in it of the casuist or the medieval mystic: in that respect his genius differed entirely from that of his disciple and biographer."[1]

Both d'Indy and M. Vallas testify, however, to Franck's passionate nature, his temper, his impatience; and M. Vallas dwells upon the conflict between the influences of the composer's wife and son, Georges, and those of his pupils: Madame Franck would have liked him to concentrate on opera and more profitable forms of the art than chamber music and organ music, and even went so far as to try to interfere with his composition; Georges, with his culture and his zeal for classical mythology, tried to turn his father away from religion; whereas Franck's pupils and disciples always pressed him to devote himself to the instrumental forms and sacred music. The composer did his best to please both sides, and seems really to have succeeded in writing what he felt inwardly moved to write. M. Vallas says[2] that he sometimes showed—in Romain Rolland's phrase—"a lovingly pagan soul"; I doubt this: Franck was always a Christian, but that no more prevented him from entering imaginatively into the story of *Psyche* than did Bach's Christianity hinder him from composing suitable music for *Phoebus and Pan*.

M. Vallas draws a much more credible picture of Franck as a human being than the pious portrait visualised by d'Indy. And in the light of it we can understand the turbulent emotions expressed in the masterly Quintet for pianoforte and strings, which Madame Franck disliked so much, and the warmth of feeling in the Symphonic Variations, the Violin and Piano Sonata, the Symphony and the String Quartet. Nevertheless religion, with a fundamentally Christian outlook, predominated in his music. His first great work was *Rédemption* (1871–2), entitled a "symphonic poem", for mezzo-soprano, mixed choir and orchestra. In its first part, amid the forces of paganism, angels announce the coming of Christ to mankind. The orchestral second part depicts, after the lapse of many ages, the joy of Christ's message. In Part III, angels bewail man's fall from grace, an archangel proclaims redemption through prayer, and a final chorus of angels and repentant human beings sing of Christ's forgiveness. The work is full of melody, and points the way to the greater heights attained in *Les Béatitudes* (1869–79).

[1] M. Léon Vallas, *César Franck*, pp. 250, 251. [2] Ibid., p. 251.

The verse libretto of *Les Béatitudes* was by Madame Colomb, the wife of a schoolmaster friend of Franck, and was based on the Sermon on the Mount. All the music which Franck was inspired to assign to Christ is supremely beautiful, but in his portrait of Satan he does not show the same mastery that he afterwards displayed in depicting the forces of evil in *Le Chasseur maudit* and *Les Djinns*. Franck was apparently too benevolent-minded to be able to maintain a diabolical character in his art for long at a stretch; musically, Satan, though more convincing in the Eighth Beatitude than elsewhere, is, like the earthly wrongdoers of the Seventh Beatitude, similar to a figure in a melodramatic opera rather than to a sinister character in an oratorio.

Franck's religious outlook found expression not only in vocal works such as the early *Ruth*, a " Biblical eclogue " for chorus and orchestra, the Mass for three voices (which includes the well-known " Panis Angelicus "), the short oratorios—*The Tower of Babel* and *The Complaint of the Israelites*—and the two later works in the same genre which we have been considering, and the fine song *La Procession*, but also in parts of his instrumental art. Both the two great solo pianoforte compositions, the *Prelude, Chorale and Fugue* and the *Prelude, Aria and Finale*, are imbued with it: the former is a kind of religious triptych, and the chorale-like character of the first two sections of the latter (whose themes recur in the Finale) sanctifies the whole work.

The other great instrumental masterpieces—the Symphonic Variations for pianoforte and orchestra, the Sonata for violin and piano, the Symphony, and the Quartet—not only express deep emotions, but reveal a spiritual character such as we find in those of Beethoven and Brahms, even though its scope is more limited than theirs; and Guy Ropartz was surely not fanciful in calling one of the leading themes in the Symphony " the motive of Faith ".

Franck's last compositions were the three beautiful chorales for organ, which form a fitting close to the creative life of a man who consecrated his genius to God, and who, largely because of that very quality of the spirit, had so profound an influence on musicians in France especially and also beyond its borders.

. . . . .

Whatever doubt has arisen on the nature of Franck's religion, there has never been any question about Bruckner's attitude. He was a devout Roman Catholic. The son and grandson of village schoolmasters, he was intended by his parents for the same profession, which comprised music for both school and church. But at thirty-one, when he became organist at Linz Cathedral, the die was cast: he ceased to be a schoolmaster and became a musician and nothing else. Subsequently he was appointed to various musical posts at Vienna University, won great distinction as an organist and devoted himself to composition. He was frequently in love in his innocent way, but never married. A naïve, simple, modest, childlike soul, with an unquestioning faith, his creative art was essentially dedicated to God, and his religion never seems to be absent long from his music. He once quaintly remarked, " When God finally calls me and asks, what have you done with the talent I gave you, my lad, I will show Him my scores and I hope He will judge me mercifully."[1] On another occasion he said, " They want me to write in a different way. I could, but I must not. Out of thousands I was given this talent by God, only I. Sometime I will have to give an account of myself. How would the Father in Heaven judge me if I followed others and not Him? "[2]

In his symphonies, romantic in feeling though they are, there is a strong vein of religious mysticism. He introduces chorale-like melodies, such as the second subject of the Finale of the Seventh Symphony, opens his Fourth Symphony with an impressively solemn passage that reflects the atmosphere of the Catholic Church, and in the slow movement of Symphony No. 6 gives us a second theme the beauty of which lies in its deeply devotional character. He inscribed his Ninth, and final, Symphony "An meinen lieben Gott"; in its long, earnest, sonorous first movement, amid the climaxes and the pauses, the music is unquestionably religious in feeling, and the Adagio, which comes third and is the last completed section of the work, is art of transcendent sublimity, in which the composer seems to be contemplating the infinite; he frequently prayed to be granted long enough life to enable him to finish the symphony; his prayer was not answered as he wished; yet there is something fitting in his having ended his life's work on so exalted a note.

Some music-lovers find Bruckner's symphonies prolix at times, though this, I suggest, is due to imperfect acquaintance with them. In any case, no such charge can be made against his liturgical compositions, which are perfectly adapted for performance in church, deeply religious in character, and direct in utterance. The Second Mass in E minor, for instance, in which the voices are accompanied only by wind

[1] Quoted by Werner Wolff in his book, *Anton Bruckner, Rustic Genius*, p. 92.
[2] Ibid., p. 104.

instruments, is simple, devout and terse in expression. The F minor Mass is more fully orchestrated, but by no means lengthy. The *Te Deum*, which only takes a little over twenty minutes to perform, employs rich orchestral resources and tremendous choral effects without any trace of ostentation, and is a moving paean of praise to God.

Bruckner's contemporary supporters proclaimed him as a Wagnerian symphonist, in opposition to Brahms. Composers have often found themselves, against their will, set up as champions against a rival with different ideals. Bruckner was content to compose to the glory of God according to his own lights, and it is in that spirit that we can listen to the unfolding of his great symphonies, lengthy though it may be occasionally, and to the concise utterance of his sacred choral works.

14

BRAHMS AND THE END OF A CENTURY

THE world of music outside the opera-house in the second half of the nineteenth century is dominated by the majestic figure of Johannes Brahms. And the reason why he towers over his immediate contemporaries is, fundamentally, a spiritual one. He is the poet of profound, noble and tender emotions, expressed in music which springs from the inmost depths of his soul. This might be said of Bruckner, but the latter had not Brahms' immense range of feeling, though even Brahms' scope is not so wide as that of Wagner. Brahms rises to greater heights of imaginative power than any other non-operatic composer of his own period (except Hugo Wolf in his more limited sphere), yet even he does not attain to the heavenly insight of Bach or penetrate into the mysteries of the universe with Beethoven's vision. But the genuineness of his attitude towards music was so intense that anything in the slightest degree showy or superficial was repugnant to him. Moreover, that the glowing colours of Berlioz, the vivid and varied kaleidoscope of the Wagnerian scores, and, still more, the rich orchestration of Richard Strauss, are so far removed from the character of Brahms' instrumental art, is due to the fact that such features as those were unnecessary in his case (though not in theirs), and, if attempted, would have hung on his Muse like an ill-fitting garment. He could voice his moods and his thoughts perfectly in the intimate terms of a chamber-music ensemble, and when he came to compose for the orchestra he unconsciously enlarged his chamber-music technique to orchestral size rather than conceived his ideas in an orchestral form from the start. The relevance of this from the spiritual standpoint is that it throws light on Brahms' character as a person and as an artist. The strength and the gentleness of man's nature, the depths of religious feeling—these called to him for expression so imperiously that it is almost as though the means employed were of secondary consideration.

He was brought up by his simple, Protestant parents in Hamburg as an orthodox Lutheran, and was prepared for confirmation by Pastor Johannes Geffcken of St. Michaelis, from whom he derived his love for the old Protestant church music. His knowledge of the Bible was prodigious and his devotion to it lasted all his life. He told his friend

Von der Leyen, " We North Germans long for the Bible every day and do not let a day go by without it. In my study I can lay my hand on my Bible even in the dark." He set Biblical texts to music over and over again—in the *German Requiem*, the *Begräbnisgesang*, the Thirteenth Psalm and the motets, the *Triumphlied*, the *Fest- und Gedenksprüche*, and the *Four Serious Songs*.

Moreover, in his conduct Brahms was a practical Christian. It is true that he was often rude and rough in his manner and could sometimes even appear unkind. That was, as it were, the obverse of his rugged, uncompromising nature. And he became outwardly so reserved, even shy, as regards his deepest feelings, that he was liable to be misunderstood. But beneath the tough exterior he was immensely kind-hearted and generous. He showed his love for his parents, his step-relations, his brothers and sisters, not by words merely but by actions. He loved children and animals, and his devotion to his friends and his impulse to help fellow human beings were so strong that, whilst denying himself everything except necessities, he gave away considerable sums of money—sometimes secretively—not only to an intimate friend such as Clara Schumann for the education of her children, but to colleagues, mere acquaintances or even strangers in the musical profession when they were in financial need. Such Christian conduct is of course to be found among Christians and Jews alike, and indeed among members of other great religions; but as a matter of history it owes its development, if not its origin, largely to Christ's influence; and when it is so conspicuous in a man who was brought up as a Christian, who was a constant reader of the Bible, and who selected texts from the New Testament as well as from the Old Testament and the Apocrypha for some of his most sublime music, it is reasonable to think that a broad, non-dogmatic Christianity was Brahms' religion.

Nevertheless, the testimony of writers on Brahms has been by no means unanimous on the subject. Both Walter Niemann and Richard Specht (the latter of whom knew Brahms personally at the end of his life) described him as a Protestant,[1] and Niemann went so far as to call him " a convinced and believing member of the Lutheran Protestant Church. Not as regards dogma, not in the letter, but in the spirit."[2] J. A. Fuller Maitland in his article on Brahms in *Grove's Dictionary*

[1] *Brahms* by Walter Niemann (translated by Catherine Alison Phillips); *Johannes Brahms*, by Richard Specht (translated by Eric Blom).

[2] Ibid., p. 182.

of Music and Musicians,[1] wrote that " the dogmatism of the churches did not appeal to him " and was silent on the question whether Brahms was a Lutheran Protestant or even a Christian at all in his religious convictions. H. C. Colles, a great authority on Brahms, stated that the composer " wrote no liturgical church music because he was not of any church ".[2] The present music critic of *The Times*, however, in an article in that paper on September 11th, 1952, went much further: with regard to the *German Requiem* he wrote that it showed " a basic insincerity in what is outwardly a noble work. Brahms was not a Christian, but a Stoic and not a very good Stoic at that, as both the *Song of Destiny* and the *Requiem* prove. In both he proclaims his fatalism in emphatic terms and then runs away for some sort of comfort to a vaguely hopeful wishful thinking. The sixth chorus of the *Requiem* is not even wishful—it is mechanical. . . ."

Many music-lovers, I fancy, must have rubbed their eyes in astonishment at reading those words, coming especially from so august a source! There is no composer in the whole history of music who is more utterly and profoundly sincere than Brahms. This deep authenticity is, indeed, the keynote of his character, both as man and artist. The notion that the *Requiem* is "basically insincere" is, frankly, incredible. It was begun with his thoughts on his dearly loved friend Schumann, who had died so tragically, was continued after the death of his mother, to whom he was devoted, and was completed in memory of the dead who had fallen in the war of 1870. The words were chosen by Brahms, with his exhaustive knowledge and deep love of the Bible, from passages in the Scriptures after the most careful and anxious thought: Matthew v, 4; Psalm cxxvi, 5, 6; I Peter i, 24, 25; James v, 7, 8; Isaiah xxxv, 10; Psalm xxxix, 4–7; Wisdom iii, 1; Psalm lxxxiv, 1, 2, 4; John xvi, 22; Ecclesiasticus li, 27; Isaiah lxvi, 13; Hebrews xiii, 14; I Corinthians xv, 51, 52, 54, 55; Revelation iv, 11 and xiv, 13. It is inconceivable that Brahms—of all people—did not mean what he said in setting such texts as these to music. The work is indeed different both in the letter and the spirit from the Roman Catholic mass for the dead. It is, however, a sublime and moving musical poem on what is fundamentally a Christian theme, albeit one which is acceptable to any who believe in a loving God: blessed are they that mourn, for they shall be comforted; for though all flesh is as grass and every man must die one day, death is swallowed up in victory:

[1] Third edition, Vol. I.
[2] *Oxford History of Music* (1934), Vol. VII, p. 360.

" O death, where is thy sting? O grave, where is thy victory?" Those who die in the Lord are blessed, they shall rest from their labours and their works shall follow them.

We think—perhaps especially—of the tranquil, spiritual grief of the opening movement; the solemn magnificence of " Behold all flesh "; the radiance of " How lovely are Thy dwellings "; Brahms' thunder as he depicts the wrath of the Last Judgment; the grandeur of the mighty fugue in which he praises God after the victory over death; the divine serenity of the final music of eternal blessing.

Reinthaler, the organist of Bremen Cathedral, with whom Brahms corresponded about the *Requiem*, suggested his making the work more orthodox by inserting a passage dealing with Christ's redemption of mankind by His death on the Cross; and pointed out that, moreover, in the last movement Brahms says " Blessed are the dead which die in the Lord *from henceforth* ", i.e. after Christ has finished his redeeming task. Brahms replied that he was writing for humanity as a whole, and had deliberately left out verses such as John iii, 16[1] but that he could not dispute or omit the " from henceforth " of his " revered poets ". This seems to show that he was seeking to compose a work on a broad, human basis which would appeal both to Christians and others.[2]

The *Four Serious Songs*, which were his last work, are settings of two passages from Ecclesiastes (iii, 19–22 and iv, 1–3), one from Ecclesiasticus (xli, 1–2) and one from the First Epistle to the Corinthians (xiii, 1–3, 12, 13). In the first three of them he sings of death as the common fate of men and beasts, as a release from oppression, as the enemy of those who prosper carelessly and as the friend of those whose strength is failing and who are in despair. The darkness which lies over these songs is at last dispelled by the radiance of the wonderful music in which Brahms, in the fourth song, has embodied St. Paul's vision of faith, hope and charity. Although Brahms jestingly accused himself of " unchristian principles ", in writing to Herzogenberg about these songs, they are a noble expression of the great conception of the passage of humanity from suffering and the valley of the shadow of death into the blessed serenity of love which reconciles the world.

There was, it is true, something of the Stoic in Brahms, but that is because some of the Stoic qualities—heroic endurance and resignation,

[1] " For God so loved the world, that He gave His only begotten Son, that whosoever believeth in Him should not perish, but have everlasting life."

[2] In this paragraph I am indebted to Mr. Ernest Newman's admirable preface to Novello & Co.'s score of the *Requiem*.

for instance—are shared by Christianity. The description of Brahms as " not a very good Stoic " is appropriate only in the sense that he was not a perfect example of a Stoic, because he was a Christian, with all the differences which exist between the two creeds. *The Song of Destiny* illustrates this. It is based upon a poem by Hölderlin, which contrasts the peaceful happiness of the celestial powers with the sufferings of humanity: but whereas the poem is entirely an embodiment of this pagan conception, Brahms, though in common with countless other Christian creative artists he is capable of entering imaginatively into the spirit of a pagan subject, shows his non-pagan outlook by the way in which, after depicting the misery of men, he ends the work with a wonderfully serene orchestral epilogue: it is as though he wishes to convey that, in spite of everything, eternal peace will be the ultimate destiny of mankind. Brahms was too much of a Christian to feel able to embody in full measure the ancient Greek conception of man dominated by a pitiless fate. Some may regard this as a weakness in him as an artist; but even if it is (which I do not admit) it is due to the tender side of his nature, the Christian outlook which guided his music and his life.

We see this again in the *Gesang der Parzen* (Song of the Fates), the words of which are from Goethe's *Iphigenie*, and in *Nänie*, set to Schiller's poem. Goethe's lines, like *The Song of Destiny*, point the contrast between the bliss of the pagan gods and the wretchedness of men cast down for their sins into the abyss of darkness; but at the end Brahms cannot resist the impulse to express in music pity for the human beings whom the gods have punished so ruthlessly. In *Nänie*, the poem of which is an allegorical ode, in an antique Greek guise, on the death of his friend, Anselm Feuerbach the painter, both words and music move from tender sorrow to comfort and peace.

Thus Brahms' settings of " pagan " themes are softened by a Christian gentleness. But in the *Alto Rhapsody* he found a subject even more after his heart. He selected three stanzas from Goethe's *Harzreise im Winter*: the first two depict vividly an unhappy young misanthrope wandering in winter through the mountains and the anguish of spirit which consumes him; the third stanza is an ardent prayer, in which the male chorus joins the soloist, beseeching the " Father of Love " to enlighten the young man's soul. Brahms was so fond of this work that he put it under his pillow at night, in order to have it always with him.

Wagner portrayed the renunciation of love musically in *The Ring*, but he certainly did not experience it in his private life! It was Brahms who did so. There can be no doubt, though many biographers have been reticent on the subject, that a deep love for Clara Schumann had grown up in his heart, and that after Robert's death the two of them had to decide whether to marry or to continue as devoted friends. That they followed the path of friendship rather than matrimony may have been partly due to the fact that Clara was thirteen and a half years older than Brahms, but for him it was chiefly a question of choosing between an all-absorbing love and the dedication of his life to composition. So sacred to him was his sense of a mission to produce the art which he knew he had the power to create, that he chose music. But it was a tragic dilemma. He fell in love idyllically with other women after Clara—with Agathe von Siebold, with Elizabeth von Stockhausen (who married Heinrich von Herzogenberg and with her husband maintained an abiding friendship for him), with Clara's daughter, Julie, when she grew up to womanhood; but he remained a bachelor, though sometimes he wistfully longed for the happiness of married life.

To this loving, warmly affectionate temperament we owe the tenderness and beauty of his many love songs; to his renunciation of wedded bliss, to his reserved nature and his suppression of his emotions, the melancholy, which has sometimes been called "Nordic pessimism", and the infinite sadness inherent in some of his music; to his magnificent virility and strength of character, the grandeur and splendour of his great Allegro movements; to the resignation and serene wisdom of his later years, the sweet, mellow tranquillity of the Trio for clarinet, violin and pianoforte and the Quintet for clarinet and strings.

Apart from his chorale-preludes for organ and one other possible exception to be mentioned, Brahms did not express religious feeling in his instrumental music, but rather the sorrow, tenderness, buoyancy, graciousness and heroism, which, whether voiced or not in his personal relationships, were engrained in his nature. The slow movement of the First Pianoforte Concerto, however, was originally inscribed "Benedictus qui venit in nomine Domini" ("Blessed is he who cometh in the name of the Lord"—Matthew xxi, 9); but according to a communication from Brahms' great friend Joachim to Kalbeck, these words were to be interpreted "Blessed be he who returns in the name of the dear lord (Schumann) to the deserted Domina (Clara Schumann) and the children bereft of their father." Now, the first movement is known to have been written under the shadow of Schumann's terrible mental illness and his attempted suicide by throwing himself into the

Rhine; but I find it hard to accept that interpretation of the original " Benedictus " inscription on the second movement: Brahms had gone at once, like a true friend, to Clara in her distress; but surely he would not have compared himself to the Messiah! Just about the time that he was composing the slow movement he wrote to Clara on December 30th, 1856 (five months after Schumann's death in the asylum) " I am also painting a lovely portrait of you: it is to be the Adagio." Nevertheless, Tovey[1] calls it " a Requiem for Schumann "; yet it does not sound like a Requiem, even though all Requiems have peaceful passages. The music does resemble an idealised love picture, and that, particularly in Brahms' case, would account for its spiritual character. May not the truth be that in painting " a lovely portrait " of Clara, Brahms was at the same time praying for her and uttering his prayer in the language which always expressed his inmost thoughts and feelings more eloquently than words could ever do—the language of music?

Brahms' instrumental works contain so many embodiments of a spiritual quality which is not directly religious, that space permits me to recall only a few examples: the noble second subject in the first movement of the Trio in C minor (op. 101); the sublime introduction to the Finale of the First Symphony; the second theme in the Andante of the Fourth, with its unconscious reminder of the slow movement in Beethoven's last quartet (op. 135), both of them achieving their effect with a similar, even rhythm and the simplest means—an extreme " legato " and movement largely up and down the major scale; the heavenly melody with which the 'cello opens the slow movement of the great Pianoforte Concerto No. 2 in B flat; the *Intermezzo* for pianoforte in E flat (op. 117, No. 1), with its tender Andante, the anxiety of its piu Adagio section, and the return to the tranquillity of the beginning.

In a sense, the question whether Brahms was a Lutheran or simply a Christian is today unimportant. Humanity is his theme—humanity in its grandeur and its distress, its joy and its loving tenderness, its laughter and its tears, its passion and its serenity, but without any reference to the sordid, degrading, or ostentatious facets of mankind. In his love music, and in the sound pictures of the beauties of nature which we find among his songs, he was a Romantic, though he was not concerned with the fairies and fantastic shapes which the Romantic movement conjured up, but with men and women as he knew them. He may not have been a devout churchman; he went back to bedrock—to the

[1] *Essays in Musical Analysis*, Vol. III, p. 117.

Bible itself; and for him, either in the background or the foreground of his thoughts, there was the presence of a loving God.

. . . . .

The close of the nineteenth century roughly tallied with the death of Brahms and with the end of the creative careers of three of his leading contemporaries, apart from those previously considered. Tchaikovsky pre-deceased him by three and a half years. Dvořák died in 1904, but nearly all his music was composed in the previous century. Hugo Wolf lived until 1903, but his tragic lunacy cut short his artistic life in 1897.

Tchaikovsky, apart from the *Liturgy of St. John Chrysostom* and some church choruses (among which the *Hymn to the Trinity* is an example of a work intrinsically devout in feeling), would normally be described as a creator of "secular" music. During and just after the Second World War there were two composers whose serious art made the strongest appeal to the British public—Beethoven's, on account of its spiritual character, and Tchaikovsky's because of its very human qualities. Tchaikovsky's music, even if most of it was earth-bound, spoke of the ordinary emotions in simple, melodious terms and with lucid, masterly instrumentation, and the fact that it did so with complete frankness and with its heart on its sleeve made it all the easier to understand.

The divinity of beauty is not present in his work to an extent comparable with its manifestation in the art of the greatest masters. Yet in certain places even his "secular" music has directly religious associations. Thus the fantasy-overture *Romeo and Juliet* opens with a solemn theme representing Friar Laurence, to which there is also an allusion during the development section. The opening and closing parts of the symphonic fantasia *Francesca da Rimini* depict with Dantesque vividness the furious whirlwind which, according to medieval imagery, ceaselessly tosses carnal sinners to and fro in the darkness of Hell.

Tchaikovsky wrote to his sympathetic friend Nadejda von Meck—the widow who out of her admiration for his music so generously helped him and corresponded with him for many years—a "programme" for his Fourth Symphony, which showed that the opening, recurrent theme was intended to represent "Fate, that inevitable force which checks our aspirations towards happiness ere they reach the goal. . . ." He told Taneyev that this symphony was a reflection of Beethoven's Fifth, and that if Taneyev had not grasped this idea, that was because he himself was "no Beethoven". The conception of an external, supernatural, obstructive influence—which was indeed shared by both composers in these two symphonies—is a religious one, even though without faith in a loving God it would not be Christian. Tchaikovsky described his Finale as a rustic holiday " where you may discover happiness among the people if you cannot find it in yourself"; this is very different from the spiritual victory of Beethoven's Finale, but it sincerely reflected Tchaikovsky's mood at that period of his life.

The " Fate " idea seems also to underly Tchaikovsky's Fifth Symphony, in which a melancholy motto theme recurs in each movement but in the Finale is transformed into triumph in the major key. This symphony is really more religious than the Fourth: the slow movement opens with solemn chords, followed by a serene and soothing melody; the Finale portrays the victory of faith over depression and misgiving.

Tchaikovsky's homosexual instincts were the tragedy of his life, and some authors have professed to find in his music a sense of guilt or sin. The issue concerns us here, because, if Tchaikovsky sinned, his sin was against God's word, and if he revealed or " confessed " his sin in his music this will inevitably have a bearing on our discussion. His homosexuality was something of which he was ashamed, he exerted great self-control with regard to it, and in spite of his exceptionally strong affection for certain members of his own sex there is no real evidence that he yielded to temptation. He even contracted a misguided and—as it turned out—most unhappy marriage with a girl who proved to be a nymphomaniac, in the hope of subduing or at least concealing his abnormality. To sit in judgment on him as a " sinner " is, I suggest, uncharitable. His perversion was a misfortune which in itself should command our pity, not our censure. If he did not indulge it, we must admire his determination. And even if he did sin in that way, that does not in itself make him a worse character than other men whose sinfulness takes different forms. Lastly, I crave leave to doubt whether those who claim to have discovered a sense of sin in Tchaikovsky's music would have done so if they had not already known of his unfortunate tendency from external evidence, or indeed whether it is possible for music to " confess " guilt; it does voice emotions and prayers of entreaty and can portray evil, but I suggest that certain critics have deceived themselves by reading into Tchaikovsky's music something which is not there and which is precluded from being there by the very nature of the art. I have met many music-lovers who did not know about Tchaikovsky's sexual abnormality—for many years I did not myself—and who, while sensing the emotionalism of some of his music (which they rightly assumed to be a reflection of his temperament), did not detect any " guilty confession " in it and are unable to do so even after learning the facts.

Considering how much of Tchaikovsky's work is cheerful, charming and light-hearted in character, and that he was one of the great masters of exquisite fairy music and dance music for ballets, too much has been made of the morbidity of his art. As a man, he was a neurotic, who sometimes indulged in self-pity; the extent to which he expressed it in his music has been exaggerated, and undue stress has been laid on the mournful ending of the " Pathetic " Symphony: at the close, we have been told, the basses sob themselves to sleep in self-pity. But if the composer had intended to produce an effect of sobbing, irregularity of rhythm would surely have been a more graphic way of conveying it; in fact, the melody proceeds down the scale with a steady tread; the evenness of the rhythm is maintained to the end, as the basses, with perfect control of emotion, utter their deep notes of sorrow. If this music is conducted and played as it should be, there is dignity in its grief; and the more that a man bears his grief with dignity, the nearer he is to God. In this symphony and elsewhere, Tchaikovsky does pour out his emotions into his art unreservedly, whether they are sad or gay; that did not prevent him from casting his music into beautiful shapes.

Certain passages in Tchaikovsky's correspondence and diary throw light on his attitude towards religion. In March 1881, after Nikolay Rubinstein's funeral, he wrote to Madame von Meck about God: " I often pray to Him with tears in my eyes (where He is, what He is, I do not know; but I do know that He exists), and implore Him to grant me love and peace, to pardon and enlighten me; and it is sweet to say to Him: ' Lord, Thy will be done,' for I know His will is *holy*." And in March 1884 he commented to her, in connection with Tolstoy's Confessions, " Every day, every hour I thank God for having given me this faith in Him. What would have become of me, with my cowardice, my capacity for depression, and—at the least lapse in courage—my desire for *non-existence*, had I been unable to believe in God and submit to His will? "

In 1884 also, he corresponded with Balakirev about religion (and about church music, as the Tsar had indicated that he would like him to compose for the Church): " How good you are! What a true friend you are to me! How I wish that that transfiguration which has been effected in your soul might be vouchsafed also to mine. I can say without the slightest infringement of the truth that I *thirst* more than ever for peace and support in *Christ*. Pray that I may be strengthened in my faith in Him."

Tchaikovsky idolised Mozart. The following is a remarkable extract from his diary, dated October 2nd, 1886: " And so what do I think of Beethoven? I bow to the grandeur of some of his compositions—but I do not love Beethoven. My attitude towards him reminds me of my childhood feelings towards the God Jehovah. I had towards Him (nor have my feelings changed) a feeling of wonder, but also of terror. He has created heaven and earth, and though I kneel before Him, I do not love Him. Christ, on the other hand, calls forth only the emotion of *love*. He is God, but He is also Man. He has suffered like ourselves. We pity Him and in Him love the ideal part of man's nature. If Beethoven holds in my heart a similar place to that held by the God Jehovah, I love Mozart as the musical Christ. This comparison does not to me seem blasphemous. Mozart was pure as an angel, and his music is rich in divine beauty."

In the same year he wrote in his diary: " I should like to set down my *religion* in detail, if only to make my faith clear to myself once and for all, to define the boundary between it and knowledge. But life keeps flying away and I don't know whether I shall manage to express that *symbol* of the faith which has recently developed in me. It has very definite forms, but I don't make use of it when I pray. I pray just as before, i.e. as I was taught."

. . . . .

Dvořák is a much less controversial figure. He presents no problem to us here. From our standpoint, his importance rests on two facts, the second of which arises from the first: (1) that he regarded his art as a gift from God, and (2) that his enormous versatility included a genius for composing religious music.

He came of humble stock, his father having been an innkeeper and butcher in a Czech village. Recognition of his musical talent led to small beginnings in the world of music, from which he worked his way gradually upwards by means of his prolific creative powers, until he attained worldwide fame. He made a happy marriage and was the father of six children, and indeed, in contrast with many other great composers, lived a contented life apart from his early struggles and the conflict which he had to face in his forties when his Austrian friends, such as Hanslick the critic, seemed to be trying to deflect him from his chosen path of a national Czech and Slavonic composer and to induce him to become more cosmopolitan by embarking on an opera with a German libretto. M. Otakar Šourek in his book *Antonin Dvořák*[1] suggests that this inward struggle found expression in certain of his works of that period and particularly in the Symphony in D minor (known as "No. 2"). This may be so, but the tragic grandeur of that symphony may equally be the outcome of Dvořák's deeply sincere nature both as man and artist. His instrumental music is, for the most part, genial, fresh, spontaneous and full of gracious melody, set forth in glowing, but never gaudy, colours. It is the product of a warm-hearted, very human personality, and it is in keeping that a man of his sympathetic character should sometimes have portrayed also the sorrows and struggles of life in his music.

Dvořák remained faithful to his ideal of voicing the character of his own people in his art, and this was indissolubly linked with his devoutly religious outlook. His creative work, with its happy rhythms, its flowing melodies, its fresh, open-air quality, is imbued with the spirit of Czech and Slavonic folk-music and with love of the Bohemian countryside. This racial quality did not prevent Dvořák from absorbing the soul of the Negro folk-tunes and spirituals, with which he became acquainted during his sojourn in America, and fusing this with his Czech musical mentality in his symphony *From the New World*, the String Quartet in F (op. 96) and the Quintet (op. 97).

Dvořák's impulse to produce characteristically national music was part and parcel of his religion, in the sense that for him it was a mission from God to compose from the heart, and his heart was with his own people. He was, however, not only loved by Czechs of all classes, but was extremely popular in Germany, Russia, England and the United States. He was, indeed, a very lovable man. Brahms helped him in his early days by commending him warmly to Simrock, the publisher, because he both admired his talent and liked him as a man. Tchaikovsky and Dvořák became great friends and loved one another's music. Dvořák also formed a warm friendship for Anton Seidl, a former secretary of Wagner's, and he greatly admired Wagner's works. The antipathies or differences which existed between Brahms, Tchaikovsky and Wagner, as artists, become, as it were, submerged in the glow of Dvořák's affection for all three.

And his versatility did not consist simply in producing chamber-music, symphonies, concertos, operas, songs, pianoforte pieces, symphonic poems, cantatas, oratorios and liturgical works, but in

[1] pp. 19 f.

creating beautiful music in all these different spheres of activity. He was a Catholic of simple piety, and his specifically religious works form an important part of his art. The *Stabat Mater* (1877) sprang from Dvořák's grief at the death of his eldest daughter, but his inspiration and his deeply religious feeling transformed this, in the opening movement, into a heartfelt musical expression of the emotions of Mary beholding the Cross; there follows a series of airs, choruses and concerted pieces in which the very loveliness of the melodies seems, as it were, to comfort the mourner; *Inflammatus* is a mystical prayer; in the last quartet and chorus, "Quando corpus morietur" (When the body shall die) the glory of Paradise is set to music which blazes with splendour, but the work ends in the utmost tranquillity. In the oratorio *St. Ludmila* (1886) Dvořák sought to combine Christian fervour and Czecho-Slavonic patriotism: there is a joyous freshness in the heathen songs of the first part, but a certain heaviness in some of the music associated with Ivan, the Christian monk; compensation for this comes, however, in the stirring choruses of the third part, celebrating the baptism of Queen Ludmila and her lover Duke Bořivoj and of the Czech people. The *Requiem* (1890) is a deeply spiritual creation, imbued with a noble sorrow at the thought of death (which Dvořák conveys by means of narrow intervals within a small compass), yet relieved by expressions of resignation, praise to God, submission to His righteous will and faith in everlasting rest for the dead. The *Te Deum* (1892), framed on symphonic lines in four movements, is not only a joyful paean to the Almighty, but with its many touches of open-air sweetness reminds us that music can be at once charming and religious. The last of Dvořák's devotional works was of a more intimate kind—the cycle of ten *Biblical Songs* (1894) composed during the latter part of his visit to America: happy though he was there, it was probably his longing for his own country and the news of his father's last illness that caused him to voice his most inward religious feelings in these simple, but beautiful, settings of various texts from the Psalms.

. . . . .

Hugo Wolf had a more intense feeling for the words and detail of the poetry which he set to music than any of his great predecessors in the art of composing *Lieder*. Consequently, though his melodic gifts did not equal Schubert's, he was unrivalled as an interpreter in song of the exact meaning of every line of the poem and not only of its general mood or sense as, for instance, Brahms was. He steeped himself in every poem that he set, so that he got to the inmost core of it, and his genius enabled him to embody it completely in musical terms. And as the poems which he selected express with almost infinite variety the diverse aspects of human nature, the result is that truth as well as beauty—two of the manifestations of God to man—are represented in Wolf's songs in a supreme degree.

Mr. Frank Walker's admirable book *Hugo Wolf* (1951) gives us a picture of an impetuous, passionate, sincere man, a devoted son and brother, with an attractive personality, but a difficult and "fiery temperament" (as his father called it) which made him his own worst enemy and caused him, on the most trivial grounds, to break friendships with people from whom he had received great kindness. In a normal person, such conduct would seem extremely ungrateful, and his behaviour towards Frieda Zerny, the beautiful singer and enthusiastic interpreter of his songs, showed little consideration for her feelings: his love for her cooled because he found her "egotistical", according to his letters to others; but the egotism was really in his own character, in the sense that he regarded his art as practically his only purpose in life—a kind of mystical gift from Heaven to which everything else must give way.

Wolf was brought up as a Catholic by a devout mother, though his father was a free-thinker. He was one of the children of the town of Windischgraz in Lower Styria (Austria), who on the eve of Epiphany were dressed up as the Kings from the East and sang outside the people's houses. On the whole he seems to have been happier and more satisfactory at the Konvikt attached to the Benedictine monastery of St. Paul in the Lavant Valley, Carinthia, than at any of the other educational establishments to which his perplexed parents sent him. At Marburg, while he was at the Gymnasium, he managed to get a position in the first violins of the orchestra which participated in performing devotional music in the town church, and got into trouble with Dr. Žager, the professor of religion at the Gymnasium, because he was absent from school mass, through playing in Hummel's Mass in D minor in the church. Žager spoke of "this damned music", and this provoked an indignant outburst from Wolf, to whom his art was sacred. No wonder that he soon left the school!

Although later in life he became a follower of Nietzsche, it is probable that when at the age of twenty-one he composed the *a capella* choruses, the *Geistliche Lieder* (April 1881), which are artistically and spiritually beautiful, he was a Christian in his beliefs. A book of poems by Wolf contained among other things dated 1881 " A moving Apostrophe, delivered on 4th September as a Morning Sermon, for it was a Sunday, the Day of the Lord, which should accord with Devotion and the Love of Mankind. Reproduced faithfully in verses with a note in conclusion by the author, which witnesses to his Christian disposition, for the moral pointed thereby is given in the words of Christ, ' Father, forgive them, for they know not what they do ' ". But in a letter to his mother dated April 29th, 1892, he called himself an " Unbeliever ", and on September 7th, 1897, he wrote to Frau Rosa Mayreder, who was also a Nietzschian, that he shared her views about Christianity, but that this did not prevent him from " appreciating its artistic sides ".[1] Mr. Walker suggests that, when in 1897 he accompanied the nineteen-year-old Margarethe Klinckerfuss into the Marienkirche at Stuttgart and reverently knelt beside her, he may have been seeking only to comfort her by praying for the repose of the soul of the dead explorer Wissemann, with whom she had been in love.

The oratorio *Christnacht* (1887) was not altogether a success; and apart from the *Geistliche Lieder*, and such works as the String Quartet in D minor, the symphonic poem *Penthesilea*, the *Italian Serenade*, the *Elfenlied* for soprano solo, women's chorus and orchestra, and the opera *Der Corregidor*, Wolf's greatness rests on his wonderful songs: in addition to the vast range and infinite subtleties of human emotions presented in these, they include a considerable number of songs on religious themes. It would be an over-simplification to contend that such songs show merely that Wolf " appreciated the artistic side " of religion. He was not—consciously, at any rate—a Christian believer; but he was also no atheist; he constantly invoked God in his letters; he wished to be buried in the village churchyard at Perchtoldsdorf which he loved so much—though when the time came he was interred in a Grave of Honour in the Central Cemetery at Vienna, near the tombs of Beethoven and Schubert. Any suggestion that so authentic an artist as Wolf was somehow insincere in setting religious poems to music would be beside the mark. By a kind of spontaneous sympathy he entered into the emotions underlying the words and voiced them wondrously in his music, and this applied just as much to the religious songs as to the secular ones.

Eduard Mörike was a Lutheran clergyman and wrote lyrics on sacred subjects, in addition to expressing the joys and sorrows of love

[1] Frank Walker, *Hugo Wolf*, p. 397.

and the beauties of nature in his poetry. The fifty-three songs in Wolf's Mörike book include several which are wholly or partly religious in character. For example, *Fussreise*, with its vigorous rhythms and open-air quality, reflects the happiness of a man walking through woods and hills, feeling that he is enjoying the bliss of Paradise, and praising the Creator of nature's loveliness; there is here something of the spirit of the little girl's song in Browning's *Pippa Passes* as she goes on her way when " the year's at the spring "—

God's in his heaven,
All's right with the world.

The first of the two songs *Auf eine Christ-blume* addresses a Christmas rose which flowers in a churchyard and which the poet sought also in the glade, by the chapel, and near the lake: he compares it in its fragrance and whiteness to the bridal robes of the Blessed Mother, and pictures an elf standing in wonder before its mystical glory; all these varied images are reflected in Wolf's imaginative song. *Seufzer* is the sigh of a monk who suffers Hell's torments because he failed to cherish God's love, and Wolf portrays this with his slow rhythm and the agony of his chromatic intervals. The gentle music of *Auf ein altes Bild* pictures, in a landscape setting, the Infant Jesus playing on the Virgin's knee; yet at the end there is a touch of grief at the sight of the stem of the Cross growing near-by in the wood. *In der Frühe* overcomes the torture and doubts of a restless night by the serenity of the morning bells. *Schlafendes Jesuskind* is the softest of lullabies for the Holy Child. *Gebet* is a simple, devout prayer. *Wo find ich Trost?* is the cry of a sinner in anguish.

Among the fifty-one Goethe songs are the delightfully childlike *Epiphanias*, written for the birthday of Frau Melänie Köchert and sung by her three little girls in the costumes of the Three Kings, and the stately *Königlich Gebet*. *Prometheus* reveals man defying Zeus in music of heroic grandeur. *Ganymed* depicts in tones of radiant loveliness the youth whom Zeus loved and who worshipped him in his own love of nature's beauty. *Grenzen der Menschheit* majestically portrays the littleness of man contrasted with the remote, indifferent, yet creative power of the Deity.

In contrast with the pagan feeling of these last three songs, the first ten *Lieder* of the forty-four in the *Spanish Song Book* (set to translations by Emanuel Geibel and Paul Heyse) are all Christian in character. In the first, second, seventh and eighth the theme is again that of a repentant sinner, which seems to have appealed deeply to Wolf, for it recurs frequently in his work and always evoked most eloquent music from him. The third song, " Nun wandre, Maria ", has an almost Bach-like accompaniment as Joseph comforts Mary on the weary journey to Bethlehem. In " Die Ihr schwebet " (No. 4) she calls on the angels to still the wind that blows through the palm trees under which she is sheltering, for her Babe is asleep. " Führ mich " (No. 5) is another gentle song, entreating Jesus to lead the worshipper to Bethlehem. In " Ach des Knaben " (No. 6), which has a tender lilt in 6/8 time, Mary expresses her love for the Infant Christ. The ninth and tenth songs are dialogues between a Christian worshipper and Jesus in His last hours, and in their profound utterance all the suffering and love which are the message of the crown of thorns and the Cross seem to be embodied.

The beautiful song " Wie glänzt der helle Mond ", to a poem by Gottfried Keller, gives us an aged woman's image of Paradise, with St. Peter at the entrance mending an old shoe.

The *Italian Song Book* is a collection of lovely miniatures to poems by Paul Heyse, and again some of them strike a religious note. I have already (in Chapter 5, page 43) referred to " Ihr seid die Allerschönste " and " Gesegnet sei "; in both, the lover finds divinity in the beauty of his beloved, and in the latter song counts this among the blessings of God's creation. " Wir haben beide lange Zeit geschwiegen " presents two lovers who have not been on speaking terms, but unutterably beautiful music depicts how angels come down from Heaven to break the spell. In " Wie viele Zeit " the lover mournfully declares in a minor key that he has spent all his time in making love to his sweetheart instead of worshipping God. But in " Und steht Ihr früh " a young man tells how his beloved went to mass and all in church marvelled at her beauty: in the music there is a combination of devotion to the loved one with devotion to God, reflected in calm, legato strains, with a note of wonder and mysticism in them. In " Wenn du mein Liebster, steigst zum Himmel auf ", a girl pictures herself and her lover after death, appearing before the Lord and being granted the bliss of living together in eternal love; the song ends exultantly.

Wolf's last work was a fragment of the music for *Manuel Venegas*, a tragic opera in which the Roman Catholic religion was to play an important part. He had only completed fifty-one pages of the first act in vocal score when his mind gave way.

. . . . .

By the end of the nineteenth century, how the scene had changed in about 300 years! Before then, God had revealed Himself largely through the medium of church music and in the freshness of madrigals. But as time went on, His finger could be traced not only in liturgical masterpieces, but also in sacred oratorios and in the wonders of instrumental art, which reached a spiritual climax in the glory of Beethoven. The divinity of beauty shone brightly in the music of the great Teutonic song writers, and God used even professed "unbelievers" such as Berlioz and Wolf to bear His message. Religion was to be found, as we shall see in later chapters, in the art of opera; in symphonies, as well as in masses and requiems.

The second half of the nineteenth century, with its discovery of evolution, seemed to undermine the acceptance of the Biblical story of creation, until it came to be realised that this still enshrined a deep, allegorical truth. Science and religion appeared in many ways to be at loggerheads, and scepticism abounded. Brahms, in composing sacred music, preferred to by-pass the Church and to make his own careful choice of Biblical texts. Wagner set up his own temple of art, even though he presented more orthodox Christianity in it than he has sometimes been given credit for.

Yet, seen in perspective, the changes, vast though they were, turn out to have been changes of medium rather than of essence. "God fulfils Himself in many ways." By the end of the nineteenth century, in spite of the bewilderment to religious minds brought about by the first impact of the recent scientific discoveries and the growth of materialism and atheism fostered by certain parts of the Marxist doctrines, God's influence had, as it were, become much more varied and subtle in its methods than in the old days of clear-cut distinctions between sacred and secular art. The next stage, which merges into the contemporary scene, will be the subject of another chapter; but before we pass to it, let us turn our thoughts to two interludes, which have a certain connection with two of the composers whom we have just been considering.

15

TWO INTERLUDES: NEGRO SPIRITUALS—THE LIGHTER SIDE OF DIVINITY

OUR reflections on Dvořák and Tchaikovsky in the previous chapter lead naturally to the two interludes which make up the present one. For Dvořák, as we have seen, was influenced by the negro spirituals in the works which arose from his visit to the United States of America. And Tchaikovsky, who had as great a genius for music of the dance as for the more serious forms, is a natural link to a short discussion on the lighter side of the divinity of musical beauty.

NEGRO SPIRITUALS

It was Henry T. Burleigh (born in 1866), a negro of New York City, who arranged the negro religious folk-songs as solos and made them popular under the name of "spirituals" in the nineteenth century. He worked with Dvořák when the latter was in the United States and thinking about the composition of his symphony *From the New World*, and he sang them to Dvořák. It is for this reason that I have postponed consideration of them until now, though of course they date from a much earlier stage than that which we have reached in our narrative.

Some of the features of the music of the American negroes seem to have come from their native Africa. Many of their tunes are written in the pentatonic (5-note) scale, which belongs to certain instruments still used in parts of Africa, and contain a peculiar kind of " catch ", which is present in African native songs. The scale and the " catch " are, however, also to be found in Celtic and Magyar folk-music. But syncopated rhythm, so far as can be traced, is specially characteristic of African music. The variety of rhythmic patterns used by the negroes is astonishing. When accompanying their dances with drums and choral singing they constantly cross the time, and this gift for broken rhythms was retained by the African negroes who were carried across the Atlantic in the seventeenth century to supply the slave trade in North America; it survived in the music which they and their descendants produced during their serfdom and afterwards, and ultimately formed the basis of the syncopated dance music of the twentieth century.

The folk-songs of the Afro-American negroes are of four kinds: the spiritual, the secular song, the work song and the "shout song". In all four there was syncopation, but the rhythmic effects were less violent and complex in the spirituals than in the secular songs.

We are, however, not concerned here with the secular and work songs, but chiefly with the spirituals. Such songs as "Go down, Moses", or "Steal away to Jesus", to take only two examples, are filled with a pathos and nobility and a devotional fervour which were the spontaneous outcome of a people who had been torn from their homes and who found solace in the great religion of the oppressed, Christianity. The rhythm of the spirituals, when they are sung by the negroes themselves, is marked by a swaying of the body for the purpose of beating out the fundamental pulse of the music, while the movements of the head seem to hit it off into smaller, irregular fragments; correspondingly, the voices play with the tune, without impairing its main character.

Mr. R. Nathaniel Dett, in his article on "Negro Music" in the *International Cyclopedia of Music and Musicians* (edited by Oscar Thompson) makes the point that, alone among folk-songs, except those of the Russian peasants, the negro spiritual sprang into being fully harmonised: in large choruses, such as church and camp meetings, there is often much doubling and filling-in of parts, the singers suiting their choice of harmony to their range; this results in crossing of parts and a kind of counterpoint.

The "shout songs", though they have almost died out, also deserve mention here, because they were quasi-devotional chants sung as an accompaniment to the movements of men and women who, after the regular church services, would form in a ring and move round faster and faster, never lifting their feet from the ground save for the rigid beating of a 2/4 time with the heel of one foot, and clapping their hands meanwhile. This music, which was too crude for any written record of it to be made, was very monotonous, and the ecstasy which it produced in those taking part in it caused many to sink exhausted to the ground.

THE LIGHTER SIDE OF DIVINITY

If we believe that all beauty is divine in various degrees, it follows that there is divinity in beautiful light music. To some people this may seem almost a contradiction in terms: in their eyes, the divine is a solemn conception, utterly at variance with lightness or gaiety whether in music or in any other sphere of life. But their premise is false; as I have remarked earlier, there is laughter in Heaven; wit, if it is not malicious or dirty, is certainly godlike; and a light piece of music may be as divine as a daisy.

Most of the great serious composers have been creators of light music: the Tudor masters, whose virginal music included dances such as galliards and pavanes; Handel, many of whose movements in the *Water Music* and the *Concerti grossi* simply captivate us by their freshness and charm; Bach, who gives us the gaiety of the dance in his suites and in some of the quick movements of the Brandenburg Concertos, and could mix his style in the course of one work without incongruity—creating, for instance, the serenely beautiful Aria of the Third Orchestral Suite and following it with a rollicking gavotte; Gluck and other composers of opera, who introduced delicate ballet music into serious, even tragic, works for the stage. Haydn throughout his career frequently brought movements of light music into his symphonies. Mozart did likewise in his earlier ones, and his greatest operas, except *Idomeneo*, are as conspicuous for their light numbers as for their serious music: even *Die Zauberflöte* has its Papageno. Beethoven wrote many waltzes for the town band at Mödling, but even apart from these he often reveals his genius for light music—in many a dainty Allegro or minuet scattered throughout the works of his first period; in the graceful Allegretto and the charming minuet of the Eighth Symphony; in the Scherzo of the B flat Trio (op. 97); and in several of the Bagatelles. Schubert and Chopin with their waltzes (even though some of Chopin's strike a deeper note); Mendelssohn in the Scherzo of *A Midsummer Night's Dream*, the *Rondo Capriccioso* and some of the *Songs without Words*; Liszt with his gay *Hungarian Rhapsodies*; Brahms with his waltzes for pianoforte, his *Liebeslieder Waltzer* and Hungarian dances; and in more recent times, the *Children's Corner* of Debussy, Elgar's *Wand of Youth* suites, and the lighter parts of the ballet scores of Stravinsky and Falla; all illustrate the same truth, that there is no sharp dividing line between light and serious music. Though it is obvious that works at either end of the scale belong to one sphere or the other, the two styles meet and merge together, and the conception of the divinity of beauty must apply to both.

Tchaikovsky's dance music, however, in his three great ballets, *Swan Lake*, *The Sleeping Beauty* and *Nutcracker*, occupies so important a place in his art as to form a natural stepping-stone to reflection on the work of composers who were predominantly masters of light music. Here, at any rate, there is no room for the suggestion that has been made about a sense of guilt or sin in Tchaikovsky's symphonic compositions. Free from any trace of sensuality, his ballet music is radiant, vigorous, fresh, delicate, and scored with unerring mastery.

When we claim that divinity in some measure may be present in light music, we do not, of course, mean that it is religious, or even that it is spiritual—but simply that because God reveals Himself in beauty, the lighter forms of beauty in their own manner show His presence. And among the composers whose fame rests mainly on their contributions to the lighter side of the art, far the greatest, in my opinion, is Sullivan, whose career happens to be contemporaneous with those of the musicians discussed in the last chapter. The music of Offenbach's comic operas is light-hearted, amusing, often charming. Charm and delicacy are also the chief qualities of the art of Delibes, and we are entranced by the waltzes of Waldteufel. The music of Johann Strauss the younger is intoxicating; it captivates us by its gaiety and energy, combined with a sensuous appeal typical of Viennese life at that period. Now, Sullivan could enchant his listeners in *Iolanthe* with fairy music which rivalled that of Berlioz and Mendelssohn, but he did not need to intoxicate them; he won their hearts by natural grace, and still does so. At some points in his comic operas he wrote below his own normal high level; at others he merely produced music suitable as a background, almost, for Gilbert's brilliant lyrics, particularly in the " patter " songs. He had a genius for musical humour, and, where the occasion called for them, he could write splendid tunes like " For he himself has said it " in *H.M.S. Pinafore* or Lord Mountararat's song about the House of Lords in the second act of *Iolanthe*; a magnificent chorus such as the Procession of Peers in the first act of the same opera; or a song of vivid imaginative power like the one about " the ghost's high noon " in *Ruddigore*. But the quality which, perhaps, chiefly distinguishes his art (apart from his exceptional gift for beautiful orchestration) is an open-air fragrance that is not to be found in the work of any of his Continental predecessors or contemporaries in the same field. We find this over and over again—in exquisite concerted numbers such as the so-called madrigal " Brightly dawns our wedding day " in *The Mikado*, or " Strange Adventure " in *The Yeomen of the Guard*; melodies of simple beauty like " Prithee, pretty maiden " in *Patience*, " I know a youth " in *Ruddigore*, Strephon's first song in *Iolanthe*, or " The sun whose rays " from *The Mikado*; in *The Yeomen*, again, Phoebe's opening song, " When maiden loves ", as she sits at her spinning wheel, and the haunting phrases of " I have a song to sing, O! "; Gianetta's song " Kind sir, you cannot have the heart " in *The Gondoliers*; women's choruses which seem to have the freshness of spring or early summer in them, such as " Comes a train of little ladies " in *The Mikado* and the one that opens the second act when the girls are making Yum-Yum ready for her wedding, or the first chorus in *The Gondoliers*, " List and learn, ye dainty roses ".

This fragrance Sullivan's creations possess in a unique degree. So far as my knowledge goes, among his successors in the world of light music only Edward German and André Messager have approximated to it—the former in his *Henry VIII* and *Nell Gwynn* dances and in parts of *Merrie England* and *Tom Jones*, and the latter in some of the music of *Véronique* and *Monsieur Beaucaire*. This particular quality, especially when it is so strong a feature, is akin to nature in her most gracious moods, and thus brings Sullivan's art, as it were, nearer to God than that of any of the other composers whose gifts lay chiefly in the same direction as his.

16

MY CONTEMPORARIES

I WAS born in 1892. Thus, ignoring early childhood, the music-loving span of my life covers roughly the present century, so far as it has gone, and enables me to include under the heading of " my contemporaries " the non-operatic art of those composers whose creative careers overlapped the nineteenth century and the twentieth, as well as the later ones.

The music of this period is, mostly, too close to us to be seen in proper perspective. Even apart from the delicacy of trying to visualise the true characters of men who are either still alive or who, though now dead, continued their activities into this century, we cannot yet assess their true significance as artists, at any rate in the case of the more recent ones; and it is fairly safe to assume that several—perhaps many—of those whom we have been regarding as eminent or even great composers will diminish in stature as time goes on and will either be forgotten completely or remembered only in name or by virtue of a few works. Previous periods in musical history are today represented by a mere handful of great creators; there is no reason to believe that posterity will deal otherwise with ours. These reflections are my justification for treating my contemporaries rather differently from their predecessors—referring to individual composers or to particular works sometimes briefly, though in other cases at rather greater length, according to their relevance to our subject, in my attempt to view the scene as objectively as I can.

I am struck by one feature particularly. In spite of the terrors and tragedies of our times, the indifference and hostility to religion, the intellectual upheaval caused by modern science and the quantity of so-called " secular " music produced, many of the finest spirits among composers of recent generations have in greater or less degree consecrated their art to the worship of God, either in the form of devotional works or of music which is spiritual in character. It will be my object in the following pages to illustrate the extent to which they have done this and the means which they have adopted.

. . . . .

Mahler (1860–1911) was born in Bohemia of Jewish parents. An unhappy childhood may well have accounted for the sorrowful outlook which frequently throughout his life found expression in his music, and also for the streak of ruthlessness which at times, as Artistic Director of the Vienna Opera, he could show towards eminent performers who did not satisfy his exacting standards. In general, he was warm-hearted and deeply interested in others, even though his concern was more for humanity than for individuals. A romantic if ever there was one, he was a man of intense emotions, yet intellectual, absorbed both in metaphysical and scientific problems. In 1895 he became a Roman Catholic; but though he could reach great heights of religious fervour, his consciousness of man's inhumanity to man, of nature " red in tooth and claw ", of the prevalence of disease and of life's sorrows and anxieties, constantly prevented him from resting in the serene acceptance of the Christian faith. He sought after God all his life, but he was never able completely to reconcile the world, as he found it, with the conception of an omnipotent God of love.

It is not surprising that the profoundly personal music of a man whose spiritual life was so intense a conflict, should present strange contrasts. At different times tragic, humorous, sad, nostalgic, almost childlike in its simplicity, or expressive of the beauties of the countryside, it could also be deeply devotional. He composed religious songs such as *Urlicht*, *Es sungen drei Engel* and *Um Mitternacht*. The Second (" Resurrection ") Symphony in C minor was completed shortly before he adopted Roman Catholicism. We know from Mahler's own notes that its opening Allegro maestoso was concerned with the problem, what is life and what is death? The strife is only relieved by a short section in a major key. The next movement, Andante moderato, is an exquisite piece of nostalgia—a gentle minuet with a slight flavour of a Viennese waltz. The so-called Scherzo, which follows, is disturbed and anxious, but the ensuing slow movement, in which a contralto voice joins the orchestra, is religious in quality and expresses faith in eternal life. The choral Finale ranges from the terror of the last trumpet and the graves giving up their dead, to the glory of resurrection; the symphony ends in spiritual triumph, a blazing sound of exultation.

In his Third Symphony Mahler originally prefixed titles, which he subsequently discarded, but which showed that the music of the first three movements was concerned with the awakening of Pan and the coming of summer, the messages of the flowers, and of the animals in

12—DQM

the forest; in the fourth movement a contralto voice enters to tell of man's grief and joy amid the stillness of night; this leads to another vocal movement, in which boys' and women's choruses join the soloist, to sing the words of angels proclaiming the joys of Heaven for repentant men; but the Finale is an instrumental Adagio, which closes this immense work with its solemn consolation.

The first three movements of the Fourth Symphony, which are also purely orchestral, are none the less intimate in character; they are, in general, idyllic, graceful or tranquil; the composer told Bruno Walter that the Andante was inspired by the thought of a tombstone in a church bearing an effigy of the departed " with the arms crossed in eternal sleep ".[1] In the last movement Mahler reverts to the use of words, which a soprano soloist is to sing " with a childlike happiness ": it tells of the joys of Heaven, with St. Peter looking on; of St. John and St. Luke bringing the lamb and the ox to gentle slaughter, and of the angels baking the bread; of the garden of Heaven, St. Peter catching fish and St. Martha as cook; and finally, of 11,000 maidens dancing in Heaven while St. Ursula laughs and St. Cecilia and her kinsfolk tenderly sing their happy, celestial music.

Mahler returned to a religious theme in his colossal Eighth Symphony, the " Symphony of the Thousand ", scored for an enormous orchestra, two large choirs, boys' chorus and eight soloists. Its first part is a devout setting of the hymn, " Veni, Creator Spiritus ". The second part expresses, with rich eloquence, yet with a complete freedom from any extravagance in spite of the tremendous forces engaged, the vision of heavenly immortality contained in the closing scene of Goethe's *Faust*.

In a sense, the Eighth Symphony marked the climax of Mahler's career. He could scarcely venture beyond it in the realm of religious mysticism. But it was not the end. When he composed *Das Lied von der Erde*, for tenor and contralto soloists and orchestra, to words by Hans Bethges translated from the Chinese of Li-tai-po and other eighth-century Chinese poets, he knew that a serious illness of the heart must bring his life to a premature close. In its six movements he sings of earth's sorrows, of autumn loneliness, of youth and beauty and even of " the drunken one in spring "; then in a Farewell the music passes gradually from infinite sadness to serene eternity. Yet even this was not Mahler's farewell to his beloved art. He returned to a purely orchestral fabric in his Ninth Symphony, and in the final long-drawn-

[1] Bruno Walter, *Gustav Mahler* (translated by James Galston), p. 120.

out Adagio he seems to be saying goodbye not only to life but to a passing age of European culture.

Mahler was once asked what his religious beliefs were, and replied "I am a musician". For him music was religion, not exactly in the sense that he was so wrapt up in the art that he thought of little else, but rather that it was through music that he communed with God.

Meanwhile the British musical renaissance had begun. With the notable exception of Purcell, there had been no really great native composers of serious music since the Golden Age of Tudor England. The naturalised Handel dominated the scene in the eighteenth century. Field and Sterndale Bennett were distinctive but minor composers. The anthems and hymns of S. S. Wesley (1810–76) still maintain their place in the affections of English church-goers; the background of Stainer's "meditation", *The Crucifixion* (1887), a simple, melodious, and devout work, was the Anglican hymn of the nineteenth century, and although it may be called old-fashioned by superior-minded people today, it retains its popularity. But Parry (1848–1918) and Stanford (1852–1924), though they also may be regarded as relatively minor composers, at any rate started a movement which led to bigger things, enabling England once more to achieve high distinction in serious art as well as in the light music of Sullivan. Parry composed a great deal of fine sacred and secular music, though unfortunately we do not hear very much of it nowadays apart from the splendid hymn-tune *Jerusalem* set to words from Blake's *Milton*, the majestic anthem "I was glad when they said unto me" which has been sung at each Coronation in this century during the Sovereign's entrance into the Abbey, and the setting of Milton's *Ode at a Solemn Music*, "Blest pair of sirens", which never seems to lose its freshness and beauty. Stanford was even more versatile, being eminent as a composer of orchestral and chamber music, operas, cantatas, songs and church music; yet today much of his work is regrettably neglected; nevertheless, with his stirring cantata *The Revenge*, his many beautiful songs, and his eloquent religious creations both in the form of settings of Latin liturgical texts and of music for the Anglican Church, he is not likely to be forgotten.

The climax of this renaissance came with Elgar (1857–1934), that virile, shy, courteous, kind-hearted, humorous Englishman who created the most glorious music that any native of this country had produced for about 200 years. Nobility, either revealed or latent, is the chief quality of his finest work. In the "Enigma" Variations, in which he first displayed the full measure of his genius, the masterly technique is equalled by the sympathy with which he portrays in musical terms the characters of his friends; and supreme among the variations is *Nimrod*, which depicts a noble person and could only have been composed by an artist with faith in all that is greatest and most inspiring in human nature. Elgar was a Roman Catholic, and the music which he created at this period of his life was the outcome of his religion and of the outlook on humanity prompted by his religious beliefs. Thus it was that the " Enigma " Variations were followed by the three magnificent oratorios, *The Dream of Gerontius*, *The Apostles* and *The Kingdom*. *Gerontius* was not only the greatest oratorio since Brahms' *Requiem*; it was the first in which any composer had ventured to picture, in music of wondrous symbolism, the passage of a human soul from death into the very presence of God. There had been many visions of Hell in music, and some attempts to glimpse Heaven. Richard Strauss' orchestral tone-poem, *Tod und Verklärung*, which had preceded *The Dream of Gerontius* by about eleven years, dealt with a man's struggles in his last illness, his death, and then, in an epilogue, his transfiguration. But Elgar's work is spiritual from start to finish: even the first part, depicting Gerontius near to death, surrounded by priests and assistants, does not concern itself with any physical conflict, but with his soul's anguish; it closes with the great hymn in which the chorus bid his soul go forth upon its journey in the name of the Father, the Son, and the Holy Spirit, and find peace in Heaven. The music of the second part, except for the vivid chorus of demons, is wholly mystical: we hear the soul serenely communing with the Angel, the glorious prayers of the Choir of Angelicals, the urgent intercession of the Angel of the Agony, the tremendous moment of the Judgment, the enfolding of the soul in the loving arms of the Angel, and the final music of celestial tranquillity. Technically and historically, the significance of *The Dream of Gerontius* is that it adapts the idea of the Wagnerian leitmotiv for the purposes of an oratorio: there are no distinct arias or set numbers; the music grows out of a few phrases which recur throughout the work just when the text requires that they should, and achieves a unity through this process of natural growth, almost like a living organism. Intrinsically, the glory of the composition lies in its deeply religious, human feeling, imbued with mysticism, and expressed in an idiom entirely personal to the composer.

From this mystical glorification of Cardinal Newman's visionary poem, Elgar turned to the conception of a great trilogy of oratorios enshrining the very heart of the Christian faith, to be set to words from the Bible carefully selected by the composer himself. *The Apostles* tells the Gospel story from the first days of Christ's ministry right down to His Ascension. As in *Gerontius*, many of the leading themes are presented in the Prologue, and thereafter they themselves or reminiscences of them reappear in the course not only of this oratorio, but of its successor. Striking musical features in Part I are the sounding of the Shofar or ancient Hebrew ram's horn in the first scene (" The Calling of the Apostles "); Mary Magdalene's prayer for mercy in the Tower of Magdala, and the eloquent tones in which she relates the turbulence within her own breast to the storm of the elements and perceives that if the raging of the sea can be stilled by God, faith can calm the anguish in her soul; and the closing episode for soloists, chorus and orchestra " Turn you to the stronghold ", set to music of great strength and tenderness. In Part II, the drama reaches a climax in the tragic grandeur with which the music symbolises Satan entering into Judas' soul, his repentance and his death. Elgar leaves the scene of the Crucifixion and the death of Jesus to our imagination. " Eli, Eli, lama sabachthani? " is movingly expressed by the muted strings. In the scene at the sepulchre we again hear the Shofar. There is an imaginative picture of the Ascension, and the work ends with a sublime Finale in which Mary, Mary Magdalene, John and Peter, the Apostles and the Holy Women, and a Mystic Chorus in Heaven, combine to voice the message of Christ's Passion and redemption of the world in a majestic pattern of leading motives transfigured by the inspiration of genius.

The Kingdom is simpler in design, in spite of the fact that fresh themes are added to those which recur from *The Apostles*. It tells the story of the Church in Jerusalem after Christ's Ascension, as set out in the early chapters of The Acts. The wonderful prelude represents the Gospel, the Apostles as the preachers of it, Peter's contrition for his denial of Jesus, the New Faith and the Real Presence in the Breaking of Bread. Then we find the Disciples and the Holy Women in the Upper Room, with Peter, John and the two Marys: " Where two or three are gathered together in My Name, there am I in the midst of them "; the music is serene and gentle, until all join in a song of praise. Peter speaks of the need to find a successor to Judas in the apostleship, and the lot falls upon Matthias. At " The Beautiful Gate " of the Temple, Mary and Mary Magdalene tell of the singing of Psalms and of Jesus' miracles of healing the sick, of which they are reminded by the presence of a lame man. In the " Pentecost " scene, Elgar vividly depicts the descent of the Holy Spirit, the appearance of " tongues, parting asunder, like as of fire ", the ecstasy of the Apostles and the amazement of the people; Peter calls the Jews to repentance and baptism, and the scene ends in a chorus of the utmost grandeur. The next part of the work, " The Sign of Healing ", after a short, peacefull introduction on the orchestra, is full of happy music—" At the Beautiful Gate " again—to describe the healing of the lame man at the hands of Peter and John in the name of Christ; but the episode is interrupted by the arrest of the Apostles by the priests and Sadducees, which is followed by Mary's profound and moving meditation. Then, in the Upper Room once more, John tells the Disciples and the Holy Women how, when he and Peter appeared before the rulers, the latter found "nothing how they might punish us". We hear of the mystical breaking of bread. And the work concludes with the extraordinarily original setting of the Lord's Prayer, followed by utterances from John, Peter and the full choir.

The remarkable feature of these two great oratorios is that, in spite of the multiplicity of leading motives, they are never used as mere labels but rather as elements in an organic design, the whole being suffused with a spiritual radiance. The words are transmuted into music, and by the mutual interplay of voices and orchestra the themes and their variants and the whole musical fabric are woven into a tissue of sound which combines symphonic unity with dramatic expression and religious feeling.

The Kingdom ends in an atmosphere of consolation and utter tranquillity. But Elgar's intention was to complete the trilogy with an oratorio dealing with the Church of the Gentiles: this was to include the conflict between the Church and Anti-Christ, the victory of righteousness in the Last Judgment and the glory of the Eternal Dawn: the sounding of the Shofar again at this point is among the sketches for the work which have survived. The oratorio was not put on paper, but the composer never seems to have given up completely the idea of doing so. W. H. Reed[1] tells how hard he tried to persuade him to resume work at it after the death of Lady Elgar, to whom he was so devoted, in 1920, but that the reply was " Oh, no one wants any more of that nowadays." Mr. Reed is not sure whether Elgar " was disabled by the beginnings of his physical breakdown or by a loss of faith in any real necessity for any more oratorio "; and he records that the composer

[1] *Elgar as I knew him*, p. 74.

did not talk about his religion, but " was obviously more sceptical generally as a widower than he had been during Lady Elgar's lifetime, and . . . turned finally to opera and secular music only " (though he did not actually compose an opera).

We are bound to accept this testimony from so intimate a friend, but it does not alter the fact that Elgar's art, whether " sacred " or " secular", throughout his career was in general imbued with a strongly spiritual character. At first sight it may be thought that this is an odd way of describing such representative works as the *Cockaigne* overture and *Falstaff*; but *Cockaigne* has its noble and tender passages, and the quality of its gaiety and vividness is a reflection of Elgar's warm-hearted attitude to life; *Falstaff*, with its broad humanity, its full-blooded merriment and humour, its dreamy interludes, its pointed contrasts between the characters of Prince Henry and the fat knight, and the pathos of the death scene, could only have been created by a man whose sympathies were both wide and deep. So it is with all the other great instrumental compositions. The " Enigma " Variations have already been mentioned. The Introduction and Allegro for strings, the most " absolute " of Elgar's works, is imbued with a splendid vigour and freshness. The First Symphony is based upon a noble motto theme, which survives the restlessness and sorrows of the Allegro and the bustling energy of the ensuing Allegro molto, reappears in the serenely beautiful slow movement, exerts its influence in the Finale and in the last pages of the work attains an apotheosis of resonant glory. The Violin Concerto transports us into a more contemplative world; Elgar described it with the Spanish words " Aquí está encerrada el alma de . . . . ." (" Here is enshrined the spirit of . . . . ."), leaving us to guess the last word; Mr. Basil Maine[1] suggests that it may be the spirit of the violin itself; be that as it may, the significant fact is that the composer was thinking of a spirit and a shrine: there is a religious flavour about the Andante, and an other-worldly atmosphere in the exquisite accompanied Cadenza in the last movement, where the solo violin, instead of playing the virtuoso in the usual manner of cadenzas, dwells, as if in a vision, on the themes of the various movements, against a soft background of strings muted or thrummed " pizzicato tremolando".

The Second Symphony (1910–11) was dedicated to the memory of King Edward VII and inscribed with Shelley's words

> Rarely, rarely comest thou,
> Spirit of Delight.

[1] *Elgar, His Life and Works*, Vol. II, p. 141.

This "spirit" is inherent in the joyous, confident entrance of the opening subject; but when this theme recurs in altered forms at other points in the symphony, it is often tinged with regret, suggesting that Elgar was conscious that the splendid era in which he had been living was approaching its end. Much of the first movement is exuberant, but in the development we encounter a sense of mysterious foreboding, even though the music afterwards recovers—for a time—its "spirit of delight". The Larghetto is a solemn, grief-laden funeral march; the Rondo: Presto has an undercurrent of uneasiness beneath its energy and in one passage is linked, thematically, to the mystery of that episode in the development of the first movement. Not until the Finale does the music attain to serenity; yet it finishes, not with the triumphant glory of the end of the First Symphony, but with a touch of wistfulness underneath its tranquil sounds.

This mood of regretful farewell, tempered by resignation, was deepened in much of the music that followed—for instance, in the profoundly moving strains which he composed in 1917 for Lawrence Binyon's poem *For the Fallen*, and in the sweet melancholy so often expressed in the Violoncello Concerto; in the soaring melody of the slow movement of this work we experience, not the nostalgia of Mahler or of Delius, but a regret that by its dignity, its exaltation, rises above the circumstances that gave it birth and reconciles man to the world of sorrows. It is this sense of resignation which underlies, too, the serenity —accompanied by sadness and yearning—of the chamber-music works that Elgar created in the same period of his life. The time for writing avowedly sacred music had, for him, gone by; but the nobility and tenderness, which sprang from his religious faith and from the depths of his being and are manifested again and again in his art, still subsisted, touched by an autumn poignancy, yet fundamentally peaceful. In his later works he had offered his genius to God through the medium of instruments, without voices, and at the time of his death he was engaged on his Third Symphony, which remained only in the form of some fragments.[1]

Among Elgar's most immediate contemporaries, the greatest French composers, in my opinion, were Fauré (1845–1924) and Debussy

[1] This section was written before the publication of Percy Young's selection *Letters of Edward Elgar* or Ernest Newman's articles on the composer in the *Sunday Times*, November/December 1956, in which the disillusion of Elgar's later years is made manifest. I do not think that fundamentally what I have written is inconsistent with them.

(1862–1918). Fauré's many beautiful love songs and settings of nature poems make him a kind of French counterpart to the great German *Lieder* writers, and in these and in his works for chamber-music ensembles and pianoforte solo he expresses genuine emotions in shapely music which possesses a Hellenic poise, a strength without violence, and an imagination controlled by the sensitiveness of a careful artist. This Greek quality has even prompted the suggestion that his *Requiem* is more pagan than Christian in character. His son, Monsieur P. Fauré-Fremiet,[1] tells us that he was certainly not a sceptic but that on the other hand he was not devout. A man can, however, be a believing Christian without being devout in the sense that (among composers) Bach or Bruckner were. Fauré was a church organist and choirmaster for many years; he composed a number of other liturgical works besides the *Requiem*; and he was a most sincere man and artist. The external evidence is, therefore, in favour of a Christian belief having been implicit in his conception of the *Requiem* at a time when his parents had recently died and he was thinking deeply about death. The question is whether the music is Christian intrinsically. It does present certain departures from orthodoxy, the chief one being that it omits the "Dies Irae", but, as Mr. Norman Suckling[2] has pointed out, Vittoria in the sixteenth century set an example in this respect. It is entirely suitable for liturgical use. Its leading characteristics are simplicity and peacefulness. With the omission of the "Dies Irae", all the terrors of the Last Judgment are eliminated. The soul passes direct to Paradise, the music is throughout serene and consolatory. But for a modern Christian the medieval conceptions of Hell and Purgatory can in any case only be regarded figuratively. Fauré's *Requiem*, it is true, is unorthodox also in containing no expression even of spiritual suffering after death; but "the peace that passeth all understanding" is beautifully conveyed in its celestial tones.

Debussy set forth his attitude to religion in an interview which he gave to a journalist representing *Excelsior* in February 1911. I quote from the extracts contained in M. Léon Vallas' book *Claude Debussy: His Life and Works*.[3]

"In my opinion, the writing of sacred music ceased with the sixteenth century. The beautiful, childlike souls of those days were alone capable of expressing their passionate, disinterested fervour in

[1] In *Gabriel Fauré*, p. 49. [2] *Fauré*, p. 176.
[3] Translated by Maire and Grace O'Brien, p. 225.

music free from all admixture of worldliness. . . . I do not practise religion in accordance with the sacred rites. I have made mysterious Nature my religion. I do not believe that a man is any nearer to God for being clad in priestly garments, nor that one place in a town is better adapted to meditation than another. When I gaze at a sunset sky and spend hours contemplating its marvellous, ever-changing beauty, an extraordinary emotion overwhelms me. Nature in all its vastness is truthfully reflected in my sincere though feeble soul. Around me are the trees stretching up their branches to the skies, the perfumed flowers gladdening the meadows, the gentle grass-carpeted earth, . . . and my hands unconsciously assume an attitude of adoration. . . . To feel the supreme and moving beauty of the spectacle to which Nature invites her ephemeral guests! —that is what I call prayer. . . ."

This pantheistic conception is implicit in Debussy's exquisite, at times elusive, but always truthful impressions of nature—the clouds, the sea, the rain falling on a garden, reflections in water. *La Cathédrale engloutie* is solemn rather than religious in feeling, as though the composer was impressed more by the submerged dignity of the building in the depths of the sea than by its sacred character. *The Blessed Damozel*, set to a French version of D. G. Rossetti's poem, was an early work, composed in 1887, and faithfully and delicately reflects the words which are gently Christian in character and afford an imaginative picture of Heaven. Debussy had not yet adapted his harmonic method to a mixture of the whole-tone and pentatonic scales, as he afterwards did. When he came to write the incidental music for *Le Martyre de Saint-Sébastien* many years later, the idiom which he had meanwhile acquired was well suited to the extraordinary mixture of Christianity and paganism contained in d'Annunzio's mystery play, in which there is a strange kind of identification of the saint with Adonis. Just before the production (in May 1911), the Archbishop of Paris declared the performance to be " offensive to Christian consciences " and Catholics were forbidden to be present. Debussy expressed his views to a representative of *Comoedia*:[1]

" Do you imagine that my works do not contain what I may call religious precedents? Do you propose to fetter the soul of the artist? Is it not obvious that a man who sees mystery in everything will be inevitably attracted to a religious subject? I do not wish to make

[1] Léon Vallas, *Claude Debussy: His Life and Works*, pp. 226 f.

a profession of faith. But, even if I am not a practising Catholic nor a believer, it did not cost me much effort to rise to the mystical heights which the poet's drama attains. Let us be clear about the word *mysticism*. You see that this very day the Archbishop has forbidden the faithful to assist at d'Annunzio's play, although he does not know the work. But let us not dwell on these annoying details. . . . From the artistic point of view such decrees cannot be considered. I assure you that I wrote my music as though I had been asked to do it for a church. The result is decorative music, if you like, a noble text, interpreted in sounds and rhythms; and in the last act when the saint ascends into Heaven I believe I have expressed all the feelings aroused in me by the thought of the Ascension. Have I succeeded? That no longer concerns me. We have not the simple faith of other days. Is the faith expressed by my music orthodox or not? I cannot say. It is my faith, my own, singing in all sincerity."

Debussy's opinion that the writing of sacred music ceased with the sixteenth century is obviously inconsistent with the facts, but these expressions of his attitude towards religion and its embodiment in music are fully in accordance with the character of his art itself.

. . . . .

The question of religious orthodoxy becomes almost irrelevant when we consider the art of Richard Strauss (1864–1949) and Delius (1863–1934). Strauss' *Wiegenlied* is a beautiful little song, bidding a child dream of Heaven and of the holy night when, through the flowers of Christ's love, the world was made Heaven for the child's mother. But for the most part, we enjoy Strauss' music for practically every quality except a spiritual one. The " Transfiguration " section at the end of *Tod and Verklärung* was intended to scale Heaven, but for all its panoply of rich orchestration and diatonic climaxes, there is a certain hollowness in the fabric. The Finale of *Don Quixote*, however, depicting the Knight's return to sanity and his death, has a majestic pathos, which is, I think, only equalled in Strauss' works by *Metamorphosen*, for twenty-three solo strings, completed in 1945, when he was eighty: this admittedly owes something to its quotations from the funeral march of Beethoven's " Eroica " Symphony and from the second act of Wagner's *Tristan und Isolde* where King Marke grieves at Tristan's apparent disloyalty to him; but it is a self-contained work of art and is a noble lament for those of the composer's fellow-countrymen who had fallen in the Second World War and had been deceived by their leaders.

Delius was self-centred; kind towards young artists who were striving to establish themselves, if they were talented, but ruthless if they were not; hard and intolerant, but charming; a man who in his youth had struggled for independence against prolonged parental opposition, and faced the paralysis and blindness of his last years with undaunted courage; contemptuous of " the herd", he was comfortably endowed with this world's goods and blessed with the devotion of his wife, his friends, relations, and servants; he spurned all institutional religion, was a devotee of Nietzsche's philosophy, and exulted in his paganism. But it was a modern form of paganism, not atheism, and just because it invested his conception of nature with a pantheistic character, it enabled him subconsciously to reflect a mystical quality in his musical nature studies as well as in his works for voices and orchestra. *Brigg Fair: an English Rhapsody*; *On Hearing the First Cuckoo in Spring*; *Summer Night on the River*; *In a Summer Garden*; the three of the "North Country Sketches" which deal with landscape scenes (*Autumn*, *Winter Landscape*, and *The March of Spring*); *A Song of Summer*; *A Song before Sunrise*—all these are not merely musical pictures of the external world: they have also a spiritual, other-worldly character, conveyed by haunting phrases, subtly shifting harmonies, and an orchestration which is at once rich and delicate. And in his compositions for voices and orchestra he is a mystic as well as a poet-musician. *A Mass of Life* was based on Nietzsche's *Also sprach Zarathustra*: it ecstatically proclaims the " will to live" and the joy of the dance, but also expresses an autumnal sadness and regret for the passing of youth, and at the close finds serenity in the thought of " eternal, everlasting, endless day"; the music voices and transcends the poetic visions of Nietzsche, and is less concerned with his philosophy. *Sea Drift* is not just a picture of the sea, but an infinitely pathetic expression of the grief of a bird for the loss of its mate; the baritone soloist impersonates the boy who "absorbs, translates" the story into human terms, and the chorus imaginatively shares his thoughts; as the music dies away on the words " We two together no more, no more", we realise that we have sensed not merely the sorrow of parting, but its mystery. In *A Song of the High Hills* Delius portrays not only the glory of the mountains, but man's spiritual exaltation at beholding them: the chorus is used as if the voices were part of the orchestra: it is wordless, because for Delius music alone, not words, could express the wonder of the vision. In his *Requiem* his paganism failed him: an attitude to death so negative as this could not inspire great music in him. But at the end of his life, in his *Songs of Farewell* for double chorus and orchestra, he showed that his powers were still undimmed, so that these pictures of land and sea and the human notes of joy and farewell are painted with all his old infinite resource and variety; and there is again a spirit of exaltation, in the fourth movement, when the chorus sing "Joy, shipmate, joy", before the final call to the old sailor to depart on his "endless cruise".

. . . . .

Holst (1874–1934) was a most lovable person. He constantly helped his young pupils of St. Paul's Girls' School or Morley College, friends in need or youthful composers, with his advice and introductions—and went on doing so even on his death-bed. He was of a very retiring nature, hated publicity, but was strongly imbued with public spirit, and had a keen sense of humour. For most of his life he battled bravely against bad sight and the pain of neuritis. He was deeply interested in Sanskrit literature, and combined much of the wisdom of Hinduism with the character of a practical, though unconventional, Christian. According to his daughter Imogen,[1] however, "he was never converted to any religion, Hindu or otherwise". He loved the music of Bach above all others, the beauties of nature, walks in the country, the Parthenon, lovely churches and the singing of great music in them. In 1916 he wrote to his friend, the musician W. G. Whittaker:[2]

> One of the advantages of being over forty is that one begins to learn the difference between knowing and realising.
>
> I realise now why the bible insists on heaven being a place (I should call it a condition) where people sing and *go on singing*.
>
> We kept it up at Thaxted about fourteen hours a day. The reason why we didn't do more is that we were not capable mentally or physically of realising heaven any further.
>
> Still, as far as it went it was heaven. Just as the average amateur's way of using music as a sedative or a stimulant is purgatory, and the professional's way of using music as a topic of conversation or as a means of getting money is hell.
>
> Of course, it's no use writing this. If you've had four days of

[1] *Gustav Holst*, by Imogen Holst (1938), p. 21. [2] Ibid., p. 48.

perpetual music you've learnt it already, and if you haven't it's about as sensible as describing the B minor to a deaf man.

Music, being identical with heaven, isn't a thing of momentary thrills, or even hourly ones. It's a condition of eternity.

In 1920, in an article in *The Quest*[1] he wrote: "... we are all Mystics, Artists and Philistines. . . . The difference between a Mystic who communes with God and the man who feels a power not himself making for good is obviously one of degree. . . . The highest Mystic is, I suppose, one who experiences union with God. Is he alone a Mystic? Or is Whitman a Mystic in his intense feeling of unity with all men, all life? . . . But it is in music that this feeling of unity shows itself most obviously and easily; I do not mean more deeply or truly. All Art is one below the surface. . . ."

Thus it is not surprising that mysticism should have played so large a part in Holst's own music—whether "secular" or "sacred", whether Hindu or Christian. The music of his choral settings of the Hymns from the Rig Veda is an apt expression of traditional Hindu devotion, yet unites the past with his own time by means of modern rhythms like 5/4 and twentieth-century harmonies and discords. *The Planets*, which is concerned with the astrological significance of Mars, Venus, Jupiter and the rest, ends with *Neptune, the Mystic*, which is a musical expression of the infinite: in this there are no themes in the ordinary sense of the term; the instruments are soft throughout; the music seems to move slowly onward, floating first on the orchestra and then taken up gently by a distant, heavenly choir until it fades out of hearing. *The Hymn of Jesus* was set to words translated from the apocryphal Acts of St. John and voices the ageless spirit of Christianity: after a soft orchestral prelude, the quiet, ethereal beginning for the chorus has a basis of plainsong (with Latin text), but after that the music is entirely Holst's individual utterance and follows the meaning of the words throughout; it is intense, radiant, exalted—until it reaches the celestial repose of the final Amens. Whitman wrote his *Ode to Death* to commemorate Abraham Lincoln's death; Holst set it to music soon after the end of the First World War and dedicated it to the memory of Cecil Coles, the young composer, "and other friends killed in action": with its somewhat sudden contrasts of loud and soft, it is remarkable how Holst contrives to produce an effect of comfort in the thought of Death as a deliverer, combined with the characteristic element of

[1] Quoted in *Gustav Holst* as an Appendix, pp. 184-94.

mysticism expressed through the medium of a gentle soprano voice and slow, high notes on the strings.

Much of Holst's art—and especially *Egdon Heath*—has an austere quality; but it is the austerity of a composer whose music, though at times it falls below its own best level, consistently follows the vision which God vouchsafed to him.

. . . . .

After Holst, it is natural to turn to the music of his great friend, Vaughan Williams (born 1872), the chief features of which are its many-sidedness, its essentially English character, and its fundamentally spiritual nature. This third element is the one that concerns us most here; but it cannot be separated from the other two, for Vaughan Williams has always been a man who sees life whole, through all its varied facets, and his art is imbued with the spirit of English folk-song and of the English Church. He has written symphonies, short orchestral pieces, concertos, chamber music, songs, sacred and "secular" choral works, serious and comic operas, music for dancing and for films, incidental music for radio plays, and has composed beautifully in all these different forms.

He often strikes a religious note in his instrumental music. Thus, one of his early works, the Fantasia for strings on a theme of Thomas Tallis, is based on a tenor melody which the sixteenth-century master wrote for Archbishop Parker's Psalter, "Why fumeth in sight ye Gentiles spight?", and is deeply devotional in character. *A Pastoral Symphony* is not only conceived in wrapt contemplation of the stillness of nature, but is invested with a mystical, religious cast, akin to that of the Mass in G minor which was created about the same time. *Flos Campi*, for viola, small chorus and orchestra, can almost be considered in this connection as an instrumental work, for the voices sing wordlessly; each of the six movements is prefaced by a quotation from the Song of Solomon, and the music is not only exquisite, but, again, mystical. In the serene slow movement of the Violin Concerto the solo instrument sings a religious meditation. The Fifth Symphony in D was originally inscribed with a note that some of its themes were "taken from an unfinished opera *The Pilgrim's Progress*", and over the "Romanza" the composer wrote the words "Upon that place there stood a cross and a little below a sepulchre. Then he said 'He hath given me rest by his sorrow and life by his death'." Vaughan Williams subsequently deleted these verbal clues, but even if they had never existed and if he had not—mercifully!—completed his lovely opera, the religious nature of the music would have been self-evident; the work is very individual, and though modern in idiom, falls gratefully on the ear; it is mostly reticent in character, except the Finale, which ends in an eloquent and at times sonorous Epilogue, summing up the whole work; even the Scherzo has a mysterious quality.

Vaughan Williams is the son of a clergyman; he edited the music of the English Hymnal, and has composed (and arranged) many fine hymn tunes and carols. And some of his greatest creations have been devotional works for voices either with or without instruments. One of the most deeply-felt of these is the unaccompanied Mass in G minor, which is mainly quiet in tone and reticent in its expression; it is, however, suitably pictorial where the text justifies this, as when the soprano voice soars upwards and depicts light at the words " lumen de lumine", or when the music represents the Resurrection after the previous solemnity and vividly portrays the " excelsis " in the voices of the Osanna.

Sancta Civitas, a short oratorio for tenor and baritone soloists, chorus, semi-chorus and orchestra, set to words from the Revelation of St. John the Divine in the Authorised Version, with additions from Taverner's Bible and the Sanctus of the Communion Service, develops the religious aspect of Vaughan Williams' art already revealed in the Tallis Fantasia, the Mass and the Five Mystical Songs to words by George Herbert for baritone, chorus and orchestra. Although it calls for big forces and contains some tremendous climaxes and frequent chromaticisms, its mysticism is fundamentally simple in conception.

Indeed, however much Vaughan Williams' highly individual style has bewildered his listeners in such works as the Fourth Symphony in F minor, with its dissonant violence, or the Sixth in E minor, with the turbulence of its first three movements and the mystery of its Epilogue, his religious music has always been filled with a noble simplicity, as in the setting of the " Benedicite ", the cantata " Dona nobis pacem ", and more recently the Christmas cantata *This Day*.

Job has to be considered separately from his other instrumental works, because the music cannot be fully appreciated apart from its association with the choreography, the drama, the stage setting and the décor, and the entire conception is imbued with the inspiration of William Blake's magnificent drawings. Vaughan Williams' score, in its strength and majesty, nobly plays its part in the composite whole.

. . . . .

The art of Sibelius (born 1865) is for the most part what the world calls "secular". For although he has composed a few short religious works and incidental music for Hofmannsthal's *Jedermann* ("Everyman") with serene and noble strains for its closing scene, his greatness rests chiefly on his orchestral tone-poems and music for voices and orchestra, the Violin Concerto, the String Quartet *Voces intimae*, and, above all, the seven symphonies. Several of his tone-poems and vocal-orchestral compositions are based on episodes from the *Kalevala*, the great Finnish national epic poem, which fired Sibelius' vivid imagination with its picturesque and magical legends; but these did not call for any sacred or mystical quality in the music. *Tapiola* is prefixed by a motto describing "the Northlands dusky forests", within which "dwells the Forest's mighty God"; but the music is not even in the broadest sense religious: it is a superb realisation of nature in its wildest mood, embodying a tremendous picture of storm and rushing wind. Nor is there a specifically religious element in Sibelius' symphonies; but the spiritual quality in them is important.

His significance in the history of music undoubtedly lies to a large extent in his immense contributions to the form of the symphony—the emphasis on organic unity, his terseness of utterance, and the development of melodies or themes from small musical cells, and so on. But behind and beyond all this are the nobility and grandeur of the music. Think of the triumphant end of Symphony No. 2, with the second subject of the Finale ascending, as it were, to Heaven in a long crescendo of exciting reiterations and culminating in a blaze of glory; the joyous optimism of the Third Symphony and the majestic music of the second section of its Finale, as the orchestra bravely builds up its melodic and harmonic variations on the "marcato" theme; the tragic, yet noble, grief and melancholy of the Fourth Symphony; and, by contrast, the radiant gladness of the Fifth—the courage and hope of its opening movement, the gentle sweetness of its Andante, and the swinging bell-like theme in the Finale dominating the music with its serenity and splendour. The Sixth Symphony is serene in a different way: by its restrained tones and cool harmonies it calms our minds, leads us into remote regions of the spirit, and, at the end, leaves us with a vista of infinity. The Seventh Symphony is a majestic conclusion to the series—one tremendous movement which yet embodies the main features that normally distinguished the separate movements of the older type of symphony, and the whole imbued with a spiritual grandeur overwhelming in its effect.

Sibelius' intense love of the beauties of nature in all its forms is, as it were, the link between his technical sovereignty in the modern history of music and the qualities of the spirit which characterise his greatest masterpieces. For their organic unity and the manner in which melodies, and even movements, grow out of tiny cells, resemble the processes of nature itself; and his love of nature is so strong that it seems to suffuse his music with a noble pantheism. God is in all nature; and the art of Sibelius, both resembling and reflecting nature in its various aspects, thereby worships God, though not in any traditional way.

His tremendous imagination and the structural aspects of his art would be enough to place him on a high pinnacle; but I believe that the main reason why his symphonies tower over so many of those of his contemporaries is this spiritual greatness which they share with the supreme symphonies of his predecessors.

. . . . .

Ernest Bloch is a citizen of the world. Born at Geneva in 1880, of Jewish parents, he has lived in Switzerland, Belgium, Germany, France, Italy and the United States. It has been said that his art is Jewish, and that in fact he is the first great composer of specifically Jewish music. The works of the Lutheran Mendelssohn do not contain any special characteristics which can really be attributed to his Jewish blood. Max Bruch's *Kol Nidrei* for violoncello and orchestra affords the best known example of his interest in old Hebrew melodies, but he was a distinguished, rather than a great composer.[1] And it is necessary to consider just what is meant by describing Bloch's music as Jewish. He only uses Hebrew elements to a small extent, and has expressed doubt whether most of the music traditionally ascribed to Hebraic sources really originated with them or was borrowed from elsewhere. The Jewish character in Bloch's art is intrinsic rather than traditional. It is not evident in all his works—not, for example, in the two symphonic poems *Winter* and *Spring*, or in *Helvetia: a symphonic fresco*, or in the string quartets and the piano quintet which are monumental expressions of profound emotions common to all mankind.

Bloch's attitude to Judaism, as conveyed both in his words and in his music, is of very special interest. He once wrote: "It is not my desire to attempt a 'reconstruction' of Jewish music. . . . It is the Jewish soul that interests me, the complex, glowing, agitated soul that I feel

[1] He himself was not a Jew.

vibrating throughout the Bible. . . . All this is in us, all this is in me, and it is the better part of me. It is all this that I endeavour to hear in myself and to transcribe in my music: the venerable emotion of the race that slumbers way down in our soul."

Anger and the thirst for revenge are not characteristic of Bloch himself, but they are present in one part of the text of Psalm cxxxvii, and the composer, as an imaginative artist, voices them with the same intensity in his setting for soprano and orchestra that he gives to the grief and despair of a down-trodden people. And his genius enters with equal conviction into the very different feeling inherent in Psalm cxiv, beautifully portraying how sea, river and mountains " bow down in fear of the Lord ".

Bloch was for some time contemplating a work based on the Book of Ecclesiastes, and eventually solved the language problem by composing a Hebrew Rhapsody for violoncello (instead of a singer), with orchestra, under the title of *Schelomo* (Solomon) to mark the traditional authorship of the Book. It is most deeply felt music, with widely spaced chords and sonorous orchestration, now pessimistic, now yearning in character.

The " Israel " Symphony, after a solemn introduction, becomes almost fierce in its tension, but passes to a mood of calm exaltation and ends with four women's voices and subsequently a baritone entreating God—" Hear Thou my voice, hear my prayer, I am steadfast "—as the music softly sinks to rest.

A religious quality sometimes appears in Bloch's chamber music—for instance, in the profound and eloquent *Poème mystique* for violin and piano, and in the six movements which comprise *Voice in the Wilderness* for piano and 'cello (the pianoforte part also exists in an orchestral form): these are, in effect, six meditations on man's existence, passing through despondency and doubt, but ending in spiritual victory.

Bloch's greatest achievement in the realm of religious music, however, is the *Sacred Service* for baritone solo, chorus and orchestra. The following is an extract from the programme note written by the composer: " The ' Service ' is a setting of Hebrew texts used in the Reform Temples of America. Most of them belong to the Sabbath morning service, and they originate from the Psalms, Deuteronomy, Exodus, Isaiah, Proverbs and other sources of Jewish spiritual patrimony. These texts embody the essence of Israel's aspirations and its message to the world. Though Jewish in its roots, this message seems to me above all a gift of Israel to the whole of mankind. It symbolises for me far more than a 'Jewish Service', for, in its great simplicity and variety, it embodies a philosophy acceptable to all men." In its five parts, the work sings the praises of the loving God, who is worshipped in "the sacredness of all things" and in acts rather than words; tells of the order of the Law, which is "to remain alive in the hearts of men"; prays that all men shall live in brotherhood, worshipping one God, whose Kingdom shall be established on earth, and that in spite of the sadness and sufferings of this world He will help them to understand the Infinite and grant them peace. The music is deeply moving, at times transcendental and mysterious, but its texture is essentially simple. Bloch's art, both here and elsewhere, may reflect the sorrows and aspirations of Judaism, but it has that universal quality which belongs to the work of a great composer.

. . . . .

Posterity may decide that among "my contemporaries" there are other great composers, apart from those hitherto discussed in this chapter. Meanwhile, it must suffice to refer to certain works which have a bearing on our subject.

The Fifth Symphony of Carl Nielsen (1865–1931) evokes big, spiritual issues with eloquence and great originality. Technically, it is a drama of vast contrapuntal forces sounding together, as compared with Beethoven's and other composers' symphonic dramas of contrasted subjects succeeding one another. It has only two movements: the first is as a struggle between "progressive" and "destructive" influences (according to the composer's own description), the latter being represented by a side-drum which eventually yields before the serenity of "progress" typified by the clarinet; the ensuing Allegro shows the potent, active forces of life and leads to a majestic expression of faith in man's constructive powers. This spiritual beauty is present again in the first movement of Nielsen's Sixth Symphony, with its tragic grandeur, but is unfortunately not maintained in the ensuing movements, which reveal the disillusionment that attended him in his last illness.

Stravinsky (born 1882), that immensely gifted and versatile man, startled the world in 1913 with the crude barbarities and harsh dissonances of *Le Sacre du Printemps*, which was yet felt to contain an elemental force that was suited to the picture of ritualistic human sacrifice. Time has accustomed us to its asperities, but this twentieth-century expression of an ancient pagan cult is so remote from our modern outlook on religion that we can scarcely recognise it as religious in any sense that the word bears today. Stravinsky voiced his true devotional feelings in the *Symphonie de Psaumes* for chorus and orchestra, " composed to the glory of God ", and in his setting of the Mass. In the *Symphonie* quotations from certain Psalms are grouped into three movements—the first a prelude based on a simple theme, the second a double fugue, with a quiet orchestral interlude, leading to the joyous hymn of praise which ends the work. The Mass, composed when Stravinsky had become a Roman Catholic, is terse and somewhat austere in character.

In the 1920s, Kodály's *Psalmus Ungaricus*, set to Psalm lv for tenor solo, chorus and orchestra, made a deep impression both in its native Hungary and in England by virtue of its rugged strength and fiery conviction; it is to be hoped that this work, the striking *Stabat Mater* of Szymanovsky (1928) and Ethel Smyth's splendidly virile setting of the Mass (1893), will not be allowed to fall out of the repertory. The music of Janáček's *Glagolitic Mass* (1926) is warm, human and mainly cheerful: it is religious but not ecclesiastical in style.

Arthur Honegger's oratorio *Le Roi David* is remarkable, partly because it seems to solve the problem, which has baffled so many composers, of combining music successfully with a spoken narrative, and partly because it vividly embodies the Old Testament spirit of the text. But in this latter respect it is surpassed by William Walton's *Belshazzar's Feast*, a moving, dramatic and richly coloured creation: with tremendous force this work presents the Almighty as a God wreaking vengeance upon a tyrant; it is the early Hebrew conception, before the notion of a God of Love had become paramount; the only softening of this stern picture is in the passage beginning " By the waters of Babylon, there we sat down: yea, we wept ", where the music is possessed by a sorrowful beauty. Walton's setting of the "Te Deum " for the Coronation of Queen Elizabeth II is a work of pageantry and worship, entirely suited for a ceremonial occasion: the loud, richly orchestrated parts of the score are forthright expressions of the words, and the soft passages are also appropriate to their texts. Yet I feel that there is a deeper spiritual quality in a composition which is not avowedly religious at all—Walton's Symphony: here, after the conflict of the Allegro assai, the irony of the Scherzo, and the expectant melancholy of the slow movement, the Finale provides a majestic and victorious answer.

Something of this same spirit is present in John Ireland's work for tenor solo, chorus and orchestra "These things shall be", set to poetry by J. A. Symonds. The joyous vision of a future time when

> Nation with nation, land with land
> Inarmed shall live as comrades free

is embodied in impressive, triumphant music, closing serenely.

Two works by Arnold Bax require special mention here: the exquisitely beautiful setting of the carol "Mater ora filium"; and the motet for unaccompanied chorus *The World's Joie*: in this, the chromatic effects convey the uncertainty and anxiety of the words "for I know not whither I shall, nor how long here dwell" and of "for we shall die"; the prayer to God "to shield us" is naturally more forthright, but slower in tempo; a fortissimo major chord ends the work on a note of hope.

Hindemith's opera, *Mathis der Maler*, is discussed in a later chapter, and the music of his symphony of the same name was extracted from it before its production. His oratorio *Das Unaufhörliche* ("The Unceasing") is based on a poem by Gottfried Benn: this is not a Christian utterance, but seems to have an affinity with Bernard Shaw's "Life Force", which—though he would not have admitted it—is really only another name for God. These human expressions of ours, fundamentally, have the same object: they are attempts to convey in the language of man the notion of an infinite, life-giving Power, which Benn, at any rate, idealises as beneficent. And Hindemith, with his stark, profoundly felt, and in many passages awe-inspiring, music, does seem to voice a conception of this unending "Divinity"—call it what you will—which has guided creation from the beginning and goes on doing so "world without end".

Nobilissima Visione is a suite from the music for the "choreographic legend" which Diaghilev commissioned Hindemith to compose in collaboration with Massine on the subject of St. Francis of Assisi. Hindemith tells us[1] that the introduction (which certainly has a religious flavour) depicts the saint sunk in deep meditation; and the Rondo, his mystic union with Mistress Poverty "... the blessed peace of unworldly cheer with which the guests at the wedding participate in the feast—dry bread and water only"; the March and Pastorale "picture the march of a troop of medieval soldiers"; and the closing Passacaglia is a "Hymn to the sun": "here all the symbolic personifications of

[1] See *The Complete Book of 20th Century Music*, by David Ewen (Prentice Hall, Inc., New York).

heavenly and earthly existence mingle in the course of the different variations through which the 6-measure long theme of the Passacaglia is transformed "; the solemnity and earnestness of this music are well suited to a ballet about St. Francis.

Hindemith's Three Motets for soprano and piano, set to New Testament texts, have a certain austere grandeur and simplicity (in spite of their angular, at times rather unapproachable, idiom), which somehow succeed in conveying the Biblical atmosphere of 1,950 years ago, even though they do not suggest the true inward gentleness and love of Christianity.

One of the most significant composers of our time is Rubbra: his symphonies evince an unadorned spiritual grandeur, which reminds us of those of Sibelius in their approach, though not in their language; for Rubbra's idiom is highly individual; his music is at once intellectual and exalted. And in keeping with his symphonies are his sacred choral works, such as the simple but impressive *St. Dominic Mass*, the brief *Song of the Soul* (in which a stream of soft, beautiful melody on the strings is set in slow counterpoint against the mystical utterances of the chorus) and the *Festival Te Deum*—a noble song of praise in which the music of voices and orchestra rolls on like a great river of sound.

The art of the prolific and talented Benjamin Britten includes several examples of religious music. His *Sinfonia da Requiem* (in three connected movements) is, I think, the only purely orchestral Requiem: in the " Lacrymosa ", syncopation in slow time seems actually to enhance the dirge-like quality of the music; the " Dies Irae " is terrifying, with its swirling rhythms and orchestral yells of horror; the " Requiem aeternam " is a soothing lullaby. *A Ceremony of Carols* is a setting of medieval texts, framed by a Procession and Recession with Latin words; the treble voices sing mystical music to the carols, interrupted by a peaceful interlude on the harp. The Festival cantata *Rejoice in the Lamb*, to words from an eighteenth-century poem by Christopher Smart, is an unequal work, perhaps because of a certain incoherence in the poetry; it combines naïveté in the cat-and-mouse episodes with moving religious eloquence elsewhere. The beautiful *Serenade* for tenor solo, horn and strings includes a gruesome dirge,[1] with a refrain " And Christ receive thy soul "; the happy music set to Ben Jonson's *Hymn to Diana* is a welcome relief after it. I regret that I am unable to join unreservedly in the chorus of praise which greeted the *St. Nicolas Cantata*, written for the centenary of Lancing College:

[1] " A Lyke-Wake Dirge " (Anonymous, fifteenth century).

it is all very well to compose simple music for school performance; but this work, in my view, does not represent Britten at his best; and much though I love waltzes, the waltz rhythm for " The Birth of Nicolas " is incongruous in a composition of this kind; the best parts, I suggest, are the delicate, unusual accompaniment on two pianos in No. 4 " He journeys to Palestine "; No 7 " Nicolas and the stolen boys " (except the final alleluias, which are poor in quality); No. 8 " His piety and marvellous works " which is simple and attractive; and the two hymns, the melodies of which, however, were not composed by Britten!

At least three of the most revolutionary composers of this century have expressed religious thoughts and emotions by means of instruments without voices. Two instances of this are to be found in concertos, each of which was its creator's last work. After Alban Berg had begun to write his violin concerto, he heard of the death of Manon Gropius and dedicated it " To the memory of an angel." She was the beautiful daughter of Gustav Mahler's widow by a second marriage and died at eighteen from poliomyelitis after great suffering. Berg was on terms of intimate friendship with the family. The first two movements are linked to form Part I of the work, and seem to express Manon's gentle character and youthful spirits. Part II opens with an Allegro suggestive of her painful illness and death, leading to the final Adagio which is religious and based on Bach's chorale " Es ist genug " from the cantata " O Ewigkeit, du Donnerwort ". In this movement Berg's music, which had been largely, though not wholly, within the 12-note system, becomes more diatonic, thus conveying a sense of divine consolation after the anguish of the preceding Allegro. It ends in heavenly peace. Berg died of a septic ulcer in his back a few months after completing this spiritual music. Little did he think that in commemorating Manon he was writing his own elegy.

Bartók's Third Piano Concerto—so much more approachable than most of his works—has a buoyant first movement with relatively simple harmonies and piquant rhythms; the Adagio religioso is even more diatonic: after a beautiful dialogue between slowly progressing chords on the piano and more flowing phrases on the strings, the music rises from quiet meditation to impassioned entreaty; ultimately the movement leads direct into the happiness of the Finale. What a wonderful ending to Bartók's musical life!

Though both these composers eventually found tonality a more suitable medium for their devotional thoughts than the 12-note system,

Olivier Messiaen (whose "Turangalila" Symphony has already been mentioned in Chapter 5) does not hesitate to assault our ears even in his religious art. In his earlier *L'Ascension—quatre méditations symphoniques* (1933) he was speaking a language which most music-lovers could understand and in which they can readily find an upsurging of the spirit. But the *Visions de l'Amen* for two pianos (1943) and the *Vingt Regards sur l'Enfant Jesus* for piano solo (1944) are indeed the strange outpourings of a religious mystic; Messiaen revels in dissonances clashing against one another, and in rapid passages in the treble competing against a slow-moving background in the depths of the instrument; at times the music turns to diatonic chords, to a meditative, serene, or even majestic, utterance, but these are moments of light in a puzzling world of harsh intensity.

From these remarkable manifestations it is a relief to turn our thoughts, in concluding this chapter, to a composition by a Swiss musician and three choral works by English composers, original in idiom, yet linked with tradition.

Frank Martin's oratorio *Golgotha* (1945–8), based on the Gospels and the writings of St. Augustine, returns to Bach's conception of setting the story of Christ's Passion to music. It is its essential simplicity that makes this work appropriate to its great subject, for which elaborate orchestration would have been out of place; and in spite of some rhythmic monotony and its austere avoidance of counterpoint, the music is moving and impressive.

In *A Child of our Time* (1941), which is largely diatonic or chromatic, Michael Tippett voiced his indignation against the hideous racial persecutions practised by the Nazis in Germany; the whole work is spiritual in character, with passages of deep pathos and tragedy. It ends on a note of hope and serenity. The composer has most convincingly sensed the universality inherent in the Negro spirituals which are woven into a score different from them both in mood and style but equally universal in appeal.

Alan Rawsthorne's short, deeply religious chamber cantata *A Canticle of Man*, for baritone, chorus, flute and strings (1952), is based on words by Randall Swingler, which brood on man's anguish and dreams; his anguish, which Rawsthorne conveys by pronounced chromaticism and unusual modulations, can only be ended by his soul being won to love; the music finishes with soft, ethereal tones.

Hymnus Paradisi, by Herbert Howells (1950), is a setting of Latin and

English texts, from Psalms xxiii and cxxi, the " Missa pro defunctis " and the Book of Common Prayer, for two soloists, chorus, and orchestra. It was dedicated to the memory of the composer's only son, but typifies something universal—the comfort that comes from faith to those who sorrow, and the eternal peace and joy of those who have endured in the heat of the conflict. Individual and modern in character, this exalted music is the product of deep conviction, conveyed by relatively simple means. With this intensely moving and beautiful creation we may fittingly end our survey of the consecration of music to God in the contemporary world.

17

RELIGION IN THE OPERA HOUSE
I—UNTIL MOZART

NO excuse is needed for treating religion in the opera house as a distinct subject, for the words pose the problem of the relationship between music and religion in its most paradoxical and provocative form. The term " operatic " has often been used almost as the antithesis of " religious ", and to apply it to a piece of liturgical music has been virtually tantamount to condemnation.

Yet this attitude is, I believe, too sweeping. In the first place, if we regard the human mind as in some measure divine—or, at least, divinely inspired—that divinity will manifest itself in opera as in other forms of creative activity, even though it only does so indirectly. Where we find a genuine expression of human emotions, which in opera takes a dramatic form, and where evil is presented not as a force to be admired or condoned but as indeed an evil thing communicated for the purpose of dramatic contrast, the work will probably contain the divinity of beauty in some degree, though without being specifically religious. This principle, once enunciated, can be seen to apply to countless non-religious operas throughout the ages, from the seventeenth century onwards. To deal with all the operas which in this wide sense are divine, or even with those only which are divine in a supreme degree, would require a whole volume.

Secondly, although opera only came into existence as recently as the end of the sixteenth or beginning of the seventeenth century, its ultimate sources were the ancient pre-Christian dramas, linked with music and religious in origin.[1] Coming down to medieval times, music was an element in the liturgical dramas which were performed in Christian churches, the words usually being in Latin but sometimes in the vernacular. These musical religious plays grew out of the church service, being performed by priests and choristers as part of the liturgy.

Thus about A.D. 980,[2] in Anglo-Saxon Winchester, a drama with

[1] See Chapter 2.

[2] In this and the following paragraphs I am indebted to a valuable article on " Medieval Music-Drama " by Mr. W. L. Smoldon in the *Musical Times*, December 1953: to his article on " Liturgical Music-Drama " in the 5th edition of *Grove's Dictionary of Music and Musicians*; and to his chapter on " Liturgical Drama " in the *New Oxford History of Music*, Vol. II.

singing was performed in Church, near the altar: the Winchester Troper and the *Regularis Concordia* of Ethelwold, Bishop of Winchester, together give the Latin text and music and stage directions. The angel appeared at the empty sepulchre, and gave to the three Marys an assurance of the Resurrection. Some of the music, sung unaccompanied, was liturgical, some of it was a "trope", i.e. an interpolation from outside the liturgy. The "trope", *Quem quaeritis* ("He whom you seek"), existed on the Continent in 920, and dramatic versions probably came from Frankish sources there. About the end of the tenth century versions of this Easter scene were performed in many parts of Western Europe.

Later, other incidents were added, such as Peter and John hastening to the sepulchre; Jesus disguised as a gardener, asking Mary Magdalene questions and then revealing His identity to her; priests requesting a guard for the tomb; Pilate's instructions to his Roman soldiers, and their march round the tomb singing stanzas in turn, with a refrain in chorus; an angel with a flaming sword; the striking down of the guard, their recovery and return to report and being bribed to maintain silence; and the appearance of a merchant from whom the three Marys buy spices. There were also dramas depicting episodes after the Resurrection, such as those of the doubting Thomas and the meeting between the two disciples and Christ as a stranger at Emmaus.

The music of these plays was monodic: in the prose parts Gregorian melody influenced the style, but the metrical portions are often non-Gregorian and "secular". A version at Tours had a large singing rôle for Mary Magdalene. Musical religious plays in church also came to be associated with Christmas. The shepherds, the Three Magi and Herod make their appearance, and sometimes the massacre of the innocents figured in the drama. The music was partly borrowed from traditional liturgy, but was mostly invented in a style resembling the Gregorian.

About 1150 there was a "Daniel" music-drama in Beauvais Cathedral, probably performed after matins on the Feast of the Circumcision (January 1st): this presented Belshazzar's feast, the writing on the wall, Daniel's interpretation of it, the arrival of the victorious Persians and the seizure of the throne by their king, Daniel in the lions' den, his rescue by the angel and his re-establishment. The music comprised a string of melodies set to Latin texts. There were solos, choruses of satraps and guards, harps, drums and other instruments.

The raising of Lazarus, the conversion of St. Paul, the Last Judgment (depicted in a French drama founded on the story of the Wise and

Foolish Virgins), and the miracles of St. Nicholas, were the subjects of other musical dramas enacted in medieval churches.

In these religious plays, with actors, costumes, gestures, and the dramatic text set to music, we can trace a vital stage in the evolution of opera from its ritualistic pre-Christian origins until its final emergence as a distinct art-form about A.D. 1600.

Thirdly, some operas have definitely religious connotations: for example, those dealing even with ancient pagan myths, such as the legends of Orpheus, Iphigeneia and Alcestis; those based on Biblical subjects; those linked with Christian beliefs but embodying non-Biblical stories, such as *Tannhäuser*, *Lohengrin*, *Parsifal*, *Mathis der Maler*, and *The Pilgrim's Progress*; and a unique opera like *Die Zauberflöte*, which is at once spiritual and symbolic, though the symbols and the ceremonies to which they relate are those of Freemasonry, not of the Catholic Church.[1] It is chiefly with these types of opera and also with any specifically religious elements in other operas that I propose to deal in this chapter and the next.

It is not necessary to spread the net more widely than this in the case of operatic music. Although divinity in varying degrees may be revealed in non-religious operatic art, the attitude of the composer and librettist is discernible largely by inference: only thus do we know their own sentiments, as distinct from those of the characters whom they are presenting on the stage; whereas in many other forms of music, such as liturgical art and most instrumental compositions, the personal thoughts and emotions of the composer are directly communicated to us: he speaks in the first person, and it has been relevant to the subject of this book to consider many non-operatic works which are deeply spiritual but not actually religious.

An old pagan myth may have little or no religious significance for the artist who is re-creating it, or on the other hand it may awaken a religious response in him in spite of its remote origin and character. For the ancient Greeks the tale of Orpheus and Eurydice occupied a place corresponding to that filled by an Old Testament story in the minds of Jews and Christians, but we could hardly expect that all the librettists and composers who created settings of the subject in the seventeenth and eighteenth centuries A.D. will have treated it as religious in character. Angelo Poliziano was the author of *Orfeo*, an entertainment rather like a masque, produced in 1472 at Mantua; Raphael painted the scenery; we know nothing about the music, but

[1] But see note on p. 205.

the poem indicates that the work was one of those that anticipated opera, as some of it was sung. Although Peri's *Dafne* (1594), as a play with continuous music[1] was in effect the first opera, the next was *Eurydice* (1600) by Peri and Caccini, and after that the Orpheus legend was set by many composers from Monteverdi in 1607 to Gluck in 1762. In the twentieth century it has been the subject of operas by Milhaud and Casella and of a ballet with music by Stravinsky. The attempt to reproduce the conversation and emotions of the characters solely by means of recitative in *Eurydice* was greatly admired by its contemporaries, but it can arouse little intrinsic interest for us, and though the opera contains pleasant choruses, its importance is mainly historical.

Monteverdi's *Orfeo* is a very different matter, for in addition to recitative he introduced expressive melodies for the soloists as well as for the chorus and developed the use of the orchestra as a means of contributing to the emotional and dramatic effect. The old story ceases to be just a legend. It becomes a tale of love so devoted that it lasts beyond the grave, of a soul tested in the crucible of obedience to the divine will and found wanting, losing the beloved one for ever, yet in the end borne to eternal rest in Heaven. And in Monteverdi's moving music this conception transcends the pagan mythology and acquires a universal meaning. The substitution of happy for unhappy endings in Greek tragic stories was introduced in the drama of the Renaissance and continued by Corneille and Racine to suit the tastes of the audiences of those days, but in Monteverdi's *Orfeo* the final variant of the original Greek legend[2] is no conventional happy ending. After Eurydice's second death, Orpheus wanders over the plains of Thrace, in hopeless grief. He calls upon nature to mourn with him in pity. Apollo (his mythical father) comes down and takes him up to Heaven, where he will behold Eurydice among the stars, and the chorus sing happily of his divine immortality. The opera ends with a dance of the celestial ballet.

Meanwhile, operas with specifically religious subjects in the orthodox Christian sense of the term were making their appearance. *La Rappresentazione di Anima e di Corpo*, by Emilio de Cavalieri, was produced in 1600 in the Oratorio de Vallicella, one of St. Philip Neri's oratories in Rome; it was a descendant of the mystery play, with choruses and dances added, and was performed like an opera

[1] Only a few fragments of the music have survived.
[2] See Chapter 2.

with scenery and acting, not like oratorios which were a later development in musical history. *Eumelio*, by the liturgical composer Agostino Agazzari, was a " dramma pastorale " which appeared in 1606, and there were several other works of the same type, such as Kapsberger's *Apotheosis of St. Ignatius of Loyola*, which was produced in the Jesuit College in 1622.

It would be far-fetched to attribute a religious character to Purcell's divinely beautiful *Dido and Aeneas* on the ground of the mythological origin of its story; or to his *King Arthur*, which is on the borderline between opera and drama with incidental music but is entirely secular in style although based on the story of a Christian king in conflict with heathen Saxons. In the late seventeenth century, opera, as it spread through Germany, was based on Biblical subjects in a succession of minor works, but eventually it acquired a secular character. Handel's operas, however divine we may find much of their music, are no more religious than those of Alessandro Scarlatti, Lulli or Rameau. He voiced the religious side of his artistic nature in his oratorios and his ecclesiastical works.

The greatness of Gluck (1714–87) rests entirely on six of his operas: *Orfeo ed Eurydice*, *Alceste*, *Paris and Helen*, *Armide* and the two *Iphigeneias*—and his music for the ballet *Don Juan*. His operas before *Orfeo* all conformed to the practice by which musical ornamentation, rather than true expressiveness and dramatic feeling, was the prevailing factor. Five of the six great operas, in which he conveyed drama and emotions in convincing musical terms, were based on ancient Greek myths. It does not follow that there is a religious quality—even a pagan religious quality—in all five: and in fact *Paris and Helen*—though a god, Erasto (Cupid), is one of the characters, and Pallas Athene appears at the end and prophesies an evil outcome from the love of the two principal persons—contains no music that is intrinsically religious, but is either charming or romantically beautiful in a style which resembles *Armide* rather than Gluck's four other " Greek " masterpieces.

The pathos and emotional depth of the music of *Orfeo ed Eurydice*, the tragic profundity of the scene with the Furies, and the delicacy of the writing in the scene in the Elysian fields, are leading features of the immortal score. But there is also a specifically religious element. As with Monteverdi, the ancient legend inspired Gluck to express something universal. The opening of the first act, with the chorus of girls and shepherds and Orpheus at Eurydice's tomb, lamenting her death in the key of C minor, is not only a moving expresson of grief, but a solemn invocation to her spirit to return to him. It is followed by a voice of heavenly comfort from the orchestra in E flat, as the chorus move slowly round the grave, strewing flowers upon it. Later in the scene, after Orpheus had resolved to descend to the underworld and bring back Eurydice, Cupid appears, tells him that the gods have taken pity on him, bids him go and prevail over the divine rulers below by means of his lyre and his singing, and informs him that he must not look upon Eurydice until they have returned to the upper world.

The music of the netherworld, which begins the second act, has a sense of religious terror which is akin to the spirit of Dante's *Inferno*—with Orpheus begging the Furies to admit him, their stern replies of "No!", his continued entreaties and their final yielding, as their voices sink to a "pianissimo" with deep utterances from the orchestra. If we find a Dantesque quality in Gluck's music for this scene we should recall that Dante's conception owed a debt to the sixth book of Virgil's *Aeneid*, which in turn went back to Homer's *Odyssey* (Book XI). That today we do not believe in the tortures either of a medieval fiery Hell or of a gloomy classical netherworld, but rather in a state of spiritual remorse, does not alter the fact that the belief in a Hell of real, even physical, horror or pain was a religious one in ancient Greece and Rome, in medieval Europe, and for a long while afterwards, and that Gluck has expressed something of this feeling in his powerful music. It is significant, too, that in the later, Paris, version of the opera he reproduced the wonderful music of the dance of the Furies from his ballet *Don Juan*, the setting of which was, of course, in the Christian era. It may seem strange that Furies, who belonged to ancient Greek mythology, should have appeared in a ballet dealing with a legend many hundreds of years later in date. Don Juan's fate obviously had a religious connotation. That the same music is supremely appropriate in both places is another example of the generalised nature of the art.

The music of the scene in the Elysian fields is of heavenly quality. A man of my acquaintance once told me that he would like this dance of the blessed spirits to be played at his funeral, and as we listen to these divinely happy melodies and the serenely beautiful music for flute and strings, we can assuredly sympathise with his wish. Orpheus' air, "Che puro ciel", with the exquisite accompaniment for oboe and strings, maintains the atmosphere of celestial peace and introduces a note of wonder.

As in Monteverdi, the sad ending contained in the later version of the old story is changed, though in a different way: instead of the idealistic, almost mystical conception which closes Monteverdi's work, Gluck's opera introduces a *deus ex machina* of a somewhat artificial kind. After Orpheus has sung his noble lament "Che faro senza Euridice", and is about to kill himself in despair, Cupid reappears and tells him that the gods have now had enough proof of his faithfulness; whereupon Eurydice is restored to life, and the opera closes happily with dancing and singing, the music of which, like that of the overture, is not on a level with the grandeur and beauty of the rest of the opera.

Gluck's *Alceste* was based on the drama of Euripides. Admetus, King of Pherae in Thessaly, is at the point of death; but Apollo, who had been received by him when banished from Heaven, persuades the Fates to spare his life provided that someone can be found to die instead of him. Alcestis, the wife of Admetus, offers to take his place and passes into the underworld, and in Euripides' version Heracles (Hercules), who visits Pherae at this time, in return for the hospitality of Admetus recovers her from Death and restores her to her husband. In the Italian version of the opera, however, Calzabigi, the librettist, eliminated Heracles and made Apollo reunite husband and wife as a token of his gratitude to Admetus and in recognition of their mutual devotion. The later Paris version defaced the work by introducing Hercules to fulfil the rôle assigned to him by Euripides and by representing him as a blustering, intemperate person, who sings an aria probably written by Gossec in Gluck's absence owing to the death of his niece.

Euripides had glorified hospitality, whereas the Italian version of Gluck's opera glorifies marital fidelity. It is the story of a wife's love for her husband, so complete as to prompt her to sacrifice life itself to save him from death, and ultimately rewarded by reunion with him. The modern religious character of the general idea does not need to be pointed out, but it is reinforced by the nature of the music of the first two acts and the beginning of the third. The sublime overture is followed by a scene of public lamentation at the imminence of the King's death and solemn music in which Alcestis prays to the gods to relax the rigour of his fate and bids the people follow her into the temple to join her prayers.

Then comes the magnificent scene in the temple, where the High Priest begs Apollo to have mercy on the dying Admetus, Alcestis prostrates herself before the image of the god, and the oracle proclaims that the King must die that day if no other will die in place of him. The people fly in terror, Alcestis decides to offer her life for her husband's and asks the gods to accept her sacrifice. The High Priest tells her that Admetus' health is now restored, and she sings the great aria "Divinités du Styx". The music of this scene is deeply impressive and religious throughout.

In the Italian version, the second act begins with an eerie scene at night in a forest sacred to the gods of the underworld. Alcestis invokes them and is answered by Death, who bids her descend into Hades with him but allows her first to return to the palace to say farewell to her husband and children: infernal spirits accompany her on her way.

In the scene in the palace, which follows, choral singing and ballet happily celebrate the recovery of Admetus, until he hears that someone unknown has submitted to death for him. Alcestis enters, he wrings the truth from her and declares that he will again offer his life to the gods or else will die by his own hand, so that he may not be separated from her. He rushes away. She prays for him, and the people lament her fate. She prepares for death, calling on the gods to bless the King and her children.

At the opening of the third act Admetus' distraction of mind is depicted. Alcestis enters with their children and begs him not to marry another wife, and so he promises. Alcestis swoons and is carried off by the spirits of the underworld. Admetus tries to end his own life, but Apollo appears in the clouds, with Alcestis, and reunites the happy pair. The weak ending, with a final chorus, does not (either in this Italian version or in the French one) obliterate the dramatic effect and, in parts, the moving religious quality of the earlier, tragic, but inspiring music.

The libretto of Gluck's *Iphigeneia in Aulis*, by Du Roullet, was founded on Racine's tragedy, which was in turn derived from Euripides. A comparison between the three versions has a bearing on the part played in them by religion. Let us first consider Euripides' drama. The Greek forces under King Agamemnon were on their way by sea to fight against Troy, the cause of the war, according to legend, being that the Trojan Paris has carried off Helen, the wife of Menelaus, Agamemnon's brother. But their ships have been delayed at Aulis by a calm, and they have been told by the priest Calchas that only if Iphigeneia, Agamemnon's daughter, is sacrificed to Artemis will favourable winds arise to carry them on their voyage. So at the behest of Menelaus Agamemnon has sent for Iphigeneia to come to Aulis as a bride for Achilles; but, on reflection, his love for her and the desire to save her life prompt him to send a second message to his wife,

Clytemnestra, to tell her to postpone bringing Iphigeneia to Aulis on the ground that the marriage has been deferred. Menelaus, however, intercepts this letter and so Clytemnestra and Iphigeneia come to the camp. Achilles arrives to ask Agamemnon why the Greeks have not sailed for Troy, and meets Clytemnestra, who hails him (to his amazement) as Iphigeneia's betrothed. During their exchange of explanations, the attendant to whom the second letter for Clytemnestra had been given comes in and, being an old servant of the house, tells her of the danger in which Iphigeneia stands and of Agamemnon's manoeuvres. Amid Clytemnestra's grief, Achilles promises to rescue Iphigeneia from her fate. Agamemnon finds out that Clytemnestra and Iphigeneia know everything, but says that he cannot fight against the goddess. Iphigeneia, despite the entreaties of her mother and Achilles, courageously offers herself for the sacrifice; but when she has gone to the altar, Clytemnestra is told that, just as Calchas was about to strike with the knife, Iphigeneia had been miraculously spirited away and that her place had been taken by a hind: the gods are satisfied, the winds arise and the Greek host is able to sail for Troy.

Racine made a number of alterations in the story. Among other things, Achilles becomes a passionate lover of Iphigeneia, and a new character, Eriphile, appears, who is Helen's daughter by Theseus and is now a companion to Iphigeneia. Achilles has taken her captive in war, and she has been brought up ignorant of her real name and birth, is anxious to know them and secretly loves Achilles. When the sacrifice is imminent, Calchas hears from the oracle that there is someone present who is a kinswoman of Helen and must take Iphigeneia's place. Eriphile does not wait, but slays herself with the knife of sacrifice. Iphigeneia and Achilles are happily married.

Du Roullet largely follows Racine's version, but omits the rôle of Eriphile altogether and presents Calchas in person (in Racine he does not appear). To that extent Du Roullet goes back to Euripides, but the net result is that the story is humanised, there is a happy ending, no final miracle, and less of the supernatural and religious element than in *Orfeo* or *Alceste*.

After the tragic and dramatically moving overture, the curtain rises on Agamemnon's aria " O pitiless Diana, in vain dost thou command this fearful sacrifice", based on the first theme of the overture. He has already sent Arcas (who, as in Racine, takes the place of the Euripidean attendant) to prevent Clytemnestra and Iphigeneia from coming to Aulis, and expresses his grief at the idea of Iphigeneia's sacrifice.

The chorus of Greeks enquire of Calchas why the goddess is angry. Calchas, appalled at the sacrifice demanded, asks the gods whether any other victim will satisfy them, and he and Agamemnon together pray to the goddess for pity. The chorus fiercely cry " Name us the victim and at once we will slay him ", and then in grave music beg the gods for mercy. Calchas assures them that a victim will that day be found, and then tries to induce Agamemnon to yield to the gods. The king, however, pours out his distress in a magnificent aria, and swears that he will not obey the gods. Calchas warns him that he will have to bow to their will, and Agamemnon sadly gives way.

The story of the remainder of the opera, apart from the ending, is mainly on the lines already indicated, so that there is little opportunity for Gluck to strike a religious note until near the close of the third, last, act, except for the fine air in the second scene of Act II in which Agamemnon distractedly veers between his love for his daughter and his awe of the gods. In the third act Clytemnestra's aria " Jove, dart thy lightning ", is at once dramatic, tragic and religious, and it is followed by a chorus of deeply devotional feeling, in which the Greeks beg the gods to be propitious and to accept the sacrifice. The ending is regrettably tame: Calchas tells the two parties—Achilles and the Thessalians on the one side and the Greeks on the other—to cease from their enmity, and declares that the gods are satisfied; Iphigeneia is restored to her parents and is to wed Achilles and the opera finishes with festive dancing and singing.

Euripides' ending leads quite logically to the story of his *Iphigeneia in Tauris*, where we find that Iphigeneia, after being mysteriously taken from the altar at Aulis, has become the High Priestess in the temple of Artemis at Tauris. Racine's and Gluck's works dealing with the Aulis legend are self-contained, so Gluck's *Iphigeneia in Tauris*, in view of the way in which his " Aulis " opera finishes, does not follow as a sequel to it. The libretto, by Guillard, was modelled directly on Euripides. Both the original Greek play and Gluck's opera show the two creators, dramatist and composer, at the very height of their powers.

The overture is merged into the first scene more completely than in any previous opera. After a short, peaceful opening, depicting the calm of the elements, the music of the storm begins, and in the midst of it Iphigeneia's voice is heard, praying to the gods to abate the thunder and to show mercy. The chorus of priestesses join her prayer, while the storm continues to rage on the orchestra and eventually dies down. Iphigeneia narrates her dream of the burning palace of Mycenae, the chorus again beg the gods for mercy, Iphigeneia invokes her brother Orestes (whom she believes to be dead), despairs of escape from the doom that overhangs her father's house and in moving accents implores Artemis to end her life. Thoas, the King, enters, hears from her that the gods have not answered their prayers, and says that the divine wrath must be appeased with blood, not tears. Two strangers are dragged in by Thoas' Scythians, who are calling for a victim. They are Orestes and Pylades, who, however, declare that they cannot reveal their names. Thoas orders that one of them is to be sacrificed.

At the beginning of Act II, Orestes refuses to be comforted by Pylades, who beseeches him to be patient. An attendant comes in and orders Pylades alone to accompany him. When Pylades has gone, Orestes gives way to despair. Then he sings in quieter music that his heart is growing calmer, but the orchestral accompaniment in threatening tones seems to speak of the Nemesis that pursues him: for he has slain his mother, Clytemnestra, in revenge for her murder of his father, Agamemnon; and even as his words cease, the Furies enter and torment him with their music and dance of terror.

Iphigeneia appears and elicits from this unknown man from Mycenae the fearful news that Clytemnestra has killed Agamemnon, has herself been slain by Orestes, and that Orestes is dead. She sings the great aria " O malheureuse Iphigénie " and, with the priestesses, a song of mourning for her brother.

In the next act, Iphigeneia is determined to free one of the two strangers to take a message to her sister at Argos. Eventually, after each has made repeated offers of self-sacrifice, Orestes is accepted for immolation, and Pylades departs with the letter, swearing to return and save his friend's life.

The last act shows Iphigeneia praying to Artemis to steel her at the time of sacrifice so that she may do her duty as priestess, though inwardly she shrinks from the deed. Orestes thanks her for her pity, and she is about to slay him when he calls out: " So didst thou die in Aulis, Iphigeneia, my sister! " Iphigeneia recognises him, but Thoas enters, rebukes her for letting Pylades escape and orders the guards to lead Orestes back to the altar. When Iphigeneia tells him that Orestes is her brother, Thoas threatens to kill them both, but Pylades with a party of Greeks arrives back in time to overpower him. Artemis enters and bids the Scythians give her image back to the Greeks. Iphigeneia and Orestes return to Mycenae.

The first two acts of this great opera, particularly, give Gluck full opportunity to express the religious side of the drama, with its prayers for mercy to the gods, the portrayal of Iphigeneia's character as a priestess, and the supernatural terror of the Furies. This religious aspect is blended with the emotional, human quality of the words and music so marvellously that the work is justly regarded as Gluck's grandest and most perfect masterpiece.

Gluck did not shine as a composer of church music, and his greatness rests entirely on his compositions for the stage. Mozart, an even greater genius, wrote beautiful music for the liturgy as well as for instruments without voices, but regarded opera as his ideal art-form. If we consider the expression of human characters and emotions by means of lovely music as essentially divine, then we can trace the finger of God even in Mozart's operatic comedies. Three of his greatest operas, however—*Idomeneo*, *Don Giovanni* and *Die Zauberflöte*—contain in different degrees a specifically religious element, harmonising with the devotional character which is to be found in the finest parts of his liturgical compositions and sometimes in his instrumental works.

The libretto of *Idomeneo*, like so many previous examples in the world of "opera seria", was framed in a setting of ancient Greek mythology, but corresponded to the Biblical story which told how Jephtha, on returning from war, vowed to sacrifice to God the first living being he met, and how this turned out to be his own daughter. Idomeneo, King of Crete, has sent Priam's daughter Ilia to Crete as a captive from Troy. She has fallen in love with his son, Idamante. Electra, Agamemnon's daughter, has fled to Crete after her mother's murder: she also loves Idamante and is wildly jealous. Idomeneo, as his fleet approaches the harbour in a storm, only escapes death by swearing to sacrifice to Poseidon the first living thing that he meets on shore. When he realises that that person is his son, he tries to save Idamante's life by telling him to take Electra back to Argos. When they are about to leave, another storm arises and a monster comes out of the sea. As the Cretans contend that someone has offended the god, Idomeneo confesses that it is he, and is willing to die. Idamante resolves to kill the monster, and Ilia and he declare their love for one another, but Idomeneo again tells him to depart from Crete. To rid the island of the ravages of the monster, the Cretans insist on a victim, and the King is obliged to give his son's name. The High Priest prepares for the sacrifice, but Idamante kills the monster. He is, however, ready to die in order that his father's vow may be honoured. Ilia offers her life in his place, but an oracle announces that the King must abdicate and that Idamante, with Ilia as consort, is to succeed him. The work ends with oyful songs and dances.

This, in a very brief form, is the plot of the opera, which inspired Mozart to compose music of tragic grandeur and passion. But there is also a touch of mystery in the overture, and, wherever the situation called for it, a religious aspect in the music that follows. Thus, after Electra's outburst of jealousy in the first act, there is an eloquent chorus of Cretans begging the gods for mercy. In the second act, when the monster appears, the people know that they are the victims of a divine curse, and when they demand who the guilty one is, the wind instruments three times echo their call in tones of supernatural terror. When Iopmeneo charges Poseidon with injustice, the orchestra rages in fury at his blasphemy. In the great quartet between Idomeneo, Idamante, Ilia and Electra, in the third act, there is an underlying feeling of mystery as though all the four characters sense that they are dominated by supernatural powers. And finally, the voice of the oracle is accompanied by the solemn sound of the trombones, which Mozart so often employs to convey a religious atmosphere. In his day, they were not normally used in the theatre, but in church.

The religious side of *Don Giovanni* is present only in the overture and in two scenes. Before discussing these, let us consider some earlier versions of the plot. The story of a dissolute blasphemer who invited a dead man to supper was current in many countries before it assumed a literary form in Spain in the seventeenth century. It is said that there was a Don Juan Tenorio at the court of Peter the Cruel, and another man of the same name, a profligate, at Seville at a later date, but these may have been legendary figures. Variations of the story have been found in Picardy, Iceland and the Azores. But its first appearance in writing seems to have been in a Spanish play, *El Burlador de Sevilla* (" The deceiver of Seville "), dated 1630 and attributed to Tirso de Molina. In this, Don Juan pursues various ladies, including Donna Anna, fights a duel with her father, the Commendatore, and kills him; later, he invites the statue of the dead man to supper and is carried off to Hell: the comic servant describes the catastrophe and then the other characters are happily married.

The story passed to Italy, and to France, where less emphasis was laid on its ethical, supernatural or religious aspect and more on its comic side, as in Molière's *Le festin de pierre* (1665). In England, Shadwell's play on the subject, for which Purcell wrote incidental music, was produced in 1676: in his preface to it, the author, who did not believe in religion, hopes "that the Reader will not be offended at the representation of those vices, on which they will see a dreadful punishment inflicted". He goes on: "I have been told by a worthy gentleman that many years ago (when first a play was made upon this story in Italy) he has seen it acted there by the name of 'Atheisto Fulminato', in Churches, on Sundays, as a part of devotion: and some, not of the least Judgment and Piety here, have thought it rather an useful moral than an encouragement to vice."

The Italian Goldoni, in the preface to his play *Don Giovanni Tenorio osia Il Dissoluto* (1736), wrote: "I thought I ought not to suppress the thunderbolt which strikes down Don Giovanni, because the wicked man ought to be punished; but I managed this event in such a way that it could be an immediate effect of the anger of God, and that it could also spring from a combination of secondary causes, directed always by the laws of Providence."

The ballet *Don Juan* (1761), with choreography by Angiolini and music by Gluck, was based on Molière but is entirely serious throughout. Elvira is here the daughter of the Commendatore, who is killed by Don Juan in the first act. The Statue makes two appearances: in the second act it enters Don Juan's house during a banquet, the guests fly in terror, he invites it to join him in the feast, and the Statue refuses but asks him to visit it in the cemetery. Don Juan does so in the third act: the Statue tries to induce him to repent, calling up a vision of his past loves, but all in vain. The Statue consigns him to the Furies, who dance to the magnificent, stormy music afterwards used again by Gluck in *Orfeo*, and carry him off to the infernal regions.

In 1787, Bertati, the librettist, produced *Don Giovanni Tenorio osia Il Convitato di Pietra* (*The Stone Guest*), an opera with music by Gazzaniga and a prologue adapted from an earlier work of his own. Da Ponte's libretto for Mozart's *Don Giovanni* followed Bertati's version more closely than any other. Mozart called his opera a "dramma giocoso" on the title page and an "opera buffa" in his thematic catalogue. This, of course, does not mean that there could not be serious, pathetic, or even tragic passages in it; but until near the end the score is largely filled with vocal and orchestral music of infinite charm and humour. In the cemetery scene, Don Giovanni is startled when he hears a voice warning him that his doom is approaching. Only then, in the darkness does he see the Statue of the Commendatore. His servant, Leporello, at his bidding invites the Statue to supper and the Don confirms the invitation. The Statue nods and answers "yes". In the final scene, Don Giovanni is at supper in his home, with music for wind instruments to entertain him, when the sinister sound of heavy footsteps is heard: Elvira, who has entered to make a final attempt to induce the Don to repent, rushes out to see what is approaching, and utters a loud scream; Leporello, who follows, screams too and comes back terrified. The Statue strides in, addresses Don Giovanni in awesome tones, and eventually invites him to come with it to supper. The Don accepts and takes the hand of the Statue. Flames arise and thunder is heard. Devils call to Don Giovanni to come down to eternal torture; they appear, seize him and drag him off to Hell.

Leporello, trembling under the table and calling on his master to refuse the Statue's invitation, has still presented a comic figure, and the opera ends with a scene in which he gives a grimly humorous description of the Don's downfall to the five other principal characters and they all sing a light-hearted sextet, settling their own future lives and telling the audience to take warning from the fate of Don Giovanni. But this does not obliterate the impression of the two scenes with the Statue. In the cemetery, the words of the Commendatore are accompanied by the trombones, used here for the first time in the opera and again, as in *Idomeneo*, associated with the supernatural. The D minor music of the scene with the Statue in the Don's house is not merely tragic, but tremendous. Once more, the trombones utter their awesome tones, and when Don Giovanni takes the Statue's hand the orchestra surges on, with sudden changes from loud to soft notes, until the flames have subsided and the devils have dragged the Don from the stage, when the music settles down again. We have had a foretaste of this supernatural effect (though without the trombones) at the beginning of the overture, which Mozart is said to have written just before the first performance and in which therefore he was really introducing music already composed for his Finale. In spite of his sub-title for the work and the character of Da Ponte's libretto, and whatever may have been his original intention when he set out to create the score, there can be no doubt that in these great passages of his tragi-comic opera he expressed the supernatural, religious element of the old story by means of powerful and impressive music.

As early as 1773 Mozart had begun to write incidental music for Gebler's play *Thamos, König in Aegypten* and completed it in 1779. The play was a failure, but the music richly deserves to be performed in a concert hall both for its own sake and because of its interesting connection with some of the music of *Die Zauberflöte*, the setting of which is also in ancient Egypt. The first chorus, which is accompanied by a large orchestra for those days—including trombones—is a hymn to the sun, impressive and solemn in character. Act V contains two noble choral songs of thanksgiving, the second of which is preceded by a bass solo. In all this music there is a distinct anticipation of the Masonic parts of Mozart's final opera composed in 1791, the last year of his life. The original idea for *Die Zauberflöte* was that it should be simply an oriental fairy tale. Schikaneder, the librettist, had in mind the story of a good fairy, a wicked magician and two lovers who had to pass through various ordeals and at last were happily united; but both he and Mozart were Freemasons, and, whatever the reason, the whole scheme was changed into an allegory: the setting was located in Egypt; Sarastro, High Priest of Isis, and Osiris, an Orator, and a chorus of priests, were introduced; the good fairy became the Queen of the Night, a vindictive woman constantly acting as their enemy; Monostatos, the unpleasant and oppressive servant of Sarastro entrusted with looking after Pamina, takes the place of the wicked magician. The libretto has been accused of being a farrago of nonsense: but except for occasional infelicities of diction, it is nothing of the kind, and the result of its embodiment in Mozart's miraculous music is that the opera forms a perfect whole, the prevailing character of which is serene and spiritual. Sarastro and the authorities of the temple stand for goodness and wisdom, as evinced in the ideals of Freemasonry. The lovers, Tamino and Pamina, have to be tested and ultimately to pass through fire and water before they can attain to happiness; both the magic of the flute and the earthly humour of Tamino's companion, Papageno, the birdcatcher, with his entrancing chime of bells, are blended into this tale of mystic symbolism.

Pope Clement VIII in 1738 condemned Freemasonry, as a religion in rivalry with Catholic Christianity. It would be outside the scope of this book to enter upon that subject, and inappropriate for one who is not a Freemason to do so. It is sufficient to say that the Order of Freemasonry is not itself a religion, although it does employ certain rites and symbols; that it is mainly concerned with human welfare; and that it admits a man " of any religion or mode of worship, provided he believes in the glorious Architect of heaven and earth and practises the sacred duties of morality." In *Die Zauberflöte*, however, for dramatic purposes it is symbolised by the membership and priesthood of a temple in which the ancient Egyptian divinities, Isis and Osiris, are worshipped, and much of Mozart's music is imbued with a religious spirit which transcends all divisions between creeds: the solemn tones of the three Genii in Act I; the sacred character of the march of the priests at the beginning of Act II; Sarastro's great aria " O Isis and Osiris ", with the chorus that follows, and the later chorus (in D major) which opens with the names of the same deities; his second aria " In diesen heiligen Hallen "; the duet of the Men in Armour who tell Tamino that he must pass through fire and water and whose melody is based on the old German chorale " Ach Gott von Himmel sieh darein "; and then later, as the lovers march through the elements, the purity of the melody on the flute, accompanied by soft drum taps and gentle notes on the trombones. In *Idomeneo* and *Don Giovanni* the trombones have only been employed at a few particular moments to convey a sense of supernatural awe; in *Die Zauberflöte* it is significant that they form an integral part of the score throughout, but there is mysticism, not terror, in their tones—mysticism and simplicity, as if to suggest that the spiritual forces of the world, mysterious though they are, yet remain utterly simple, just as all the music of this last and greatest of Mozart's operas is filled with a divine simplicity.[1]

[1] Ann Lapraik Livermore, in her article " *The Magic Flute* and Calderón " in " *Music and Letters*", January 1955, traces certain resemblances between Calderón's *El Purgatorio de San Patricio* (" The Purgatory of Saint Patrick ") and the libretto of *Die Zauberflöte*, which point to a Christian background behind the Masonic associations of Mozart's opera.

18

RELIGION IN THE OPERA HOUSE II—FROM BEETHOVEN TO WAGNER AND BEYOND

THE tendency of librettists and composers of operas to look to Greek mythology for their subjects, which had persisted since the early days of the genre, abated towards the end of the eighteenth century. Mozart did not return to that source after *Idomeneo*; and when Beethoven was searching for a story for an opera, his choice went eventually in favour of a modern theme. At one time he thought of setting *The Return of Ulysses*, and the fact that he contemplated an opera on the subject of *Macbeth* shows that at that stage he might have been interested in a tale containing a strong admixture of the supernatural; but he wrote to Collin that he was prejudiced against anything in the nature of a fairy tale type of libretto, containing magic " and that sort of thing ", and it was in consonance with his whole conception of his art that he should choose a subject of an essentially human kind, embodying great nobility of character, courage and fidelity, and reflecting his own religious attitude towards life. A story containing any supernatural elements in which he did not personally believe, would not have appealed to him sufficiently to inspire him to actual creation. When the suggestion of setting *Faust* to music was made to him in 1822 by Rochlitz (with the authority of Breitkopf and Härtel, the publishers), he replied " Ha! That would be a piece of work! That would be worth doing "; but the idea did not materialise.

The libretto of *Leonora* (as Beethoven would have liked his opera to be called) was one of the " rescue pieces " which had become the vogue about that time—stories in which a prisoner was set free from bondage. Cherubini's *Water-carrier* was one of these, and its librettist, Bouilly, was the author of an opera *Leonora* with music by Gaveaux. Bouilly had been in charge of a department near Tours during the Terror of the French Revolution, and drew on his experience for incidents in both these works, but in *Leonora* he shifted the action to Spain. Von Sonnleithner made a German version of this for Beethoven, who found in it a subject after his heart: a heroic tale of a wife's courage and devotion in rescuing her husband who is a political prisoner. There was no room for superstition in such a story, but Divine Providence, in which Beethoven profoundly believed, plays a vital part in it. The libretto was later revised, and improved, by G. F. Treitschke, and it is in this, its final, form, as *Fidelio*, that it was bequeathed to posterity.

In the first act, when Leonora realises the depths of tyrannical villainy in Pizarro, the governor of the prison, and is left alone on the stage, she bursts into the recitative beginning "Abscheulicher" ("Thou monstrous fiend"), with its stormy musical setting, but this rapidly gives place to a vision of hope; then the tender "adagio" passage in E major, "Komm Hoffnung", leads in turn to the Allegro con brio, in which she sings of the inner voice that is now guiding her in her heroic enterprise: in this great music Beethoven portrays supreme human courage inspired by faith in God and by love and devotion to her husband. In the wonderful dungeon scene of the second act, Florestan's song of grief, illumined by the image of "ein Engel, Leonore", who will lead him into the Heavenly Kingdom, is followed by the dramatic, spoken duet between Rocco, the jailer, and Leonora, as they dig the grave to the accompaniment of mystical music on the orchestra, and the tense music of their duet in A minor, "Nur hurtig fort". The key changes to A major for the trio "Euch werde lohn in besseren Welten, der Himmel hat euch mir geschickt", as Florestan pours out his gratitude to Heaven for sending them to him. But he does not recognise his wife in the darkness and in her disguise, until Pizarro has entered and threatened both Leonora and Florestan with immediate death; when she reveals who she is and has placed herself between her husband and the tyrant and pointed a pistol at Pizarro, the trumpet call rings out announcing the arrival of the Minister, Don Fernando. It is characteristic of Beethoven that the beautiful melody of the prayer of thanksgiving, which follows, is played on the orchestra, with the four solo voices sounding above it. "O namen—namenlose Freude", the subsequent duet between Leonora and Florestan, is a song of transcendent joy and gratitude to God for his mercy. This mood is carried over into the final scene, in which public rejoicing—"O Gott! O welch ein Augenblick"—is blended with the ecstatic happiness of the two principal characters.

Beethoven composed four overtures for his only opera. *Leonora No. 1* may have been written for a performance at Prague which did not materialise or it may actually have been the first overture composed for the opera but withdrawn before the first performance as being not significant enough. Even this overture, however, contains a good deal of the character of the opera itself, with the noble solemnity of its introduction, the vigorous bravery of the Allegro, the anticipation of Florestan's aria, and the ebullient joy of its closing passages. But it is easily surpassed by the sublimity of the overtures *Leonora No. 2* and *No. 3*. It would be irrelevant to our present purpose to discuss the structural differences between these two great overtures. Both of them embody the basic ideas of the opera in music of profound spiritual grandeur. In *Leonora No.* 3 the hymn of thanksgiving appears twice: after the first distant sounding of the fanfare on the trumpet, it is heard in B flat, as in the second act; when the trumpet call comes nearer, the hymn tune is repeated in G flat—a particularly beautiful change of key. The final Presto is even more thrilling in its joy and ecstasy than the ending of *Leonora No. 2*. When Beethoven finally revised the opera, he felt that either of these two tremendous overtures would have overshadowed the comparatively light character of the opening part of his first act, and therefore composed the cheerful *Fidelio* overture to start the proceedings.

Religion plays a very small part in the operas between *Fidelio* and Wagner. Those of Schubert range from ballad—and magic—operas to Italian style "grand opera", and the subjects did not afford scope for the devotional mood expressed in his liturgical music and in some of his songs. Weber was a composer of romantic operas first and foremost: they contain supernatural and magical elements, but the religious note is struck only in certain passages of *Der Freischütz*, such as Agathe's prayer and Max's song "Hatt denn der Himmel mich verlassen?" Zamiel, the wild huntsman, is no doubt an embodiment of the devil, but his part is spoken, not sung. The scene in the Wolf's Glen is, however, graphic in its portrayal of gruesome terror, and can be compared with the representations or glimpses of the infernal regions which various composers from Monteverdi onwards have vouchsafed to us and which accord with the religious belief in Hades or Hell that persisted through the ages. Rossini in his *Stabat Mater* introduced an operatic style into the liturgy: he did not reverse the process. Bellini's *Norma* is the tragic story of the High Priestess of a druidical temple; most of its music is not religious in character, but in "Casta Diva", where she prays to the Moon goddess for the return of the Roman leader, Pollione, whom she loves, the gentle moving phrases of the melody reflect, in their own delicate, exquisite fashion, the emotions of the character.

It is remarkable that of Berlioz's three operas, *Béatrice et Bénédict* should be the one that does not include any religious music: for though he called himself an unbeliever, he was (as we have seen) constantly setting devotional words, and in Shakespeare's *Much Ado About Nothing*, on which this opera was based, the church scene at the interrupted wedding of Claudio and Hero, and the Christian character of Friar Francis, are essential parts of the story; but they do not figure in Berlioz's work, which is simply a beautiful comic opera. *Benvenuto Cellini*, however, the libretto of which is a dramatic version of the life of the great sixteenth-century sculptor, does contain in its third act some beautiful music for a religious procession, accompanied by a prayer which Teresa (his beloved) and Ascanio (his apprentice) utter for his safety. Some of the music of *Les Troyens* is also religious: in "La prise de Troie", the Trojan march and hymn, which recur throughout both parts of the opera, first appear in solemn form sung by the priests and the people, with a majestic orchestral accompaniment. The scene in which Andromache, Hector's widow, and her son Astyanax lay their offerings on the altar, the boy is blessed by King Priam, and the two of them move away, is accompanied by quiet effects on the orchestra and a moving melody on the clarinet. In "Les Troyens à Carthage" we have the Carthaginian hymn sung by the chorus, the recurring march with its sacred call to duty, the invocation of the priests of Pluto to the gods of the underworld to bring vengeance on the departing Trojans, and the final transfiguration of the march with harp accompaniment. These religious moments contribute to the grandeur of the whole conception.

The year 1813 saw the births of Verdi and Wagner. Both of them devoted their genius mostly to opera, both expressed Christianity in their art; but Verdi, whose personal character was more truly Christian than Wagner's, did so by composing liturgical works, few in number, but several of them of great beauty, rather than by introducing religion into his operas, which he only did incidentally.

For example, *Nabucco* (Nebuchadnezzar), though dealing with a Biblical subject, is intrinsically more dramatic than religious, but there is a genuine devotional character in the moving prayer of Zachariah, the High Priest of the Jews, at the beginning of the second scene of Act II, when he beseeches God to speak to the heathen through his lips; in Nebuchadnezzar's entreaty to Jehovah for forgiveness in the first scene of the fourth act; and in the proclamation of faith in Jehovah which he and the chorus of Babylonians sing in the final scene.

I Lombardi aroused difficulty with the Archbishop of Milan when it was first written because it represented some of the rites of the Church on the stage, and the heroine's prayer is one of the features in this early opera of Verdi's that still maintains its appeal.

In *Il Trovatore*, the scene in the cloister of a convent contains a beautiful effect when the chorus of nuns sing their unaccompanied song, just before the entry of Leonora. In the penultimate scene, the priests' " Miserere " chant has an ecclesiastical flavour, which provides a moving background to Leonora's notes of anguish in a minor key and the prayer in the major sung by Manrico behind the prison bars.

In *La Forza del Destino*, " Madre, pietosa Vergine ", the melody of which comes in the overture, is sung by Donna Leonora as she kneels near the convent by moonlight, in Act II, and the priests are heard chanting from inside the building. Her duet with the Father Superior; the scene which follows between her and the Friars; her song " Pace, Pace " in the last act; and the closing trio of the opera; all these are imbued with religious feeling.

Aïda is a story of Egypt in the time of the Pharaohs, and there are passages of a devotional kind in the course of its lovely score. At the end of the first scene Aïda prays to Heaven in moving tones to take pity upon her. The next scene shows Ramphis, the High Priest, before the altar of the temple of Vulcan at Memphis, with other priests and priestesses; their chant, with its descending and ascending intervals of three semitones, has an oriental flavour, and so has the sacred dance which follows. The chant returns in the wonderful double scene at the end of the opera, sung by the priests and priestesses in the temple, while Aïda and Radamès utter their last music together in the tomb below.

In the final act of *Otello*, when Emilia has left Desdemona after the affecting farewell between them, Boito (as librettist) and Verdi have made an addition to Shakespeare in the form of an " Ave Maria " which Desdemona sings to the accompaniment of muted strings; it has a marvellously soothing effect after the heartrending music which has preceded it.

Now, Wagner produced one non-operatic religious composition, *The Love-feast of the Apostles*, for male voices and orchestra, but it is not of great intrinsic interest apart from the place which it occupies in his artistic development. On the other hand he introduced more Christianity into his stage works than any composer of operas before him. This may seem strange in view of the character of the man. He was the most egocentric person among all the great composers. He had an inveterate thirst for physical luxury. He proved ungrateful to Meyerbeer, who—whether from simple generosity of heart or from calculating motives or from a mixture of both—had been extremely kind to him. Wagner's anti-semitism, too, was clearly incompatible with a truly Christian spirit. Yet he was loved and honoured by many fine people among his contemporaries, and his religious beliefs were unquestionably sincere. It is necessary to insist on this, because he has been attacked not only for excelling in the composition of erotic and voluptuous music but even on the ground that he wrote *Parsifal* with his tongue in his cheek. Nothing could be further from the truth; and however much his art may be disliked by some people, his integrity as an artist cannot fairly be disputed.

Wagner's own attitude towards Christianity requires to be considered carefully.[1] At the beginning of his essay *Religion and Art* he quotes an extract from a letter written by Schiller to Goethe: " In the Christian religion I find an intrinsic predisposition to the highest and noblest, while its various manifestations in life appear to me so repulsive and insipid because these are only abortive representations of the highest." He begins the essay itself: " One may say that where religion becomes artificial it behoves art to rescue the quintessence of religion by apprehending the figurative value of the mystical symbols which religion would have us believe in their literal sense, and by revealing the hidden depths of the truth of these symbols by means of an ideal representation."

He wrote a lot of moonshine to the effect that the human race had been degenerating steadily for thousands of years, partly because it had been eating the wrong food, and partly because it had lacked the guidance of Schopenhauer's philosophy. And he thought that the will to live must complete itself in the will to redeem and that this was to be achieved by a return to the principle of pure Christianity via music.

Yet, stripped of a certain amount of nonsense and verbiage, Wagner's conception of Christianity, though not sectarian, did not differ much in essentials from that of countless other Christians of his own day and ours. He was not the only one to hold that the Church had in fact done evil things in its history, for example by means of the Inquisition,

[1] In this and the following two paragraphs I am specially indebted to Mr. Ernest Newman's great *Life of Richard Wagner* and have taken the liberty of reproducing certain translations of short extracts from the German which appeared in it.

the burning of heretics, and the actions of some of the medieval Popes. Where he went wrong was in not giving it credit for its innumerable acts of goodness. He believed in pity for the poor and oppressed, in renunciation, and in regarding Christ as the centre of our existence. During a great part of his life he had the absurd—and un-Christian—notion that the Germans were superior to all races, but in 1879 he wrote to Konstantin Franz that he thought Germany would have relapsed into barbarism by the middle of the next millennium, and that the salvation of the world lay only in Christianity. He was greatly concerned because Germany had come to worship militarism and commercialism.

It is in the light of these facts that we can consider the religious elements which in various forms and different degrees are present in each of the series of Wagner's greatest operas starting with *Der Fliegende Holländer* and ending with *Parsifal*.

Wagner was familiar with the legend of the Flying Dutchman before he embarked on the voyage from Riga to London on his way to Paris in 1839, which stimulated his imagination to compose the vivid music of the sea that is so conspicuous a feature of the score of his opera. The story was confirmed to him by the seamen when the ship put into a Norwegian port. It told how Vanderdecken, the captain of an Amsterdam vessel, swore to round the Cape of Good Hope in spite of rough weather, even if he had to beat about till the Day of Judgment; how either the Devil or Heaven (according to different versions) accepted his challenge and, as a punishment for his blasphemy, condemned him to sail till Doomsday, unless, when his ship reached harbour once every seven years, he should meet a woman who loved him so devotedly as to sacrifice her life for the sake of his redemption. In his first aria in the opera, in the key of C minor, against a shimmering background in the 'cellos and basses and impressive notes on the trombones, the Dutchman asks the angel of God for salvation and goes on to tell of his only real hope, that when the Day of Judgment ultimately comes, amid the sounding of the trumpets of God, he himself will attain the mercy of destruction. In the second act Senta sings her ballad, telling of the curse upon the Dutchman and vowing that if the angel of God guides him to her she will redeem him by her devotion. We hear the theme of redemption; and at the end of the opera, when she has thrown herself from the cliff into the sea and the Dutch phantom ship has sunk with all the crew, the souls of Senta and the Dutchman in visible form rise to Heaven, and this same theme is transfigured, as it had been at the close of the overture, by a musical apotheosis. No doubt there is something autobiographical in the figure of the Dutchman, with whom Wagner identified himself as a wanderer through the world hoping for the unselfish love of the ideal woman. But on Senta's part the sacrifice of her life for the sake of the man to whom she has sworn her devotion is a religious act in harmony with the Christian ideal of love. Christ's name does not occur in the libretto, but the conception inspired Wagner's music. This redemption idea did not figure in all the earlier versions of the story, and it is significant that Wagner should have adopted it and should have made it the focal point of his opera. In different forms and degrees it reappears in *Tannhäuser*, *Lohengrin*, *The Ring* and *Parsifal*.

Tannhäuser is second only to *Parsifal* in its specifically Christian character. Wagner wove the story of the opera from many strands, which, either in medieval legend and tradition or in his own, possibly subconscious, imagination, had become associated with the historical Tannhäuser, a thirteenth-century Minnesinger. Anyone coming to the opera for the first time may well wonder at a libretto which includes the goddess Venus side by side with medieval Christian beliefs. The deities of Nordic mythology, which had long dominated the minds of the German people, were ultimately defeated by Christianity, though traces of them survived in other forms; but they were not the only pagan divinities with which the Christians had to contend: thanks to Roman infiltration, the Germans had acquired a knowledge of the Latin gods, and the legend of a mountain in Thuringia inside which Venus, the Roman goddess of carnal love, held sway, is told in the *Tannhäuserlied*, a fifteenth- or sixteenth-century ballad. This describes how the knight, Tannhäuser, was a slave to the voluptuous delights of Venus, escaped when he invoked the Virgin Mary, and implored pardon of the Pope, who, however, declared that his staff would put forth green leaves before Tannhäuser should attain grace; the knight, therefore, believing that there was no welcome for him in Heaven, returned to the arms of Venus; soon afterwards the Pope's staff started by a miracle to produce green shoots, and he sent to find Tannhäuser in vain: the knight remained in the Venusberg, and the ballad ends by consigning the Pope's soul to eternal damnation!

There was an old Italian legend (described by the French writer Antoine de la Sale early in the fifteenth century) about a Sibyl who held court inside the Monte della Sibylla, in the Apennines: an adventurous German made his way into the place and after enjoying its delights for nearly a year found that the Sibyl and her beautiful companions turned themselves periodically into snakes; so he departed to Rome to confess his sin for having stayed in so wicked an abode; the Pope, in order to make an example of him, angrily ordered him from his presence, but afterwards relented and tried to trace him; the German, however, had returned to the joys of the Sibyl and her ladies. It may well be that this Italian story found its way into Germany and was either the origin or one of the origins of the Tannhäuser legend or became somehow intertwined with it.

The tale of the Contest of Song at the Wartburg, which occupies so important a place in Wagner's opera, had nothing to do with the story of Tannhäuser until Wagner welded them together. Wagner's Elisabeth, the niece of the Landgrave, was partly derived from the thirteenth-century St. Elisabeth who was married to Ludwig IV, King of Thuringia, in her childhood and exerted a saintly influence over him until his early death. In the second act of the opera she saves Tannhäuser's life when he is threatened by the knights, and at the end her death brings him salvation.

Thus in Wagner we have the conflict between sacred and profane love; the devotional element, represented by the Pilgrims; and the final redemption.

From the start, the composer sets the religious aspect of the opera by beginning the overture with the song of the Pilgrims, which, within the limitations of the type of four-square melody characteristic of his early period, is a fine tune, devotional in quality; it rises to a climax, accompanied by a triplet figure on the violins (which Wagner called " The Pulse of Life ") and then dies away. Any suggestion that Wagner was more adept at writing erotic than noble music is negatived by the countless examples of his equal mastery elsewhere in expressing spiritual grandeur and the fact that the Venusberg music, in its revised form, was composed for the Paris version sixteen years later, by which time he had finished *Tristan und Isolde*, and therefore shows him at the height of his powers: he realised then that something wilder and more voluptuous than his original music for this scene was needed to provide the requisite contrast to the other, spiritual elements of the score. He paints the picture in vivid colours, and surrounds Venus with supernatural beings associated with classical mythology—nymphs, naiads, sirens, bacchantes, satyrs, fauns and Cupids, with the Three

Graces revealing visions of Jupiter's amours, the Rape of Europa and Leda and the Swan.

When Tannhäuser, wearying of all these allurements, calls upon the Virgin Mary, the Venusberg disappears and he finds himself in a sunny valley. He hears a shepherd playing a pastoral melody on a pipe and singing the praises of Holda, the Nordic goddess of spring: this episode is not only like a breath of fresh air after the heated atmosphere of the previous scene: it was an artistic touch on Wagner's part to provide this interlude before the song of the Pilgrims which follows: it acts as a kind of stepping-stone between the pagan delights of the Venusberg and their expression of Christian devotion: without it, the change would have been too abrupt. The sound of the shepherd's pipe is still heard at times during the Pilgrims' chant; and as they make their way across the stage and pass gradually out of hearing, Tannhäuser echoes their music of repentance and prays for forgiveness.

In the second act, after the Contest of Song, when Tannhäuser has disgraced himself by his song in praise of Venus, Elisabeth utters a plea to all the company that his life may be spared. In an impressive chorus the minstrels hail her as an angel from Heaven, and he prays to God for mercy. The music of the Pilgrims is heard in the distance; and at the bidding of the Landgrave, the knights and the minstrels, Tannhäuser, to the strains of the theme of Atonement, rushes away to accompany them to Rome and to ask the Pope for divine pardon.

The instrumental prelude to Act III, which depicts Tannhäuser's journey, is mainly religious in character: the Pilgrims' song, the theme of Elisabeth's entreaty on his behalf; another one describing his misery; and the solemn but joyful music to which later he tells Wolfram, the minstrel, about the grace vouchsafed to the other pilgrims—all these in turn are unfolded before us. Then in the valley of the Wartburg we see Elisabeth at prayer. Wolfram, who also loves her, enters and prays for her. The Pilgrims return, singing their chant; Elisabeth watches them as they go by, and when she finds that Tannhäuser is not with them, she sings her beautiful prayer, beseeching the Virgin to admit her spirit into the Kingdom of Heaven. After she has ascended again to the castle of the Wartburg, and Wolfram has sung his air to the star of evening, Tannhäuser staggers in, and tells him of his tragic pilgrimage, his sufferings on the journey, his confession of his sins and the Pope's harsh judgment. He now seeks only the Venusberg: a vision of it appears to him; but when Wolfram invokes the name Elisabeth, Venus and her train disappear. A funeral procession enters, bringing the corpse of Elisabeth; Tannhäuser utters a prayer over it, and dies. Younger pilgrims come in, carrying the Pope's staff which has put forth green leaves, and singing a hymn of praise for the sinner's redemption. All the company join in the original Pilgrims' song, which began the overture, while the motive of "The Pulse of Life" is again heard on the violins.

Thus the whole opera—both the drama and the music—is predominantly religious, and Christian, in spirit: the allurements of Venus and her train are presented entirely for the purpose of showing the power of goodness and faith to overcome them.

The background of *Lohengrin* is partly historical, partly legendary, and partly religious. Henry the Fowler, King of Saxony, has come to Antwerp to try to persuade the Brabantines to join him in resisting the Hungarian invaders. He finds Brabant in a turmoil. Gottfried, son of the late Duke, has mysteriously disappeared, and his sister Elsa has been accused of murdering him by her guardian Telramund, who is married to Ortrud, daughter of the Prince of Friesland. Telramund claims rulership of Brabant through his wife's right. It is agreed to settle the issue by combat between Telramund and any champion who may appear on Elsa's behalf. A knight arrives in a boat drawn by a swan and offers to be her champion. Elsa promises to wed him if he wins the fight and never to ask him his name or origin. He defeats Telramund, but spares his life. Telramund and Ortrud plot to recover their lost honours, and Ortrud urges Elsa to ask the forbidden questions. Telramund accuses the Knight of sorcery. Nevertheless the marriage is duly celebrated, but when Elsa is alone with her husband she cannot resist the impulse to ask him who he is. Telramund and his companions break into the marriage chamber, and the Knight kills him. When the body of Telramund is borne before the King, the Knight speaks of the cause of his death and of Elsa's broken promise, and tells his own story: far away is the Castle of Monsalvat, where the Holy Grail is guarded by its Knights; Parsifal is King of that land, and he is Lohengrin, Parsifal's son, a Knight of the Grail and thus gifted with supernatural power against which nothing could prevail so long as the secret of his origin was not disclosed; now that Elsa has obliged him to reveal it, he must return to Monsalvat. The swan reappears, drawing the boat. Ortrud reveals that the swan is Gottfried whom she had transformed. In response to Lohengrin's prayer, the dove of the Grail descends, and Lohengrin loosens the swan, which is transformed back into the human form of Gottfried. Lohengrin enters the boat, which the dove draws away. Ortrud collapses with a cry, and Elsa falls dead in Gottfried's arms.

Wagner, in framing his libretto, drew to some extent upon the French epic *Le Chevalier au Cygne*, but much more upon the story of Lohengrin as told in Wolfram von Eschenbach's early thirteenth-century epic *Parzival*, in another medieval poem called *Der jüngere Titurel*, and above all in an anonymous German epic *Lohengrin* written about 1260.

The religious elements in the story and the music are those connected with the Holy Grail; and the prelude to the opera, according to Wagner's own description, represents the growing glory of a vision of the Grail, which, when it reaches its height, consecrates the beholder to its service and is then gradually borne aloft by the angel host. This conception is miraculously depicted by ethereal music on the violins, later reinforced by the woodwind, with the brass, kettledrums and cymbals crashing in at the climax of the vision, which ultimately fades away in the celestial harmonies on the violins with which the prelude had begun. Whenever the stately theme of the Grail is heard throughout the opera, and the Lohengrin motive expressing knightly purity, the music takes on a mystical cast, in contrast to the sinister character of Ortrud and the evil and hatred which she instils into the mind of Telramund. This supernatural, religious quality in the score reaches its consummation in Lohengrin's narration in the third act; and the opera ends, as it began, with the mysticism of the Grail music while he gradually disappears from view.

The greatest of Wagner's creations were still to come. In none of these, however, except *Parsifal*, does religion play so large a part as it does in *Tannhäuser* and *Lohengrin*, but in *Parsifal* it is the mainspring of the drama and the music.

Tristan und Isolde is a human tragedy with a mystical cast. The legend is of great antiquity, and Wagner with his usual skill condensed the innumerable elements which had come down to him from so many sources into a greatly simplified form, suitable for his purposes. Tristan may, at some stage in the remote medieval past, have figured as a semi-divine hero, but the mystical element in Wagner's treatment of the story does not depend on this. In his music-drama the love of Tristan and Isolde does not begin with the drinking of the potion. It is made clear to us in Isolde's narration to Brangäne in Act I, that when Tristan was lying, wounded, in Isolde's care she was on the point of killing him in revenge because she had recognised him as the conqueror of her betrothed, Morold, but that when their eyes met her heart had melted in pity and the sword had dropped from her hand. From that moment their love had come into being, and the potion only released the barriers which had held it in check. On Tristan's side it had been restrained by his devotion to his uncle, King Marke, for whose sake he was unselfishly escorting Isolde to Cornwall, and on her side by her anger against Tristan for the death of Morold and for his action in bringing her as a bride for the weary and aged King. They were destined for one another by Fate, and if their love could not be continued in this world, then they must pass through the valley of the shadow of death together, so that they might be united in the next world in love eternal.

This unearthly linking of love and death is contained in the very opening notes of the prelude. It is the dominant idea—poetical and musical—which pervades the drama from start to finish. It underlies Isolde's reference (in her discourse to Brangäne early in Act II) to the love goddess, Frau Minne, who holds life and death in her hand and controls Isolde's destiny. It is reflected in the mystical duet between the lovers, when they contrast the lies and falsehoods of this world of ours, which they call "Day" and regard as their enemy, with the other eternal world of "Night" in which true love can continue without ending. This love music is indeed ecstatic, but it is also exalted; and exaltation is the quality that inhabits Isolde's "Liebestod" at the end of the drama, as she sings of the waves of sound which are reuniting her to Tristan in death that will be life everlasting, and symbolise, too, the mystic joy of the universe.

The conception of a predestined love ordained by Fate between man and woman may not be strictly Christian, but it is in essence religious. The devoted loyalty of Brangäne to Isolde; the staunch, self-sacrificing fidelity of Tristan's servant, Kurvenal; the nobility of King Marke, who speaks in sorrow, not in anger, to Tristan when he finds the lovers together, and afterwards, when he has learnt the whole truth, seeks, too late, to give Isolde in marriage to him[1]; and the mystical idealism of the love between Tristan and Isolde as expressed both in the words and in the exalted music that Wagner created; all these things show what a complete misconception existed in the minds of those who found something "immoral" in this tremendous masterpiece.

[1] This is actually stated in Wagner's text, which, moreover, contains no indication that Isolde had ever become King Marke's wife.

The score of *Die Meistersinger* contains a great deal of divinity, but very little expressed religion. This beautiful work is a tale of simple love and friendship, of jealousy and kindliness, of fellowship and good humour, of pedantry and broad humanity, told in music which is by turns mellow in its wisdom, tender in its emotions, humorous in idiom, dignified in utterance, warm in sympathy, sunny and genial in its outlook. The characters are those of ordinary men and women. Alone of Wagner's great operas, it includes no supernatural elements. A religious passage occurs immediately after the prelude, on the rising of the curtain, when the congregation in St. Catherine's Church, Nuremberg, are singing a chorale of great beauty, accompanied by an organ on the stage, but even in the course of this we hear on the orchestra anticipations (already presented to us in the prelude) of the music later associated with Walther's love for Eva, as he gazes at her and she modestly glances at him in return. The G major theme with which the citizens of Nuremberg pay homage to Hans Sachs in the final scene of the opera, and which has been heard previously in the prelude to Act III, is described by Wagner as the solemn song with which the historical Sachs greeted Luther and the Reformation; the words are not sacred, but the music is hymn-like in character.

By contrast with *Die Meistersinger*, *The Ring* is full of beings who are in some degree either superhuman or other than human. They are all pagan gods and goddesses or the offspring of gods by a mortal or immortal mother, or else they are giants or gnomes, Rhine-maidens or Norns. The Siegfried legend, which sprang from the German Rhineland, is of unknown antiquity; it was popular in the fifth century, and also became associated with the historical defeat of the kingdom of Burgundy by the Huns in A.D. 437 and the death of Attila, " The Scourge of God ", in 453, on the very night of his marriage to Ildico. The story travelled northward to Scandinavia and was ultimately embodied in the *Volsunga-saga* in the twelfth century; a later version of it was contained in the *Thidrek-saga*; but it attained its complete form in the German epic, the *Nibelungen-lied*. Wagner used materials from all these pagan sources. In his First Sketch for *The Ring*, written in 1848, he conceived three contesting forces in the world, none of them human: the race of Giants, lazy, stupid and concerned only for their own physical security: Alberich, the dwarf, greedy for wealth and dominion and able to subjugate his fellow Nibelungs by his superior cunning; and the Gods, who are actuated by a desire to save the world both from the evil ambitions of the

Nibelung and from the slothful materialism of the Giants. Yet the Gods cannot themselves achieve that noble object, because there is a moral defect at the heart of their power: the golden Ring, which confers power to rule the world, has been wrested from Alberich by guile and force which they have exercised. He has laid the curse of death on everyone who shall acquire it. It has been yielded by the Gods in payment to the Giants for their labour in building the castle of Valhalla, from which the Gods had hoped to govern the world beneficently, and has been left by the Giants in the custody of a dragon. Thus the Gods cannot recover it without committing another wrongful act, and can only win liberation for the world by creating a semi-divine hero who by his free-will can bring about that redemption which their original sinful act has prevented them from achieving—by restoring the Ring to the Rhine-maidens, who had been robbed by Alberich of the gold from which he subsequently fashioned it, and thus rendering it incapable of further harm.

Now, if it had been practicable for Wagner to create his great tetralogy in this form, which would have invested the story with a moral grandeur through the lofty purpose which inspired the Gods in their ultimate objective, the music might have acquired a more deeply mystical or religious character in addition to the infinite variety of its other qualities. But the conception embodied in the First Sketch, in so far as it differs from the final version, proved too vague, too symbolic for presentation on the stage. When Wagner came to closer grips with his vast subject, the scheme took a more concrete shape, but lost something of its elevated character in the process. The symbolic part played by the entire race of Giants in the original version was no longer realised when transferred to two Giants only; the beneficent purpose of the Gods had disappeared, and in its place we have the figure of Wotan, dominated by a thirst for world power and ready to make a contract with the Giants which he did not even mean to fulfil—to exchange Freia, the goddess of youth, health and beauty, in return for their labour—and then to evade it when the time came.

In *The Ring*, as we have it, Wagner shows us the flaws and weaknesses of the worship of the old Teuton deities. He presents the overthrow of Wotan's kingdom by the power of mortal love and heroism, and exhibits in music, words and spectacle, the ultimate downfall of this very imperfect theocracy and of its mighty castle in the clouds. In this general theme of the collapse of a pagan religion, and of its yielding place to a higher and purer order of things, we may perceive a religious allegory. The emphasis on the evil power of gold, too, is a frequently recurring theme in the Bible, and reflected, for example, in Romeo's words to the Apothecary in Shakespeare's *Romeo and Juliet*[1]

> There is thy gold, worse poison to men's souls,
> Doing more murder in this loathsome world
> Than these poor compounds that thou mayst not sell.
> I sell thee poison, thou hast sold me none.

Again, we find in *The Ring*, the redemption idea that recurs in Wagner's operas. Sieglinde in Act III of *Die Walküre* tells Brünnhilde that for Siegmund's sake she will save the child (Siegfried) that she bears in her womb, responding to the Valkyrie's appeal in the great musical motive of "Redemption by love", which returns in the orchestra in the last act of *Götterdämmerung* and brings the whole tetralogy to a serene and majestic close.

But in spite of these factors, we find in the vast drama and wondrous music of *The Ring* everything else in greater measure than a specifically religious element—profound and subtle characterisation, the beauty and the storms of nature, the glamour of old legends, the loves, hopes, sorrows and tragedies of beings who are other than human, yet endowed with human attributes and emotions. It could not be otherwise; for the religious ideas inherent in the theocracy of Wotan and the other divinities in the story, especially as unfolded in Wagner's ultimate version, were far removed from his own beliefs. Gluck could discover in certain aspects of the ancient Greek religion something sufficiently in common with his personal convictions, or at any rate akin to his own outlook, to enable him to enter imaginatively into their spirit and so to produce music which was a sympathetic reflection of it. Wagner could not compose truly religious music for his *Ring* story, except to the limited extent which I have tried to indicate. The subject which enabled him to do this in full measure was the Christian legend of *Parsifal*.

Parsifal was the first opera which was religious from beginning to end. It is not even necessary to exclude Klingsor and the Flower Maidens from this description; for they present the vital element of contrast to the sacred character of so much of the music and words not associated with them. Without Klingsor, symbolising the forces of evil, and the Flower Maidens who are the embodiment of temptation,

[1] Act V, scene 1, lines 80-3.

there would have been no drama, no conflict, and Wagner's spiritual purpose would not have been revealed. They are as essential for his design as the pictures of the wicked and of Satan in the Bible.

Neither in the twelfth-century French poem, *Li Contes del Graal*, by Crestien de Troyes, nor in Wolfram von Eschenbach's *Parzival*, is the Grail depicted as the Cup from which Jesus and His disciples drank at the Last Supper, nor is the spear, that figures in the story, identified with the weapon with which Christ's side was pierced as He hung from the Cross. Wagner was more indebted for his dramatic scheme to *Parzival* than to any other source, and in Wolfram's great poem the Grail was the magic stone which restored the phoenix to life from its own ashes and kept a sick man alive for a week after he had looked at it; its only connection with Christianity was that its powers were renewed every Good Friday by a white dove descending from heaven with a wafer in its beak and laying this on the stone, which was thus enabled to provide food and drink in rich abundance to the Knights of the Grail. The idea that the Grail was the Cup of the Last Supper and was also the vessel in which the blood of Jesus that flowed from the wound caused by the spear was preserved, is a later addition to the story, which Wagner adopted. It was Wagner himself who first represented that sacred spear as the one with which Klingsor, the evil magician, wounded Amfortas, the King of the Knights of the Grail, so that he could only be healed by the touch of that self-same weapon. And the fullness of the character of Kundry, as depicted in the music-drama, is also mainly Wagner's creation—a strange being, anxious in the depths of her soul to serve the Grail, yet long prevented from doing so because she once tempted Klingsor and has thus fallen under his spell and is obliged to perform his will; but after his overthrow repentant and ultimately baptised and pardoned.

Wagner has not only welded the many ingredients of the old Parsifal story and the legend of the Grail into a wonderful unity through his characteristic skill in selection, but has infused the whole with a deeply religious spirit of Christian mysticism. This mystic quality is conveyed in the very first motive with which the prelude opens, by means of an intentionally vague rhythm and a melody at first unaccompanied; later in the opera it is associated with the administration of the bread and wine in the Hall of the Grail, but in part also with the suffering of Amfortas and the spear. From this and the motive of the Grail, which is based on the traditional "Dresden Amen", and the stately motive of Faith, the entire prelude is woven.

The story is allegorical. Parsifal, portrayed in the first act as a "guileless fool", who fails to ask Amfortas what ails him, and only learning wisdom through experience, really personifies Christianity, triumphing over Paganism as represented by Klingsor. Thus Parsifal, by regaining the sacred spear, is able to redeem Kundry and to heal the wound of Amfortas, and at the end is proclaimed King of the brotherhood in his stead. The score of the opera is a wondrous fabric of motives, constantly transformed according to the needs of the drama and the deep meanings which Wagner's genius infuses into them as the mystical story unfolds itself. The wild Kundry motive, the sinister music of Klingsor, the seductive strains of the Flower Maidens, and some of the religious themes which appear in the opera, do not figure at all in the prelude; but others are transmutations of those which have first been heard in the prelude in their simplest form. Parsifal himself is portrayed by a motive expressive of knightly gallantry. The Transformation music is majestic and awe-inspiring, with its solemn rhythm, accompanied by the bells of the castle of Monsalvat and afterwards entwined with the motive of Faith and the Grail. When Kundry in the second act tells Parsifal of his childhood and how his widowed mother, Herzeleide, had brought him up in the forest in the hope that he might remain safe from the perils and madness of the world, and how she had died of grief when he wandered away and did not come back to her, the music becomes infinitely tender and pathetic. In the third act we have the serene beauty of the Good Friday music and the ethereal close of the opera in the Hall of the Knights, when the themes of the Grail, Faith and the Sacrament are entwined upon a pattern of celestial arpeggios. These are only some of the passages of transcendent loveliness which are to be found in this deeply religious music-drama.

Parsifal has been attacked on the ground that it portrays, or even defaces, mysteries which ought not to be revealed in any theatre. There is no substance in these objections. Even apart from the ritualistic origins of ancient Greek drama, religious drama in the Christian era is of great antiquity and has achieved a significant revival in the present century in the works of T. S. Eliot, Dorothy Sayers, Christopher Fry and others. There is, therefore, no reason why religious opera, also, provided that it treats its subject sincerely and reverently, should not have its place. *Parsifal* was the first entirely religious opera to be composed; the example which Wagner set has been followed in our own time by Vaughan Williams and almost as completely by Hindemith; but before we deal with them, let us glance at the occasional treatment of religious elements in operas by composers born later than Wagner and Verdi.

Gounod, although he wrote sacred oratorios in the last period of his life, was gifted chiefly as a composer of charming love music, entrancing waltzes and tuneful marches: his Mephistopheles in *Faust* is more a pantomime demon than a sinister Devil, and the profound character of the story is not to be found in his opera. Yet do not let us be too hard on him! His religious feeling was entirely sincere, although it did not strike deep; and so in the church scene in Act IV, when Marguérite kneels to pray and hears the voices of Mephistopheles and the invisible demons, the music which she sings and the *chant religieux* accompanied by the organ are appropriate in their setting; in the trio in the last scene of the opera Marguérite's ecstatic entreaty to the angels to save her from the powers of darkness is telling in its effect, and so is the final chorus of the angelic host. In *Roméo et Juliette* Gounod introduces an ecclesiastical element into his score by beginning the prelude to the third act with a fugue, which strikes the right note for the scene in Friar Laurence's cell, and the music associated with the Friar is suitably solemn, just as Sutermeister's is in his opera on the same subject produced in 1939.

Bizet's *Carmen* is not usually associated in people's minds with religion, for all the divinity of beauty in its wonderful score. But Micaela's song in the third act, when she comes to seek out Don José at the smugglers' retreat in order to persuade him to come to his dying mother, is largely a prayer to God to grant her courage: it is generally regarded as one of the gems of the opera. Micaela does not figure in Prosper Mérimée's novel and was the creation of the librettists, Meilhac and Halévy; the original story exemplified the truth that the wages of sin is death, but the introduction of Micaela, whose sweetness and purity act as a foil to the fiery allurement of Carmen, added to the tragedy of passion, rivalry and revenge, a conflict between sacred and profane love. Bizet showed the many-sided nature of his genius by not only depicting the irresistible attraction of Carmen, the life and colour of early nineteenth-century Seville and the beauty and stillness of the mountains, but also by giving to Micaela, whenever she appears, some of his loveliest music.

Two other French composers brought religion into the opera house —Massenet with his *Thaïs*, *Hérodiade* and *Le Jongleur de Notre-Dame*, and Saint-Saëns with *Samson et Dalila*. It is strange nowadays to reflect that the last-named work was at first banned from the stage of Covent Garden because it dealt with a Biblical subject: anything more innocuous it would be hard to imagine, and the opera is chiefly notable for its lyrical qualities and its spectacular effects rather than any very devotional feeling. This and Richard Strauss' *Salomé* are exceptional in being based on Biblical episodes. But Strauss did not shine primarily as a composer of religious music; and perhaps it was characteristic of him that in choosing a story from the Bible he should have turned to Wilde's version of it and produced an opera which is masterly in its pathological handling of a bestial subject but certainly not religious in character.

The historical Boris Godounov was probably not guilty of the death of Ivan the Terrible's little son, Dmitri, but both in Pushkin's play and Moussorgsky's opera, *Boris Godounov*, he is presented as a murderer who is haunted by his guilty conscience. The real protagonist, however, is the Russian people, and it was in keeping with the national character of the tragedy that it should have a religious background. In the Prologue the first scene is the courtyard of a monastery near Moscow, where the people have assembled to entreat Boris to become Tsar in succession to Feodor, who has just died. Stchelkalov, the Clerk of the Douma, urges them in moving accents to pray to God to enlighten the soul of Boris. A chorus of Pilgrims enters, singing a hymn to God for the protection of Russia, on their way into the monastery where they are to beg Boris' sister to try to persuade him to accept the throne. The scene changes to the courtyard of the Kremlin, with a crowd of people occupying the space between the two Cathedrals of the Assumption and the Archangels. There is a mighty clanging of bells. Boris has accepted and is acclaimed by the people and the nobles, who are moving in stately procession to the Cathedral of the Assumption. Boris himself touches a note of sadness and anxiety, and asks the people to kneel in prayer before the tombs of the Russian Tsars and then to feast as his guests.

The religious atmosphere of the drama and the music is never absent for long. In the first scene of Act I, in a cell of the Monastery of the Miracle, Pimen, an old monk, is writing the last page of his history of Russia—a task which God assigned to him—while Gregory, who is to become the pseudo-Dmitri and Pretender to the throne, sleeps near him: when he wakes, Pimen tells him the story of the murder. Monks are heard uttering their prayers behind the scene.

In the opening scene of Act II, when Boris, in his apartments in the

Kremlin, sings his fine aria, musing over the sorrows and disappointments of his reign, he tells how he has been haunted by the vision of the dead Dmitri and beseeches the Almighty to save him. Later, after he has been warned by Prince Shuisky of the rising of the Pretender, the same apparition presents itself to his guilty imagination, and he entreats God to have mercy upon him. The music of this scene is of tremendous power and grandeur.

In the last act, the crowd hail the pseudo-Dmitri as the Tsar whom the Lord has rescued. When Boris is uttering his dying song, he prays to God to pour down His saving grace and love upon his innocent children, and begs for divine forgiveness.

If there is a religious background for *Boris Godounov*, religion may be said to be in the foreground of Moussorgsky's other historical opera, *Khovanshchina*. As a matter of history, before the time of Tsar Boris, the Russian Christian Church, being Byzantine in form, was governed from Constantinople; but Boris, in order to win the support of the clergy in Russia, set up a Patriarchate at Moscow in the middle of the seventeenth century. Nikon the Patriarch introduced many revisions of the liturgical books and reforms of the ritual, which split the nation and the Church into two main bodies—the Old Believers, who clung to the traditional form of worship, and the Reformers. Feodor, the eldest son of the Tsar Alexis, died without issue, and was succeeded by the ten-year-old Peter (afterwards " the Great "), his brother Ivan being of feeble intellect. Their half-sister, Sophia, became Regent and, in order to support the claims of Ivan, organised a rebellion of the Streltsy, a regiment of Guards most of whom were Old Believers and who were led by Prince Ivan Khovansky. Later, when the regency ended, Peter crushed the " Khovanshchina " revolt, and ultimately many of the Old Believers committed suicide rather than accept the changes introduced by one whom they regarded as Anti-Christ.

Moussorgsky's opera combines this story of religious strife with a tragic love interest, and the many beautiful passages include music that is ecclesiastical in character, such as the chants sung by the chorus of Old Believers.

Holst's *Savitri* (composed in 1908), an episode from Mahabharata, contains only three characters: Satyavan, a woodman; Savitri, his wife; and Death. It shows how the mysticism of the Hindu religion can appeal to an unconventional Christian like Holst. After Satyavan has died, Savitri welcomes Death in simple tones, against the distant sound of female voices blending with the music of a flute; in a dialogue she strives with Death for the restoration of her husband's life, and ultimately her love triumphs: Satyavan is restored to her, she tells him how one of the Holy Ones has visited and blessed them, and the little opera ends in the mystic calm of unearthly harmonies, as Death fades into the darkness.

Religion—thank goodness!—sometimes enters into strange places. Alban Berg's *Wozzeck* is a masterly, sordid curiosity, written in a free chromatic style which is not in strict 12-note technique but approximates to that. It has a gripping, emotional intensity and is for the most part harshly dissonant, whether the music is loud or soft, the nastiness of the drama being aptly conveyed by a nasty, atonal, cunning score. Yet even in this work there are two passages which yield some spiritual nourishment. One is the scene where Marie in her remorse seeks consolation in the Bible and, thinking of Mary Magdalene, prays for God's mercy: here the strings play quietly and almost ethereally until Marie bursts into an emotional "fortissimo". The other passage is the orchestral interlude before the final scene, when the composer, though still writing in a dissonant idiom, pours out his compassion for the wretched human beings whom he has been portraying, in music which rises to eloquence.

Busoni, who went back to the original German puppet-play for the plot of his opera, *Doktor Faust*, had been brought up a Catholic, but had parted company with the Christian faith. The music, traditional in character in many respects, yet revealing the individuality of its creator's mind, is mystical and full of spiritual and symbolical undertones. His Faust seeks from Mephistopheles not merely wealth, power and sensual enjoyment, but freedom and genius to comprehend humanity. In the course of the opera there are several passages containing a Christian reference: the chorus of invisible spirits in the Second Prologue, singing the Credo and Gloria as a background to Faust's signing of his pact with Mephistopheles; in the next scene—an ancient Romanesque chapel in the Minster—Gretchen's brother, the soldier, at prayer; even the quarrel between Catholic and Protestant students at Wittenberg, which Faust succeeds in stopping; and the singing of "Ein' feste Burg" that follows. Faust seduces the Duchess of Parma, but their dead child is really a symbol of his own will, though at first he does not realise this. In the last scene we hear off-stage the chorus in church singing of Judgment Day and telling Faust that God is sometimes a God of vengeance and punishment and will not hear his prayer.

He has, in any case, forgotten how to pray, and can remember only the runes of his magic. The figure of the Crucified Christ changes into that of Helena (Helen of Troy.) (Busoni's manuscript was left unfinished at this point, and the music was completed by his pupil Jarnach, who knew his intentions fully). Faust cries out that there is no grace in Heaven, but before he dies he succeeds in bequeathing his life to the dead child, who is to carry forward his eternal will. Busoni, like his Faust, had come to regard religion as futile; but his opera is supernatural from start to finish.

Benjamin Britten's operatic tragedies contain various elements of religious significance. In the second act of *Peter Grimes*, when the curtain rises, church bells sound, and an organ voluntary played in church behind the scenes. The service of Matins acts as a background to the human drama which is being enacted on the stage. The choir and congregation sing a hymn to organ accompaniment; we hear the prayers and responses, the Gloria and the Benedicite, the Credo and the end of the service. Meanwhile, Ellen Orford is questioning Grimes' apprentice, the boy John, and notices his torn jacket and bruised neck. Grimes comes in, telling John to come to work, even though it is the Sabbath day, and when Ellen tries to restrain him he strikes her and as the boy runs from him and he follows, his last words are: "So be it. And God have mercy upon me." The solo voices and the orchestral tissue in this scene are interwoven with the music of the church service in a masterly fashion.

In *The Rape of Lucretia* (the libretto of which is by Ronald Duncan, adapted from André Obey) a pre-Christian story of outrage and death is given a Christian interpretation in the Prologue and Epilogue. At the end of the Prologue, the Male and Female Commentators, who act as a chorus, sing a solemn melody to the words

> Whilst we as two observers stand
> Between this present audience and that scene
> We'll view these human passions and these years
> Through eyes which once have wept with Christ's own tears.

In the Epilogue, the Female Commentator, to the accompaniment of a reminder of the funeral march theme, asks:

> Is it all?
> Is all this suffering and pain,
> Is this vain?
> Can we attain
> Nothing but wider oceans of our own tears?

The Male Commentator answers:

> It is not all.
> . . . For now He bears our sin and does not fall,
> And He, carrying all, turns round
> Stoned with our doubt and then forgives us all.

The solemn melody which was heard at the end of the Prologue returns (with different words) at the very end of the opera.

In the fourth act of *Billy Budd*, Billy lies pinioned between two cannon, awaiting his execution. In an air of lyrical and religious beauty he sings farewell to " this grand rough world " and gains fresh strength from the vision of " the far-shining sail that's not fate ". In the execution scene, which follows, his last words to the noble Captain, who has reluctantly accepted the verdict of the court martial, are " ' Starry ' Vere—God bless you." In the Epilogue we find Captain Vere, now an old man, tortured by the thought of his failure to save an innocent life, though earthly laws had prevented him; then he remembers Billy's last words of forgiveness, and he too visualises " the far-shining sail ".

Act I, scene 2 of *Gloriana* ends with a prayer by Queen Elizabeth, left alone on the stage after she has dismissed Essex from her presence: it begins with a monotone against shimmering strings, rises to a passionate climax of entreaty to God, then sinks again to monotone and fades away with a soft " Amen " as the curtain falls.

Hindemith's opera *Mathis der Maler* deals with the life of the great fifteenth-century painter Mathias Grünewald (now known as Mathis Gothart Nithart). Hindemith wrote the libretto himself and set it against a background of the beginning of the Reformation and the Peasants' War in Germany. One of the leaders of the peasants' revolt induces Mathis to join them in their strife against feudal oppression, but this causes a conflict in Mathis' soul between two contesting human motives, both of them intrinsically righteous—the artist's urge to devote himself to the development of his God-sent genius and the social impulse at a period of crisis to participate with his fellow-men in their struggles. The noble story moved Hindemith to compose spiritual music, which, while at times dissonant, is often melodious and is full of profound emotion and conviction. Counterpoint, of which he is a special master, plays a large part in the technical means employed, but never for a merely intellectual purpose.

The rebellion is crushed; the leader of the peasants is killed; Mathis escapes with Regina, the leader's daughter, into the woods and describes to her one of Mathias Grünewald's actual pictures, " The Concert of Angels", the music for which is contrapuntal and as seraphic as the painting that inspired it. Regina falls asleep; from the darkness a representation of another of Grünewald's pictures, " The Temptation of St. Anthony", emerges, with Mathis himself impersonating the saint: the music is wild and violent, but in the end spiritual forces triumph in a majestic "Alleluia". As Regina dies, a short, slow-moving entr'acte is played, entitled " The Entombment " after the actual painting by Grünewald—with oboe, flute and violins in turn depicting the impressive scene. Although the opera has shown the defeat of the peasants, the spiritual victory rests with Mathis, who at the end leaves the employment of his patron Prince Albrecht von Brandenburg, the Cardinal Archibishop of Mainz, and with his paint-brushes, pencils and colours goes forth into the world, alone.

Luigi Dallipiccola's opera *Il Prigionero* in a prologue and one act (four scenes) is a grim tale of the Spanish Inquisition. The " warder " tells the prisoner of a means of escape, but it turns out to be a trick, an example of " torture by hope ": for the " warder " is the Grand Inquisitor himself and at the end gently leads him to the stake. The dialogue is largely declamatory and makes some use of the 12-note scale, but the religious chorus (off-stage) dominates the last scene and softens the harshness.

Vaughan Williams' "morality", *The Pilgrim's Progress*, is in effect a sacred opera based on Bunyan's great work, which has been a dominant influence on him throughout his career. The scene of " The Shepherds of the Delectable Mountains " (Act IV, scene 2) was produced as a separate one-act opera some twenty years before, yet fits with perfect fusion into its place in this very beautiful "morality". The celestial passages hark back at times to the Fifth Symphony, by actual reminders, and in idiom and general spirit to the " Tallis " Fantasia, *Sancta Civitas*, the " Pastoral " Symphony and the *Serenade to Music*. They are handled by means of Vaughan Williams' characteristic use of extremely legato writing in the upper parts of the strings, moving steadily, offset by solemn notes on trumpets and horns, with woodwind speaking eloquently in harmony and the voices soaring " above " the instruments. The serenity and, at appropriate times, the exaltation which this music expresses, are suitably contrasted with the modern dissonances and richly coloured orchestral effects used for the " Vanity Fair " scene, the sinister discords of the music associated with Apollyon (though he himself sings largely in monotone) and the quaint barn-dance of Mister and Madame By-ends: their superficiality, hypocrisy and snobbery are deftly matched by the humorous, ironical music.

One comment on this work has been that the theatre is not the right place for it—just because it is genuinely religious. The contents of this chapter and the previous one may have provided some food for reflection on this view. Religious art need not be confined to churches, synagogues, chapels, temples and mosques. A concert hall may become transmuted if great liturgical music is nobly performed in it, and a musical " morality " may fittingly be composed for production in an opera house.

19

CONCLUSION

THE D flat is "really sublime", Saint-Saëns remarked about the "pianissimo" note on the lower strings with which Beethoven begins the storm music in his "Pastoral" Symphony. Sir George Grove's comment[1] is: "This depends on the interpretation given to that tremendous adjective. But sublime or not, it is very impressive." The "impressiveness" or "sublimity" depends partly on the softness of the note, partly on its remoteness from the key of F which immediately precedes it.

The word "sublime" has been used a number of times in this book, without any attempt to define its meaning. It is necessary to do so for three reasons: (1) in my view, sublimity has a religious connotation; (2) there is no justification for leaving undefined a term which in the past has caused much discussion and, indeed, controversy, but which I have assumed—by using it—to be relevant to our subject; and (3) the nature of the sublime will be found to have a bearing on one of the most vital issues which this book must attempt to answer—the question of the relationship between the spiritual quality and the artistic value of a piece of music.

It is unlikely that the word "ὕψος" had for Longinus the same associations as "sublimity" has for us, and indeed, as Mr. E. F. Carritt[2] mentions, both Wordsworth and De Quincey pointed out that he applied it to animated, lively, energetic composition—"or, if you will, elevated writing" added Wordsworth.[3] Many thinkers since Longinus' day have tried to interpret the term. Early in the present century, A. C. Bradley[4] defined the sublime as a species of the Beautiful, distinguished from other kinds by "exceeding or even overwhelming greatness": this quality, according to him, produces in us first a negative stage of being checked or repelled (which I do not think fits every case) and later, a rush of self-expansion or uplifting which are positive

[1] *Beethoven and his Nine Symphonies*, p. 217.

[2] In *The Theory of Beauty*, p. 220.

[3] *Letters of the Wordsworth Family* (edited by Knight), II, p. 250; "Milton", De Quincey's *Works* (Black, 1862,) VI, p. 317.

[4] In *Oxford Lectures on Poetry*.

feelings of union with the object. One of the instances which he takes is that of a sparrow defending its young against a dog which seems to it "a huge monster", in an incident recounted by Turgeniev; Bradley calls this bird " sublime "; the word is usually associated with objects of great size, but here the smallness of the sparrow is essential to its sublimity, and this consists in its love and courage, which *are* great. Mr. Carritt[1] agrees with Croce that the concept of sublimity is too vague to have any philosophic value. In any event it is both a moral and an aesthetic term, and in the case of Turgeniev's sparrow it is applied by Bradley in its moral sense.

In the strictly aesthetic field, clearly there can be nothing above and beyond the greatest degree of the beautiful; but if we believe that beauty is divine, the supremely beautiful object of nature or work of art, which we call " sublime ", reveals the majesty of God in all His glory. It arouses in us a feeling of awe, which we experience, too, when confronted with something terrible and gigantic—such as an earthquake—and not beautiful at all. But the sublime object also evokes love, wonder, and even worship—not in the idolatrous sense of worshipping something other than God Himself but in the sense of worshipping Him through the revelation of Him in the sublimity of the object. We are impressed and moved by it in a more exalted way than by other objects which are also beautiful.

When we reflect upon instances of music which we are inclined to call sublime, we get some insight into the relationship between spiritual quality and artistic value. For the sublime moments in music are at once supremely beautiful, in the strictest aesthetic sense, and also arouse awe in our minds; and the two features are directly connected; indeed, they can scarcely be distinguished from one another. Many will agree with Saint-Saëns that that D flat in the " Pastoral " Symphony is sublime, but will perhaps be prepared to apply the term also to the whole of the tremendous " storm " section which it begins. And examples of sublimity are even more frequent in Beethoven's Third Period: the slow movements of the last sonatas and quartets are built upon sublime melodies and maintain that quality throughout their length: the same applies to that of the B flat Trio (op. 97) which is on the borderline of the Second and Third Periods in its majestic, mystical outlook; the *Missa Solemnis* is sublime from first to last; so, too, are the first and third movements of the Ninth Symphony, the great melody in the Finale and the variations upon it (except at those

[1] *The Theory of Beauty*, pp. 247 f.

moments at which sublimity would have been out of place); and the term is even applicable, I suggest, without an undue stretch of language, to the Scherzo, which is filled with a divine energy so abounding and, in the Trio, a happiness so serene, that we can but revere the mind that created it. Think, too, of the opening and closing choruses of Bach's St. Matthew Passion, and indeed the wondrous music in which the whole of the tremendous drama is unfolded, and the great reflective choruses, solos and concerted numbers which accompany it in its course; the majesty of the Mass in B minor, and particularly the glorious entreaty of its "Kyrie", the mystery of the "Incarnatus", the solemn tragedy of the "Crucifixus", and the supreme revelation of the divine power in the " Sanctus "; if these things are not " sublime", then indeed there is no meaning in the expression.

Most of the examples of musical sublimity are to be found, in my view, in the art of Bach and Beethoven, though of course there are many instances in the works of other composers too, which will occur to each music-lover according to his judgment. The term can hardly be denied, I feel, to the greatest of the choruses in Handel's *Messiah*, to "He shall feed His flock", to the slow movement of Haydn's *Sunrise* Quartet or his *Seven last words on the Cross*; to the " Qui tollis " of Mozart's Mass in C minor, the Piano Concerto in C minor, the Fantasia for piano in the same key and the first three movements of the G minor String Quintet; to the Adagio of Schubert's Quintet for Strings in C or to *Die Allmacht*; to Brahms' *Requiem*, the introduction to the Finale of his First Symphony, the slow movement of the Fourth, and the melody for 'cello in the Andante of his Piano Concerto in B flat; to Wotan's Farewell to Brünnhilde in the third act of *Die Walküre* or the closing scene of *Götterdämmerung*; and—I venture to add—to the chorus that ends the first part of *The Dream of Gerontius*.

But sublimity is more frequently to be found in the music of Beethoven and Bach than of any other composers, and this fact (if my readers agree with me that it is a fact) is, to say the least, not unconnected with their supreme position among the masters of the art.

The awe and reverence which we experience in contemplating a sublime object, are religious in character. (An atheist is scarcely entitled to use the word " sublimity "; he probably would not wish to do so.) It is for this reason that the nature of the sublime and the examples of it throw light on the relationship between artistic value and spiritual quality. But the presence of a spiritual character in a composition does not, of course, necessarily mean that it is sublime; it may not arouse awe in us.

Imagination; technical power; a sense of structure; all these are enormously important elements in a masterpiece. But the greatest works are also imbued, in the widest sense, with a spiritual quality which is distinct from the divinity inherent in all beauty and is, as it were, an offshoot of it. If a composition contains all the other factors that go to make up greatness, but is not spiritual in character, it is to that extent less great as a work of art; and conversely, its greatness is enhanced by the quality of the spirit. The slow movement of Beethoven's *Sonata Pathétique* is spiritual (without being sublime): its greatness largely consists in this fact. It is fair to compare the opening movements of Tchaikovsky's Fourth Symphony and Beethoven's Fifth, because Tchaikovsky himself said that his work was based on an idea similar to Beethoven's; but Beethoven's Allegro is imbued with a spiritual grandeur wholly, or almost entirely, lacking in Tchaikovsky's; and it is this element, much more than its finer structural mastery, that makes it greater music.

This spiritual character—whether or not it takes a specifically religious form—has permeated the music of all the greatest European composers from John Dunstable and Guillaume Dufay down to the present day. Thus it is reasonable to suppose that their greatness is dependent upon it in a very large measure. If we say that much of the music of Byrd, Franck, Elgar or Bloch, for instance, is more spiritual than that of Wagner, how do we account for the fact that we do not regard them as being on the tremendously high level that our artistic judgment bids us place him? The answer must be that he excels them, fine musicians though they are, in imaginative power and scope, in emotional range, in the width of his musical architecture, in gigantic technical mastery. When these qualities are united in one man in such supreme degree as they are in Wagner, and are moreover combined, as I have tried to show, with a much larger measure of spiritual character than has sometimes been conceded, even though the latter is less pronounced than in those other composers, there is the reason why we set him on a higher pinnacle. It is, however, precisely because Bach and Beethoven surpass him on the spiritual plane, whilst being equal with him in other respects, that they are even greater composers than he.

When we say that musical greatness is in a large measure dependent upon spiritual quality, we are in effect saying that it arises largely from the inspiration of God. For unless we believe in God, there is no meaning in the use of the word " spiritual " and in that case our whole scale of values would be upset. Spirit is soul, and the soul is either immortal or non-existent; and because it is a spiritual entity, it cannot be destroyed by any physical cause, but only severed from the body at death. If we believe that there is such a thing as a soul and that therefore it survives death, we are thereby acknowledging a faith that is common to most religions, and are virtually committed to belief in the existence of God: it is possible to conceive that God exists but that none of his creatures has an immortal soul; what is inconceivable is that they survive death but that there is no God: that would be a meaningless philosophy.

In spite of the atheism of the materialists and the scepticism of some exponents of the theory of the expanding universe, it has come to be recognised in our day far more strongly than at the time of the appearance of Darwin's *Origin of Species*, that science and religion do not conflict but are complementary to one another. Science has discovered that there is no such thing as inert matter. It looks almost as though there is a spiritual element in apparently materialistic substance. Cosmology, however, is concerned with the physical universe; it cannot give us much information about spiritual things, nor tell us whether the soul of man exists, what its nature is, or whether it is immortal. What cosmology does—and what concerns us here about it—is to give us a picture of a universe majestic in its immensity, mysterious in its workings, wondrous in its orderliness arising out of chaos, and continually evolving. This picture is itself evidence of the existence of a supreme Creator, working with a purpose and caring for that which He creates. It may be asked, what has this to do with our subject? The answer is, everything. For if there is no God, then my book has been written in vain. The majesty of the expanding universe, the very beauty of its conception, as well as the loveliness of its countless manifestations on the earth below and in the heavens above us, attest the existence of a Creator. And in this process of proof, music plays its part.

In the Spanish Chapel of the Church of Santa Maria Novella in Florence, one of the frescoes painted by Andrea da Firenze in 1355 represents the apotheosis of St. Thomas Aquinas and Theological Philosophy. He is surrounded by angels, the Apostles and Prophets, and crushed at his feet are three leaders of heresy and false philosophy. The fourteen female figures below are the earthly and celestial sciences which adorned the saint, and under each one is some great representative of that science. Now, among the sciences is music, shown as a beautiful young woman, dressed in green and holding a small organ. It is the only one of the " fine arts " depicted and its representative is not Jubal, the first musician mentioned in the Bible, but his half-brother Tubal-Cain, who is described in Genesis iv, 22 as "an instructor of every artificer in brass and iron "; in the fresco he is shown beating out sounds on an anvil, that being conceived as one of the origins of music. It may be that music was included in the picture because it was used by the Church to praise God. The painter of the fresco did not include painting, sculpture, architecture or literature in his scheme; and in the pictures and statuary which adorn Christian churches throughout the world, you will find countless representations of angels singing and playing musical instruments, rather than figures engaged in the creation or practice of other arts.[1] Perhaps it is not too fanciful to see in this inclusion of music as a science in the Florentine fresco, represented by an instructor of artificers rather than by a creative artist, an image of it as a kind of link between the physical universe and the world of the spirit.

Through the infinite compassion of Bach's greatest New Testament masterpieces, through the apocalyptic vision of his and Beethoven's sublime settings of the Mass, through the myriad-minded glory of Beethoven's Ninth Symphony, the grandeur of his last sonatas and the eternal mysteries of his final quartets, I seem to behold the universe stretching endlessly into space under the guidance of a loving God. A devout old clergyman of the Church of England once said to me: " We cannot really understand the nature of the Almighty." Some modern philosophers have said that He must be a mathematician. Freemasons call Him "The Great Architect of the Universe". He is also the Great Musician.

[1] In the fresco in the Spanish Chapel, rhetoric is included, probably because it is needed for preaching; but rhetoric, being utilitarian, is not what is known as one of the " fine arts ".

INDEX